How Managers Have Learnt to Lead

How Managers Have Learnt to Lead

Exploring the Development of Leadership Practice

Steve Kempster

*Head of the Business School
the University of Cumbria, UK
and Professor of Leadership*

palgrave
macmillan

First published 2009 by
PALGRAVE MACMILLAN

Palgrave Macmillan in the UK is an imprint of Macmillan Publishers Limited, registered in England, company number 785998, of Houndmills, Basingstoke, Hampshire RG21 6XS.

Palgrave Macmillan in the US is a division of St Martin's Press LLC, 175 Fifth Avenue, New York, NY 10010.

Palgrave Macmillan is the global academic imprint of the above companies and has companies and representatives throughout the world.

Palgrave® and Macmillan® are registered trademarks in the United States, the United Kingdom, Europe and other countries.

ISBN-13: 978-0-230-22095-9   hardback
ISBN-10: 0-230-22095-9   hardback

This book is printed on paper suitable for recycling and made from fully managed and sustained forest sources. Logging, pulping and manufacturing processes are expected to conform to the environmental regulations of the country of origin.

A catalogue record for this book is available from the British Library.

Library of Congress Cataloging-in-Publication Data

Kempster, Steve, 1961–
How managers have learnt to lead : exploring the development of leadership practice / Steve Kempster.
     p. cm.
Includes bibliographical references and index.
ISBN 978-0-230-22095-9
1. Leadership. 2. Management. I. Title.

HD57.7.K473 2009
658.4'092—dc22   2008050867

10   9   8   7   6   5   4   3   2
18   17   16   15   14   13   12   11

Printed and bound in Great Britain by
CPI Antony Rowe, Chippenham and Eastbourne

This book is dedicated to my sons, Chris and Rob, for their distractions, to Sarah for her patience and to my parents, John and Alison, for their leadership.

Contents

Tables

Figures

Foreword

The great majority of books on leadership are about key principles. Very few examine leadership development and even fewer examine how we learn leadership. Often these books are read by people who are interested in finding a new approach to leadership, a way of leading that seems more appropriate for the circumstances of today. Yet I sense that the polemic suggestions and recipes on offer within these books fail to grasp how an individual may assimilate and distil such wisdom into being able to lead in the complexity of the specific situations people face. Undoubtedly, the authors expect people to learn through translating and applying the ideas but perhaps this underestimates processes of learning. In essence I would argue that there is a major disconnect between the arguments of what leadership is and our understanding of how we learn to practice leadership. This book refreshingly seeks to bridge this disconnect by connecting leadership and learning through the notion of practice – captured by Steve's argument (in Chapter 1) that both are two sides of the same coin.

It is interesting that the book is about *managers* learning to lead. Whatever we think about the difference between management and leadership, it is almost certainly true that most people become managers before they become leaders, whether they are in large public and private sector businesses, or small businesses where people learn first to work *in* their business and then need to learn to work *on* their businesses. In all contexts, learning to move on from management to leadership is a major part of the challenge. This challenge is further accentuated by people's histories prior to becoming managers. For example, about two-thirds of people who become managers have done something else – like being an engineer or some other specialist to do with the product or service of their organisation, before moving on to management (Williams 2001, 2002). The importance of prior activities is explored in Chapter 3 in terms of identity change and an argument is outlined that learning, the development of practice and our sense of identity (as, for example, engineer, manager and then leader) are interrelated. In recent work (Pedler et al. 2004) we have argued that management is often the career step before leadership. Steve's argument is, I believe, sympathetic to this by seeing this transition as being shaped by a trajectory in which we engage with others that helps to shape our learning. In this sense we move from being an engineer to 'becoming' a leader. The continual learning associated with this notion of 'becoming' is explored in the book in chapters 3, 5 and 8 and usefully anchors this process to embedded relationships within situations enacted through particular roles. So leadership is often taken on by people following career trajectories involving quite a lot of change, and therefore demanding considerable learning along the way.

A central theme of this book is that leadership development takes place through 'natural' processes, an early theme of my own work (Burgoyne and Stuart 1977 and Burgoyne and Hodgson 1983). However, these 'natural' processes do not always work to the extent, or as quickly, as we would like. Using the example of health, this takes place through natural processes, like the working of our immune systems. For the most part we sustain a healthy balance through mechanisms that we are unaware of. In Chapter 8 Steve explores what such mechanisms might be that shape our leadership learning that occur naturally. However, we do get ill from time to time and often need medical interventions to get better. Should interventions (such as leadership development programmes) adopt a content expertise and suggest specific practices to be undertaken to develop 'healthy' leadership. Or should a process perspective be offered up that can be seen to be going with the grain and facilitating the natural mechanism? Work we did for the UK Government (CEML 2000) identified that best practice process interventions were significantly contextualised. In Chapter 9 Steve spells out how such best practice interventions can be aligned with underlying mechanisms to greatly enhance and improve the likely effectiveness of the intervention.

Another central interest of mine is the evaluation of leadership development initiatives. Steve mentions a paradox to leadership development (in Chapter 1) and this soundly resonates with me. Why do hard-headed business people seem to be willing to invest substantially in something that they are not sure works, or understanding of how it works. Using the health analogy again, it's a little like medieval medical practices and the liberal use of leeches regardless of the patient's condition and situation. In this sense for too long leadership development has been for the most part an 'act of faith'. In part such an act of faith (described in Chapter 4) is as a consequence of the equivocal issue of understanding what leadership is captured by Barker's (1997) question: 'How can we train leaders if we don't know what leadership is?' But is also a consequence of limited attention to understanding leadership in particular contexts reflected in the purpose of this book. As a consequence Steve's related question of course is: 'How can we train leaders if we don't know how they learn to lead?' The comprehensive review of leadership, learning and leadership development in chapters 2, 3 and 4 provide us with a useful synthesis of discussions related to both these questions.

But there is a final question that continues to exorcise me and returns us back to a most fundamental issue: are leaders born or made? Clearly the whole book is based around the view that leadership can be learnt, and provides ample evidence for this. Steve carefully takes us through research and literature (chapters 2, 3 and 4) explaining what we currently know and illustrates gaps in our understanding argued to be as a result of tacit learning - learning we cannot express. In Chapter 6 he helps us to think about our own tacit learning through lived experience and invites us to compare this to four cases drawn from different contexts – outlined in Chapter 7. His argument seems plausible and convincing and I think his explanation provides a most fertile ground for further and deeper exploration – and in many ways provokes us to consider the policy and practical implications for leadership development interventions. However, are leaders born or made?

My own view on the oldest question in the leadership debate comes from evolutionary psychology (Nicholson 1998, 2000): the will to manage and lead may be largely innate, but the ability to do it well is learnt. In everyday terms, this translates into the American Airways HR slogan: recruit for attitude, train for skill. The common ground between Steve and me is that we can all be '*better*' at leading. This book provides a firm foundation for us to understand more deeply how we can '*become better*'.

John Burgoyne
Professor of Management Learning at Lancaster University
Management School and Henley Business School

Preface

This is not another book on leadership. Rather, this book explores 'leadership learning' and seeks to answer the question: how we do we learn to lead?

For what seems a fairly fundamental question there is a dearth of books exploring this area. There is no shortage of books providing insights into the nature of leadership and even more on solutions and prescriptions to enhancing leadership skills and behaviours. The common assumption behind these laudable texts is that if they were to be read and their arguments enacted, our leadership practice will be the better for it. Is it as simple as that? Do these texts reshape our leadership practice? The evidence, which will be outlined in this book, suggests we may be looking in the wrong direction. Perhaps we should look first at the foundations, how we learn to lead, and then build upon this.

In a sense there is a certain paradox here. The thousands of books that have been published are in response to an almost inexhaustible demand to improve leadership, but little attention to exploring how such leadership is learnt. Leadership and leadership learning are inextricably linked – like two sides of the same coin – they both inform the other. Why then has leadership learning been so overlooked? This puzzle drew me into a study of some eight years, the outcome of which is this book. I recall thumbing through notable leadership texts that said very little on leadership learning. I did literature searches and found few investigations into this area. However, I was struck by four pieces of published and frequently cited work: Burgoyne and Hodgson (1983), Davies and Easterby-Smith (1984), McCall and colleagues at the Center for Creative Leadership (1988) and Cox and Cooper (1989). The reason for being 'struck' was partly that these authors were speaking about the area I was interested in; and in particular that three of the four sets of authors were at Lancaster University Management School – colleagues. Ironically answers seemed to be so very close at hand. Bribing them with coffee, discussions began. There was good news and bad. The bad news was that although this was an area they thought rich enough to be explored, they had been distracted by other aspects and their careers had taken them away from developing these contributions. The good news was the encouragement they gave to explore further. They felt

now, more than ever with the present zeitgeist of leadership, that processes of leadership learning warranted a deeper exploration. I have also
met with some of the folks from the Centre for Creative Leadership
who have continued to pursue good work in this area – which will be
examined in Chapter 4.

This book then is a follow-on from the collective activities of these
researchers and is also, in a sense, a companion in a complementary
way to the current work in this area, notably by McCall (1998) in his
book entitled *'High Flyers'* and McCauley, Moxley and Van Velsor's
(2003) *'Handbook of Leadership Development'*.

Building out from my Ph.D., this book draws from a theoretical base
to establish the foundations of the subject – what is known about how
managers learn to lead – in the form of Part II. Part III uses this foundation to look inside the 'black-box' of leadership learning and goes
beyond notions of 'learning from experience'. Drawing out from 40 in-
depth interviews, four cases are outlined to enable comparison between
managers in public and private sectors, women and men managers and
the employed and the self-employed. In conclusion a contextual explanation is provided that compares leadership learning between the public and private sectors, between male and female managers and between
the employed and self-employed. The insights from these four groups
allow an explanation to be put forward that addresses the fundamental
question: how do we learn to lead?

If we understand how leadership is learnt, and how such learning
differs between individuals and groups, then our focus is more oriented
towards the practice of leadership as it is constructed in particular contexts. A corollary to this, and a perspective that runs through this book,
is that there is no universal approach to leading. Leadership is learnt
in an idiosyncratic fashion through our lived experiences, particularly
drawn from the contexts in which we participate. With a local understanding, practice can be developed in tune with the organisational
context. The benefits of understanding processes of leadership learning
are many:

- We can understand and place emphasis on local contexts and the
  development of local practice.
- We can illuminate the way that individuals are shaped by their contexts and yet also shape the ongoing practice of leadership for the
  next generation.
- We can explore how leadership learning differs greatly between men
  and women, and between the employed and the self-employed.

- We gain insight into enhancing individual leadership practice.
- We can start to consider the notion of designing leadership apprenticeship for people commencing their journey towards practising leadership.
- We will begin to enhance leadership development interventions and begin to get an appropriate return on the billions invested each year.

This book addresses all of the above themes; themes that are generally only lightly addressed in the general leadership texts. There are some very good texts that explore management learning as a broad inclusive topic; but few that seek to unearth the difficult to reach almost imperceptible phenomenon that is leadership learning. The conundrum is how to make visible processes influencing leadership practice that are so difficult to recall and express, as they occur unnoticed by managers affected by them. Perhaps, in part, this explains why there has been such limited academic attention to this area. This limited scholarly interest is asymmetric to the interest from practitioners whose desire for improved leadership practice is palpable in all walks of life. Within organisations leadership is seen almost as a panacea to arrest organisational malaise and stimulate change. In the UK the most current pronouncement on skills development, in the form of the 'Leitch Report' (2006), has greatly amplified these calls for enhancing leadership skills. However, I sense a certain déjà vu: the implementation of quick short-term universal solutions with associated prescriptions at considerable cost that have very limited impact. If we wish to advance leadership practice we need to start at the beginning – how we learn to lead.

Someone reading this book could be an undergraduate student shortly to commence their leadership learning apprenticeship. It could be an experienced manager part way through their management career wishing to refine their practice and understand new influences helping or hindering their development. Or perhaps a senior manager wishing to reflect back over their lived experience and understand how their leadership practice has been constructed and appreciate the ongoing impact they have on the next generation of leaders. Or it might be someone about to commission a leadership development programme or evaluate past interventions and seek to enhance their understanding prior to further investment. Or it might be a HR professional revisiting recruitment and selection processes. Certainly it seeks to extend our understanding and to encourage further research into this most important area. This book speaks to all these agendas.

My journey to understand how managers learn to lead has been enlightening. Not just from an academic sense, but also in terms of enabling me to make sense of the many experiences I have encountered that I had previously not understood or been aware of. I hope the book helps you with your journey in understanding leadership learning and developing leadership practice.

Acknowledgements

A big thank you to the 40 managers who took part in this study; your candid and in-depth reflections on your experiences have provided such wonderful insight. In particular, my grateful thanks to the four case managers who allowed their stories to be told. I must also thank the hundreds of managers and students who I have had the wonderful privilege of working with. Your comments, questions and practical experiences have been a reservoir I have drawn from. My thanks to Sir Chris Bonnington. I have worked with Sir Chris on a number of occasions and his generosity of time and consideration to individual needs is a benchmark for many of us. I am most grateful for the time you have given me to help me with this work.

Thank you to my colleagues at Lancaster University Management School for your friendship and support over the last 15 years. In particular I would like to thank Cary Cooper, Vivien Hodgson, Mark Easterby-Smith and John Burgoyne. It was through their collective works related to this area that provided so much foundation to the ideas within this book. John Mackness has been a most special friend during these 15 years who seemed to always think there was more that could come from me.

Colleagues outside LUMS who have been ever present in shaping my writing: Ged Watts, Brad Jackson and Ken Parry. Their deep friendship and encouragement has meant so much, along with the wisdom that has been so freely given.

A special thank you to Sarah Gregory. How much can you thank someone for kindly reading, re-reading and reading yet more drafts!

Part I

1
Introduction: How Do Managers Learn to Lead?

This book seeks to develop an explanation of managerial leadership learning. The term 'leadership learning' is limited in common usage, yet my argument in this book will suggest that it provides a most important focus by which we can gain a better understanding of leadership practice and thereby enhance leadership development interventions. In this book a study of leadership learning will seek to understand underlying influences that shape a manager's knowledge acquisition and behavioural orientation towards their leadership practice.

A ten-year review of research published in the *Leadership Quarterly* succinctly summarised the situation on leadership development research: 'We do not know enough about how organisational systems develop leaders' (Lowe & Gardner, 2000: 495).

Such a comment is most revealing in terms of research orientation. The study and understanding of leadership has led to a voluminous output of research, and there are estimated to be in the region of 15,000 publications with the word leadership in the title (Grint, 2005), most of which focus on the nature and characteristics of leadership. However, despite such high levels of academic interest in understanding the phenomenon of leadership, there is a relative dearth of specific research aimed at understanding processes that shape managers' understanding of organisational leadership.

There is a certain irony that relatively limited scholarly attention is oriented at processes influencing leadership learning when an industry has been created servicing a seemingly inexhaustible demand for developing the next generation of organisational leaders. For example, it has been estimated that investment into leadership development in the US exceeded $60 billion in 1998 (Fulmer & Wagner, 1999).[1] Practitioner demand for leadership development research reflects a desire to understand whether such significant investment is creating organisational leaders. At the time of writing this book such answers were still a long way off. Lowe and Gardner (2000) emphasised that since House and Howell's (1992) call for greater understanding of 'how organisational systems enhance the efficiency of leadership development efforts' very little has been learnt (Lowe & Gardner, 2000: 495).

The thrust of the argument from Lowe and Gardner is not that we don't have a broad understanding of how managers learn leadership; rather there is a degree of consensus towards informal development. But this understanding is at such a high level that it restricts explanation. For example, it is generally understood that learning of leadership and management is shaped by hardships, line experience and notable people[2] (McCall, Lombardo & Morrison, 1988) and it is accentuated by organisational contexts, offering greater scope and diversity of experiences (Davies & Easterby-Smith, 1984; Conger, 2004). Similarly it is generally accepted that informal activities rather than formal interventions are predominant in influencing leadership learning (Conger, 1998, 2004). And finally, best practice leadership development interventions orientate around contextualised informal activities such as mentoring, coaching or a variety of stretching assignments in a range of contexts (James & Burgoyne, 2001).

However, Lowe and Gardner (2000), echoing concerns of a number of commentators (such as Bryman 1996, 2004; Parry, 1998; Conger, 1998, 2004; Day, 2000; and Burgoyne et al., 2004) are concerned that little is understood of the contextual processes influencing both leadership and leadership learning[3] at the level of lived experience. Similarly these commentators have argued that historic methodological approaches to understanding leadership and leadership development have been associated with quantitative analysis. A resounding call has been made for qualitative research as the method of choice for studying leadership and leadership development (Conger, 1998, 2004; Bryman, 2004), enabling situated nuances to be revealed that are otherwise obfuscated in the numeric aggregates associated with quantitative methodologies.

A guiding assumption that has shaped the arguments of this book has been an acceptance that leadership learning will be a complex process, idiosyncratically experienced and that a qualitative understanding at the level of lived experience is necessary if an understanding, at a deeper level than is currently known, is to be obtained. Although an individual focus is argued to be appropriate for revealing contextual depth, it may be possible to discern common underlying processes shaping leadership learning drawn from a collection of individual experiences. It is thus the intention to develop a deeper understanding of leadership learning and the processes influencing such learning, from a group of managers taken from a variety of contexts. In essence, a broad and fundamental puzzle is infused into the structure of the book:

> At the level of lived experience, are there common processes influencing leadership learning of managers; or is their idiosyncratic experience of a variety of contexts so varied that explanations can only be given at the level of the individual?

Chapter structure

To give light to this puzzle and to the notion of underlying influences on leadership learning we will first look at the lived experience of a famous mountaineer. The examination of this experience will provide a glimpse of influences on leadership learning that will be significant to an explanation of leadership learning. Additionally the mountaineer's story will introduce three contexts:

- Theoretical review of extant theorising on leadership, learning and leadership development – the interrelated nature of these three areas.
- Methodological perspective shaping qualitative research into managerial leadership learning – why such an approach is required.
- Policy environment in which leadership learning is situated – the leadership panacea.

These three contextual perspectives are drawn together through a personal narrative where I outline my interest in leadership learning. This practical and theoretical blend suggests a conundrum: Why do we invest so much into leadership development when we appear to know that we are looking in the wrong direction?

Leadership learning: Lived experience of Sir Chris Bonnington – Interview conducted 22 January 2003

I was introduced to Sir Chris Bonnington by a mutual friend. His achievements in the world of mountaineering are legend; both in terms of his climbing ability and, significantly, in terms of his leadership of expeditions. It is towards that context that the interview was oriented. Sitting at his desk in his first floor study overlooking the North Cumbria fells, his dog wrapped around his feet, Chris answered the opening question (the same question posed to all interviewees in this study): How do you define leadership in terms of your experience of leading?

> Leadership is getting a group of people to work together to achieve an objective in its simplest form. Effective leadership is sustainable. For example a bad leader, a sharp leader, a dishonest leader can be effective but not in the long run – bad is not sustainable. Sustaining is practical and lasts because of an ethical base, with integrity and humanity built in.

Examining this definition a few days later, it was most striking that the key aspects identified (such as a sustainable ethical base, integrity and humanity) could be seen in various combinations within different aspects of his leadership experiences. What was less clear during the interview was Chris's awareness of the variety of influences by which these aspects had been learnt. It is not the intention of this review of the interview to describe the vivid, exciting and dramatic stories that were clearly the milieu of experiences that construct Chris's biography. Such stories of mountaineers and business leaders are abundant, including in the various books that Chris has written. What is less abundant is an understanding of the opaque, embedded underlying influences shaping leadership learning that are so difficult to describe yet affect the development of leadership practice.

Underlying influences on leadership learning

The analysis of the interview identified seven key themes that appear to have influenced Chris's understanding of how to lead drawn from his lived experience, namely, notable people, role enactment, situated learning, identity development, performance capability, aspirational desire to lead and the role of formal training.

Limitations of formal training

The extant literature surrounding leadership learning concedes that formal training and development appear to be limited in terms of dominance in shaping peoples leadership practice (McCall, 2004; Conger, 2004). This was explicitly the case for Chris. Although he had been to Sandhurst for officer training, he commented on the low significance of such training in shaping his approach to leading. Recalling a very early leadership incident in the military, as an officer in charge of a troop of tanks, he commented that despite all the training given to

him it simply did not provide the necessary knowledge to deal with
people:

> I didn't listen to them, I used my status, using the 'pips on my shoul-
> der' barking orders. It took a year to undo the damage. I learnt that
> anybody with power can tell people what to do. The only way was
> to get people to want to do things. Also I learnt to be upfront and
> honest. I learnt that a tank crew was similar to three men on a rope:
> you have to be on good terms with people, but they know you have
> the final say.

Chris was emphasising that the aspects he was formally taught played
little significance in the way he was supposed to lead. The quote highlights a key aspect of leadership learning as being informal and highly
contextualised. Chris initially recalled only limited value in terms of
leadership learning while at Sandhurst until he began to reflect on
prominent people he engaged with – most particularly his observation
of officers who were both good and bad.

Notable people

Throughout the interview Chris cited numerous individuals with whom
he had interacted. Mostly they were climbers but on prompting he
recalled those at Sandhurst and latterly those in non-climbing contexts.
Regarding the climbing context, some were considered poor at leading, others he admired for their leadership qualities, but learning from
both was most apparent. Of importance was a strong sense of respect
not only for their knowledge of and talent for climbing but also for
their ability to engage with and hold the trust of climbers and sherpas
alike. The voluminous number and range of people within Chris's lived
experience of leadership was most striking; and most salient was his
admiration of the leadership capabilities of John Hunt[4] – a point to be
returned to later. Striking though was the limited expectation Chris had
that I wanted to know about these people and their influence on him.
I had a sense that he had not considered this aspect as most salient in
his awareness of how he had learnt to lead. Much more prominent were
the impact and developmental role of enactments as crucibles shaping
learning (Bennis & Thomas, 2002).

Learning through critical role enactment

There was a clear defining watershed episode within Chris's mountaineering career in the form of becoming the leader of his first expedition.

Reflecting on his first and subsequent expeditions he commented on leadership responsibilities, particularly regarding those who have been injured or died on his watch:

> I have to accept the fact that a high proportion of the expeditions I have led have had casualties and a number of fatalities. It's a burden that I do not bear lightly yet it is one that I can accept, since the risks involved are something that the entire team accepted in their desire to achieve success on the mountain.

This sense of responsibility enriched and emphasised a process of learning through enactment. Chris described a chronology of expeditions and events continually moving backwards and forwards between incidents and episodes reflecting on learning from observing others and applying such learning in the action of his own leadership. The continual cycle of observing and enactment is only part of the story of Chris's learning. The next important aspect of leadership learning that was arguably more underlying and much less conscious to Chris but nevertheless present in his narrative was the notion of situated learning.

Situated learning through participation

Extending beyond learning through enactment was a clear demonstration of learning through participation with others. Chris described intricate details of learnt customs, rituals and practices that enabled him to be part of a community. Through such participation he came in contact with notable people and the nature of mountain leadership became visible and subsequently accessible to Chris. Importantly, participation provided access into a shared and common body of knowledge of what is expected when leading a mountain expedition. Situated learning is associated with notions of 'becoming' a full member of a community including identity construction associated with that community (Lave & Wenger, 1991). Within the mountaineering community the intense participation and specific role enactments enabled Chris to 'become' a leader in his own eyes and those of his community.

Identification with leadership

His personal identification with the role of leader appeared as a central feature of his identity. Certainly through the narrative in the interview he expressed a coherent story of himself in leadership roles. For example, within his excellent range of published books on mountaineering he provides many insights to his personal association with leadership.

Chris was most comfortable with the notion of himself as a leader and in the latter stages of his career he has become chairman of the British Mountaineering Association and recently Chancellor of Lancaster University and non-executive chairman of Berghaus, a major outdoors clothing company. He emphasised though that such identification particularly related to contexts in which he is regarded as having knowledge and a reputation for leadership.

Performance capability as leader

Successive enactments and comparison of his performance with that of others illustrated a sense of continued feedback. After leading his first expedition he sought feedback for a book he was writing and this had a big impact:

> It made me feel not so self-satisfied but this was important for me. Openness to feedback illustrates strength of self-confidence and growing self-awareness. Poor leaders shy away from feedback and are not comfortable with others and are seemingly insecure about themselves.

The notion of judging his leadership performance was a repeating theme throughout the telling of numerous stories of enactments where failure and success were compared. Later in his career, Chris commented on the importance of confidence to lead and having the confidence of the team to know, for example, when to delegate or when to gain consensus. Talking about a particular expedition he commented:

> It's important to work from a basis of consensus while avoiding running it by committee. Having consulted and listened I made my plans and then, where possible, called a meeting and asked for comments, reserving the right of final decision to myself. My effectiveness as leader was helped by the fact that I was climbing at around the same standard as my peers. It's hard for a leader to run an expedition from Base Camp.

He went on to comment about his earlier desire to be leading by being out in front and repeatedly finding excuses to be shaping the route and losing touch with what's happening to the rest of the expedition:

> The best position for the leader of a large expedition is at the camp immediately below that of the lead climbers. Here he can keep in

touch with what is going on in front and have a good feel for how supplies are flowing up the mountain. This was the position adopted by John Hunt at the crucial stages of the 1953 Everest expedition and it still seems a sound one on more technical climbs.

An aspiration to lead

Most strikingly at the very end of the interview, Chris laid great emphasis on the impact that John Hunt had on his perspective of leadership. He stressed that Hunt had been one of the most influential figures to him, role modelling the importance and significance of leadership, to achieving the success of climbing Everest. In his early formative years he read Hunt's account of mountain leadership in great detail and hoped to become capable of fulfilling this function, hence the criticality of leading his first expedition. Chris commented that his role in leading the successful Everest expedition of 1975 had strong echoes of Hunt enabling Hillary to reach the summit: 'Neither of us made it to the top ... on that occasion.'

The interview was abruptly concluded at this point with the arrival of someone at the door and his dog signalling, with appropriate barking, that my time was up. In hindsight this final reflection appears to be most salient to his lived experience of leadership learning and it was a disappointment that this deep reflexive moment was abruptly concluded. It is interesting to note that this significant formative influence did not emerge until the latter part of the interview. This suggests that some influences within an individual's lived experience may be significant, yet not necessarily prominent unless made salient through structured and reflexive conversation (Cunliffe, 2002).

Throughout the interview there was a clear sense of recognising the importance of the role of the leader; not only reflected in the context as a mountaineer but also in his previous military context, and certainly in his latter context as a university chancellor.

Contextual influence

The lived experience of Chris's leadership learning is an illustration of situated learning (Lave & Wenger, 1991), where learning to lead is forged through participation in particular communities at particular points in time. His perspective of learning was shaped by the ethos and values of climbing. For example, values of strength, discipline, hardship, perseverance and perhaps historic associations of the heroic leader (Barker, 2001) were prevalent in the narratives that surround mountaineering and (so I'm told) abound as prevalent discourses within this community. Further, the circumstances of the leader in this context are also very different from organisational contexts. The earlier quote related to bereavement, describing the risks involved in leading expeditions, is a clear example of contextual expectations of specific contexts.

A significant proportion of the context of Chris's engagement in mountain climbing and expeditions was in the afterglow of Hunt's successful expedition of Everest, reflecting a sense of his experiences coming out of a time of heroic exploits through the sixties and seventies. His desire not to follow a managerial career or a career in the army reflected a spirit of the age for freedom and exploration and this came through strongly in the interview and reflects his narrative identity (Ezzy, 1998) in his books. In essence, Chris's leadership learning is greatly influenced by the context of his time and the community of practice (Wenger, 1998) in which he participated. The contextual experiences of leading in distinct communities at particular points in time will be shown to be of great significance to learning how to lead for the managers who participated in this study.

Summary

The purpose of providing analysis of the underlying influences on Chris's leadership learning and the context in which this occurred is to illustrate and provide a first qualitative glimpse of a range of themes that shape the arguments of this book. First, and most striking, is the dominance of informal and naturalistic influences shaping leadership learning. Although Chris felt he had learnt to lead, he explicitly commented that he had not been taught to lead; in fact he stressed that the process at Sandhurst did not influence his actions. Rather it was the milieu of events, incidents and episodes in contact with others, in particular circumstances, that shaped his approach to leading. The informal and underlying influences are not necessarily apparent. For example, Chris was not clear on how notable people had influenced his leadership practice; he was aware that they had but did not place emphasis on processes of observational learning at the time, and arguably did so only through the interview process as a result of a constructed reflexive conversation. The argument in this book, which is of importance (to me), is that even Chris who personifies a leader identity and who sees himself justifiably as being able to speak on the subject, resulting in spellbound audiences, is not prominently aware of the underlying influences and how these may have combined to shape his leadership learning.

Second, the analysis of Chris's lived experience illustrates the rich depth and nuances of research that is required in order to understand better the opaque nature of the phenomenon that is leadership learning. This learning occurs within the milieu of life and often we cannot put our finger on the underlying nature of the influences that constitute this complex process. Arguably, and very understandably, such opaque influences may lead us to suggest that leaders are born and not made.

It is hoped that this brief examination provides a useful illustration of the style, structure and emphasis of the discussion, revolving around underlying learning processes and their influence, set within contexts. These ultimately shape the contributions to and arguments of this book that people do learn to develop their leadership practice but they are often simply unaware of how this occurred.

Theoretical context informing on leadership learning

The theoretical terrain that informs on leadership learning is constructed from three aspects: the constructed nature of leadership, management learning and the perspectives of leadership development. This discussion will be related to Chris's story.

Constructed nature of leadership

The image of leadership created by Chris reflects a number of perspectives that are developed in Chapter 2, for example:

- Leadership centred on a heroic, gifted and charismatic individual able to induce transformational change through follower-enhanced motivation, commitment and enhanced collective self-efficacy.
- Leadership as a process of attribution from followers.
- Leadership as a romantic myth where society constructs and constitutes acts of leadership to sustain institutionalised notions of control.

To an extent Chris exhibited all of the above perspectives in the interview. Certainly the gifted hero is at the centre of the story, as is the attribution of followers confirming his identity as leader. Similarly the notion of leadership as a societal construct, constituted through the telling of stories, is strongly echoed by the example of Hunt, and in fact in the telling of Chris's own story. In essence, the vignette of Chris reveals the complexity of the constructed nature of leadership and difficulties of understanding the phenomenon that is constituted both universally and locally (Sjostrand, Sandberg & Tyrstrup, 2001). Such complexity creates problems for efficacy of leadership development interventions. Barker emphasises the point by stating the following:

> How can we train leaders if we don't know what leadership is ... People who emerge from these training programs rarely become what anyone might define as good leaders.
>
> (1997: 343)

Barker develops an argument for a need to understand the social system in which leadership occurs and how it is socially constructed. Emphasising again the importance of context and the need for contextualisation, James and Burgoyne comment:

> Leadership development is not separate from the philosophy of leadership in the organisation ... there is clearly no one size fits all.
>
> (2001: 10)

Chris's perspective on leadership is heavily influenced by contexts in which his leadership experience has been enacted. The crucible of his leadership learning has been through mountaineering: the people he has engaged with, the expeditions he has led and the situated nuances of the language, norms, values and ethics of mountain leadership. Leadership in Chris's world may have resonance for us, but the complexity of mountain leadership perhaps is not capable of being expressed. The learning, often tacitly absorbed, may only be inferred – but to enhance inference necessitates a qualitative, in-depth understanding of the contextual and systemic processes influencing such leadership learning.

Leadership and management learning

Although limited scholarly attention has been given to understanding processes by which leadership is learnt in organisational contexts, there is ample discussion on the broader theme of management learning, and it is from such work that this book will draw upon to utilise concepts, models and metaphors that may help reveal processes shaping leadership learning.

The foundation for work on the informal development of managers began in the late seventies, in the UK, by Burgoyne and Stuart (1977) built by Burgoyne and Hodgson (1983), Davies and Easterby-Smith (1984), Cox and Cooper (1989), Marserick (1988) and Marserick and Watkins (1990). The findings of this group have become central citations for subsequent papers and texts on leadership development. In parallel and of a complementary nature was research entitled *Lessons of Experience*, published in North America (McCall, Lombardo & Morrison, 1988) which cited and built upon Davies and Easterby-Smith's (1984) research, and was further extended by McCall (1998, 2004) and Hill (2003). Both groups of scholars on either side of the Atlantic confirmed that managers appear to learn how to manage and lead through informal in-depth line experiences rather than through formal development interventions; Chris's experiences echo this point.

However, all of the above-mentioned studies did not seek to separate leadership learning from management learning. It may be that similar or identical processes do shape leadership learning and management learning, but there is a dearth of specific empirical studies on leadership learning at the level of lived experience that clarifies this issue.

Leadership development: Practitioner's gold shoe searching for an academic Cinderella

> There is considerably greater interest among leadership development practitioners but surprisingly little scholarly interest in the topic.
>
> (Lowe & Gardner, 2000: 495)

Lowe and Gardner (2000) are emphasising the point that practitioner activity is ahead of academic study. In a sense, the limited level of research activity has not established academic foundations that inform on leadership development practice. Arguably the reverse is the case with practice leading the debate. The interest in leadership development reflects a sense of asymmetry between practitioners and academics:

- External consultants and HRM managers seek to develop interventions to create leadership; they both have a vested interest in the necessity of succeeding and matching stakeholder expectations of developing a cadre of leaders that can stimulate growth and arrest malaise and decline. Enormous investment of resources, most particularly time and money, are consumed in creating programmes of development whose efficacy is highly equivocal (Barker, 1997). Conger confirms that leadership development is impoverished in its depth of contextualised application, questioning the processes utilised in training programmes for being outdated and doubtful in terms of efficaciously producing leaders; he comments:

The art of leadership development is still in its infancy.

(1998: 57)

- Academics show relatively little desire to understand the processes and systems shaping leadership learning (Conger, 1998). Lowe and Gardner (2000) outline areas for future activity that seek to understand how leadership is developed within organisational or societal systems. The encouraged area of focus of Lowe and Gardner is on,

the understudied processes by which organisational systems can enhance development ... By learning more about systematic developmental processes, researchers can strengthen the link between leadership development systems and required managerial competencies and thereby enhance practice.

(2000: 495)

A similar process perspective is implored by Day (2000), who, along with Conger (1998), is highly doubtful whether programmes, described as leadership development, have been distinguished from management development. As a consequence they both suggest that the lack of efficacious outcome is reflected in the limited focus on leadership generally and specifically to understanding how leaders learn leadership (Day, 2000).

Summary

Leadership is a contextually shaped process, and leadership learning draws from such contextualisation. Studies from management learning suggest that there is a consensus that managers learn informally within their contexts and through the activities they participate in. We do not, however, know whether leadership learning is distinctively different from management learning. Despite the enormous industry in leadership development and desire for the enhancement of leadership skills, the academic community has not been particularly exercised to understand the phenomenon of leadership learning. This may, in large part, reflect historic research orientations towards large samples and quantitative examinations when there is a palpable need for contextualised appreciation of underlying influences on tacitly acquired leadership practice.

Methodological context of leadership learning

The predominant approach to leadership and leadership development research has been positivist, seeking to build or disprove theories that are capable of being consistent and replicable across all situations. Alvesson and Wilmott (1996) argue passionately that in the past, historic positivist epistemological perspectives have led to limited progress in defining and developing understanding of both leadership and processes of leadership learning. These approaches have been criticised for their 'snap shot' (rather than developmental) and reductionist (rather than systemic) perspectives.

Such criticism of positivism has generated a call, coherent with that described under the preceding section on understanding leadership, for a process and systemic perspective at the contextual level of the individual (Yukl, 1989a; Bryman, 1996, 2004; Parry, 1998; Conger, 1998, 2004), constructing a detailed understanding through qualitative research approaches (notably Parry, 1998; Conger, 1998).

A *process* perspective is considered within this study to be a systemic interaction of phenomena that appear to influence leadership learning. The word *process* has been emphasised as it is significant to this book. It focuses our attention on interacting influences occurring over an extended time span. The temporal feature of a processual perspective is central to leadership learning through lived experience. The examples provided by Chris illustrate such processual influences, namely notable people, events and incidents, situated learning within particular contexts, aspirations to lead and identity construction in 'becoming' a leader. Examining leadership, Chapter 2, concludes with an argument that leadership can be seen as a process. As such arguments will be developed illustrating that leadership and leadership learning are two sides of the same coin – each constructs the other.

Previous studies on leadership learning have not sought to understand and explain this phenomenon in a systemic, temporal and contextualised manner. The arguments of this book will build from 40 separate narratives of lived experience which explore and reveal influences on individual learning. These narratives of managers will be grouped into public, private and self-employed, as well as a comparison of processes influencing leadership learning between men and women. Such influences on individual learning will be compared across the groups in order to identify similarities and contrasts from which explanations will be developed in reference to the contexts from which they are drawn.

Prior to exploring the research questions that this book answers, it is important to outline the broad contextual environment in which the study is situated – the importance of leadership to organisations and to policymakers.

The environment influencing leadership learning

Many organisations view leadership as a source of competitive advantage which they have been and will continue to invest in, developing both the human and the social capital within their organisations (Conger, 1996; Drath, 1998; Moxley, 1998; Day, 2000). Leadership is seen as a key ingredient for future success and ranked first as a priority for organisations (CIMA, 2000). The scale of investment into leadership and management development has become an industry in itself with enormous impact on organisational resources. Numerous commentators echo the perceived importance of leadership to organisational success (Conger, 1998; Lowe & Gardner, 2000; James & Burgoyne, 2001; Fulmer & Wagner, 1999) in both the US and the UK.

In the UK, the Council for Excellence in Management and Leadership (CEML)[5] carried out a substantial programme of work with the following overall aim:

> To ensure that the UK is able to develop the managers and leaders of the future to match the best in the world. To sustain the UK's competitive performance, we must achieve this in both the public and the private sectors.
>
> (CEML, 2002: 2)

The Council's remit was to identify key issues for management and leadership in order to develop a management development strategy for the UK, which incorporated such issues as embedding management and leadership development in small businesses; recommendations for the development of management and leadership skills in individual career development; and a strategy for developing management and leadership skills in the UK. The recommendations (CEML, 2001) focused on disseminating best practice through centres of excellence; establishing leadership best practice networks; expanding the provision of leadership and management modules in 'Investors In People' (IIP), undergraduate and MBA programmes; and encouraging small and medium enterprises' (SME) involvement and interest. The various reports (about 30 have been published) and associated recommendations quintessentially reflect a dominant perspective of developing leaders through formal and quasi-formal interventions.[6]

In essence the need for leadership development was firmly established. The recommended solution was to continue with the formal approaches. In part this can be understood from a pragmatic perspective in terms of being able to communicate clear and feasible interventions regardless of issues of efficacy. Thus CEML's interpretation sought universal solutions to a complex contextualised problem.

This issue of contextualisation is echoed by Conger (1992, 1998 and 2004); Day (2000) and Lowe and Gardner (2000), who maintain that interventions based on best practice of one organisation will invariably require amendment to reflect another organisation's internal context. For example, James and Burgoyne suggested that differences between public and private sectors were seen to be substantial in limiting direct utilisation of best practice interventions from the private to the public sectors without such contextualisation (2001).

In a similar and reinforcing manner, research into leadership development has been most critical of formal interventions on grounds of efficacy (Wexley & Baldwin, 1986; Conger, 1998; Day, 2000; and Lowe & Gardner, 2000) and an associated issue of measurement (notably Burgoyne et al., 2004; but also Day, 2000; and again Lowe & Gardner, 2000). Equivocal issues of efficacy are encapsulated in a sense of belief that it is a good thing to be investing in leadership development. Burgoyne et al. (2004) are critical of such a belief syndrome and argues that it is too often the norm for programmes to be implemented without regard to designing evaluation in the initial programme structure. It is perhaps understandable that significant questions repeatedly occur concerning issues of efficacy of interventions when we do not have a detailed understanding of how underlying influences shape leadership learning and the construction of leadership practice in particular contexts.

CEML similarly examined issues of leadership development in small business (CEML, 2002, building upon Perren & Grant, 2001) and identified that there was a major issue of mismatch between demand and supply (ibid.; CEML, 2002). Although explicit actions were recommended, particularly aimed at stimulating interest among small business owners, interventions reflected similar approaches utilised in large organisations, that is, mentoring and formal management courses. The issue of limited empirical understanding of leadership learning of owner managers was perhaps even starker than that of employed managers.

Finally, James and Burgoyne (2001) comment that dissemination of leadership development may be problematic, and the most significant intervention may simply be engaging people to think about the causes shaping leadership behaviour and identifying appropriate forms of behaviour that suit the context.

Summary – a paradox

Thus, drawing together the elements so far presented in this chapter highlights a paradox. Despite concerns over the efficacy of leadership development programmes, billions continue to be invested into leadership development intervention; yet there is a general consensus that managers appear to learn management and leadership through informal, accidental, naturalistic, everyday activities of their lived experiences.

The context is thus, of significant demand for the development of leadership within organisations from employers and politicians. Leadership development intervention remains transfixed towards formal approaches despite strong evidence that such programmes (even those identified as best practice) have significant question marks associated with efficacy – there remains very limited return for the investment. The scholarly consensus is that we learn leadership through naturalistic experiences that occur over a long period of time; akin to a form of apprenticeship (Kempster, 2006). Leadership learning and subsequent leadership practice is embedded in contexts. If we could understand more clearly the underlying influences on leadership learning within organisations, through an in-depth sectoral empirical study, we may be able to re-evaluate our thinking on addressing leadership development in particular sectors and thus, rethink design interventions.

How have managers learnt to lead?

Study evolution

The paradox described earlier has caused me concern for a number of years and was the catalyst for this study. In 1999 I had the good fortune to discuss with colleagues Julia Davies, John Burgoyne, Vivien Hodgson and Mark Easterby-Smith their interrelated work on leadership and management learning. The sense of dominance of informal naturalistic processes to leadership learning made great sense, personally, and had significant resonance in light of personal lived experience of seeking to lead my own business.

Delving more deeply into the extant literature only further enhanced the presence of this paradox and it was reassuring to read other commentators' concerns that research needs to be focused more deeply into lived experience to reveal more about underlying influences shaping leadership learning.

The calls for qualitative research ran concurrent with growing significant practitioner disquiet in the efficacy of the investment into leadership development in terms of developing better leaders. The CEML studies greatly helped to bring the research area into sharp focus. The need for leadership development in the UK was striking – yet CEML did not explore the underlying naturalistic influences on leadership learning. Did this reflect stakeholder interest; or perhaps the case had not been explicitly researched to argue for a systemic explanation of underlying influences on leadership learning … and notably how such an explanation can inform practice.

I had a strong personal need to know more about leadership learning and to be able to apply such knowledge to intervention design. The purpose of this book is to address the following:

- Explore, in depth, the influences of leadership learning at the level of lived experience and seek to reveal how leadership learning can be understood from a systemic perspective that draws upon underlying dynamics within particular contexts.
- Connect the insights of leadership learning with policy application and inform on leadership development interventions at the practitioner level.

Further these aims can be seen to relate closely to the underpinning puzzle: *At the level of lived experience, are there common influences on the leadership learning of managers; or is their idiosyncratic experience of a variety of contexts so varied that explanations can only be given at the level of the individual?*

More specifically there are questions that need to be answered if an explanation is to be given of how mangers learn to lead in different contexts. Explicitly:

- *What influences shape leadership learning and how do these operate?*
- *How does context affect such influences on leadership learning?*

By addressing these two questions an argument will be suggested that explicates the emergence of a common set of underlying influences on leadership learning, as well as contrasting different experiences of leadership learning between men and women, and between the employed and the self-employed.

Overview of the book

The book is essentially divided into three parts (Part I is this introduction). Part II examines what we currently know about leadership learning. Part III extends this knowledge by exploring leadership learning of 40 managers from a variety of backgrounds. The book is written to be read either from cover to cover (for the complete and griping unfolding story); or for someone to select aspects they wish to understand in greater depth. For example, if someone wishes to compare their own lived experience of learning to lead with others experiences in the public or private sectors, or between men and women or between the employed and the self employed, Chapter 7 is structured to allow selection of relevant cases to the area of interest. To help in such a process of comparison, Chapter 6 has been written to enable someone to explore their lived experience of leadership learning in the same way as the managers examined in this book. Building from such a process of personal comparison, the explanation of leadership learning in Chapter 8 can be further critiqued along with the recommendations for deepening leadership learning outlined in Chapter 9. It may be with this heightened personal reflection that the theoretical arguments outlined in Part II could be revisited to explore: what is leadership and can we learn this? (Chapter 2); how do we learn? (Chapter 3); and what is understood about leadership development? (Chapter 4).

To provide further guidance each chapter is briefly introduced below.

PART II

Chapter 2 – What is leadership? Can it be learnt?

A discussion unfolds which argues that leadership can be seen as a process of influence and that such influence is shaped from four perspectives: leader, follower, situation and relationships. The learning of these leadership perspectives is complex in the sense that it is constructed from both universal perspectives, such as implicit leadership theories, and local, contextualised meanings. An integrative model is suggested to illustrate the integration of these four perspectives as systemic process perspective of leadership.

Chapter 3 – How do we learn?

The practice of leadership is learnt in situations. This chapter seeks to understand how such individual learning of a social phenomenon may occur. It builds out from an individual perspective to embrace experiential, observed and situated learning, identity, salience and memory. The chapter illustrates how individual learning of leadership is centrally a process of social exchanges within particular situations.

Chapter 4 – What is understood about leadership development?

The chapter outlines the case for the predominance of naturalistic informal development and illustrates a practitioner movement from formal towards structured informal activities. The conflation of literature on leadership and management development is highlighted affirming the need for specific attention to leadership learning. The chapter concludes by suggesting that there is a consensus that leadership learning is learnt through experiences but that there is a lack of in-depth understanding of the underlying causes shaping such learning.

Chapter 5 – So what do we know about leadership learning?

A short chapter that is a synthesis of the discussion from Chapters 2, 3 and 4. It draws the discussion together with a model of leadership learning. This model will be revisited in Part III.

PART III

Chapter 6 – How to reveal leadership learning

This chapter explains in detail the construction of a method for enabling managers to reveal their lived experience of leadership learning. Too often qualitative research has been labelled as 'journalism' and lacking validity (Silverman, 1997) and it has been a central concern that the arguments of the book are constructed on a robust methodological foundation. Without which it would be problematic in terms of validity to address an explanation of how managers learn to lead. The chapter briefly explores how four groups are constructed and examined; these groups are the public sector, the private sector, women managers and owner-managers. The chapter has been structured to encourage and guide someone to undertake the process outlined to help themselves explore their leadership learning.

Chapter 7 – Exploring leadership learning through the four cases

The four groups are examined in turn from the perspective of an individual case. This is to allow someone to examine the detailed experience of a manager and, if they so wish, compare this to their own lived experience. It is hoped that these cases would stimulate reflection and perhaps provide a vicarious learning opportunity – particularly for people at the earlier stages of their leadership careers. The four cases are compared and reveal a clear set of influences on leadership learning that are prominent with employed managers but less apparent in the lived experiences of the owner-managers. Again the most prominent contrasts are between the men and women and significantly between the owner-managers and the employed managers.

Chapter 8 – Towards an explanation of leadership learning

The chapter is spilt into two parts. Part A examines processes of leadership learning in greater detail by integrating evidence for the findings into intrapersonal and interpersonal processes influencing leadership learning. Both sets of processes are drawn together to create an explanation of underlying common processes argued to be an emergent property that through its integration, is more than the sum of its parts. Through Part A an explanation of the identified underlying influences shaping leadership learning are addressed and synthesised in a model to illustrate the argument. Part B seeks to contextualise the discussion to identify how the different contexts of the groups modify an explanation of leadership learning. Most striking is the different explanations of leadership learning of women managers and the owner-managers. The chapter concludes by addressing the low-level influence of formal interventions to leadership learning; this conclusion provides a link to policy and educative practice described in the final chapter.

Chapter 9 – Conclusion

Drawing together the arguments and explanations from Chapter 8, the final chapter summarises the explanation of how managers learn to lead and outlines arguments illustrating significantly different experiences of managerial leadership learning between men and women and between employed and self-employed managers. The policy and educative opportunities that emerge from this study are outlined, as are suggestions to guide individual development for graduates and experienced managers. Additionally an insight is provided for HR managers to consider the method used in this book as an alternative to the ubiquitous psychometric instruments for recruiting and selecting leaders. Finally, an example of leadership development practice is included, the LEAD programme. This illustrates the application of the ideas from this book on leadership development of 67 owner-managers.

It is hoped that by the end of the book someone will have been able to explore their own lived experience of leadership and deepened their understanding of how they have learnt to lead through applying the ideas from the book. It is further hoped that they would be in a position to have identified aspects that may help further advance the development of their leadership practice.

What do I mean by leadership practice?

The word practice has been mentioned many times so far in this opening chapter and will be mentioned many more times throughout this book. It perhaps seems axiomatic as to what this means, but a brief clarification may be useful. Generally, practice is defined as a local activity which generates specific outcomes. Practice and culture are interrelated (i.e. both informing and being informed by the other) but the two are not the same phenomenon (Schatzki & Knorr-Cetina, 2001). Practice can be understood both as explicit activities and routines as well as the tacit and implicit assumptions that guide local action (Orr, 1996).[7]

Building on these points, in this book I use the term practice to relate to the microactivities of action. Such activities are shaped through cultural and social assumptions and beliefs at both a societal and local (organisational) level. Practice draws on technical as well as social knowledge. It is both a skill and an identity, perhaps even a craft – learnt formally and informally – but predominately through participation in local contexts: akin to an apprenticeship. Leadership practice is thus, the day-to-day enactment of seeking to lead in a particular context. With forward reference to Chapter 2, and the definitions of leadership that will be given, oriented towards a socially embedded relational process, I suggest that such a process could be seen as 'sense-giving'. In this definitional context, leadership practice is the everyday enactment of seeking to influence peoples understanding, assumptions, expectations, aspirations and purposes about the context in which they operate and the work they undertake.

The emphasis on exploring contextualised lived experience to be outlined in Chapter 6 describes the method used to enable the managers interviewed to begin to understand the interrelationship of their leadership learning with their leadership practice. In essence, they saw that both were 'two sides of the same coin' – one informing the other.

Part II

2
What Is Leadership?
Can It Be Learnt?

Warren Bennis has wonderfully captured the essence of leadership as being 'like beauty, it's hard to define but you know it when you see it' (1989: 1). Our ability to judge what is beautiful is learnt through our lives but we struggle to understand how such personal judgment is acquired. The complexity of the phenomenon of leadership and the obscurity of the sources from whence it is learnt tend to lean our orientation to suggesting the people who are born to lead. This chapter will outline the case for the argument that leadership is a socially constructed process and, as such, it is learnt through our social interactions. Leadership appears not to have certainty of definition but is ever present in daily usage and is understood, constructed and practiced in an idiosyncratic way. In this sense, leadership practice is learnt, but importantly, not necessarily in a conscious manner. The inability of scholars to agree on a universal definition is testimony to this socially constructed and learnt process.

There are considerable ranges of theories drawn from combinations of variables that often compete for attention as an explanation of leadership, reflecting the positivist epistemic origins of leadership research.[1] Paradoxically, such enormous research energy has generated a degree of confusion in search for truth about leadership through a concentration on specific areas that are of interest to academic specialists (Steers et al., 2000).

Earliest debates have been on the individual leader, in terms of attributes and behavioural traits that contribute to, or seem to be associated with, effective leadership. During the past 20 years, there has been increasing recognition of the sterility of this approach, criticised for its snap shot (rather than developmental) and reductionist (rather than systemic) perspectives (Alvesson, 1996). An alternative paradigm has emerged in the field of social construction, where the focus has shifted from generic individual qualities to leadership as a process of social influence and a systemic view of the actors and the context involved in leadership (Dansereau et al., 1995; Hunt & Ropo, 1995; Yukl, 1998; Emrich, 1999; Parry, 2001; Bryman, 2004; Grint, 2005; Jackson & Parry, 2008). The emergence of alternative perspectives and methodological approaches from a social constructionist perspective (Sjostrand et al., 2001) gives hope to building some fundamental transitions in thinking (Overman, 1996) that may bear fruit in terms of revealing more of the learnt and constructed phenomenon of leadership.[2]

Traditional approaches to the treatment of leadership tend to follow a broadly chronological structure moving from the earliest theories on leadership and progressing to current perspectives – most notable in this respect are the popular texts of Bass (1990) and Yukl (2001). It is the intention of this chapter to draw together a considerable range of literature, often from a number of competing paradigmatic perspectives, and adopt an unconventional examination of leadership.

This chapter will examine leadership from three perspectives: leader, follower and situational. Through these perspectives it is argued that the extant literature can be examined within a holistic integrated framework to avoid 'leadership déjà vu' (Hunt & Dodge, 2001) and perhaps create as Weick (1995) describes 'vu jade' (never seen this before). Further, through such holistic integration, theories that may have previously appeared disconnected and competitive can in fact be seen as complementary explanations of leadership. Finally, a holistic appreciation will give a greater integrated understanding of leadership and how its practice is enacted and situated.

Such integration is represented as a framework guiding the discussion of three perspectives of leadership illustrated in Figure 2.1; this framework will appear at the start of each section as a symbolic signpost.

The use of a centric perspective allows thematic discussion to develop, and arguably cohere together, around key elements constituting leadership, namely leader, follower and the situation. However, it needs to be noted that it is not the intention of the integrative framework to create a scientific explanation or metatheory of leadership, but rather to illustrate that leadership can be seen as oriented around these predominant themes and illuminated from a particular lens (Morgan, 1986).

The chapter is structured into four sections: leadership definitions; leader-centric; follower-centric; situation-centric concluding with an

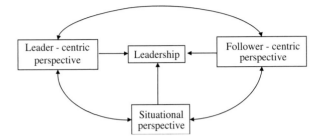

Figure 2.1 Conceptual framework of Chapter 2

integrative, processual and holistic perspective of leadership. The chapter progression follows a broad movement from leadership as a universal concept towards leadership being locally constructed. A dominant perspective that runs throughout the chapter is that leadership is a social construct that is sustained and elaborated by successive generations (Archer, 1995). For it to be sustained (and elaborated) it must be learnt – not necessarily in a conscious manner – but learnt nonetheless. It is from this viewpoint that the chapter is written.

Prior to examining the three centric perspectives of leader, follower and situation the chapter first explores leadership definitions.

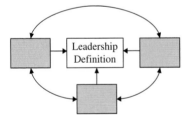

Definitions of leadership

> There are almost as many different definitions of leadership as there are persons who have attempted to define the concept.
>
> (Bass, 1990: 11)

The phenomenon of leadership is argued to have global presence, but appears to have a variety of attributes and is elusive in definitional clarity (House et al., 2004). In this book I argue that such variation is contextually derived. There is an emerging consensus that at a very high level of abstraction, leadership is argued to be a 'social and relational influence process that occurs within a social system' (Parry, 1998: 87; consolidating discussion from a range of commentators. In addition, such a view has been more recently echoed by Osborne, Hunt & Jauch, 2002; Bess & Goldman, 2001; Zaccaro, Rittman & Marks, 2001). Key aspects of significance are the emphasis on social, contextual, proc-essual and relational aspects of leadership. This sense of consensus is mostly informed by a leader-centric perspective. Barker (2001) seeks to extend the influence process beyond cause and effect leader–follower relationships to a view of leadership as a more systemic interconnected process of complex reciprocal relationships of people and institutions, process and outcomes (Barker, 2001).

Thus the phenomenon of leadership, whether it is centred on the individual as leader, follower or constituted from the social situation, may be perceived to be captured in the following two definitions that are broadly systemic and centre on influence and interaction:

> The process of making sense of what people are doing together so that people will understand and be committed.
>
> (Drath & Palus, 1994: 4)

> Leadership is an interaction between two or more members of a group that involves a structuring or restructuring of the situation and the perceptions and expectations of the members.
>
> (Bass, 1990: 19)

Both definitions emphasise notions of shaping interpretations of the situation. As such leadership can be strongly argued to be a process of sense-making (Smircich & Morgan, 1982; Pye, 2005). I would go further and suggest that leadership is more a process of 'sense-giving'; it is seeking to shape the sense-making processes of others. Viewing leadership as sense-giving embraces leader, follower and situational perspectives of leadership. For example, sense-giving may well ema-nate from a hierarchical leader. Equally it may come from the problem solving of the follower – giving emphasis to ideas of distributed lead-ership. Leadership as sense-giving goes beyond the individual leader or followers; for example, it speaks to notions of embedded practices providing certain individuals with authority to shape sense-making of others.

The next section will address the leader-centric perspective.

Leader-centric perspective

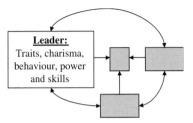

Bass (1990) claimed that the origins of discursive evidence related to leadership extend back to the Egyptian civilisation illustrated by hieroglyphics for leadership (Seshemet), leader (Seshemu) and follower (Shemsu). The first English word for leader appears to be *ledere*, which is formed from the Middle English *leden* meaning 'to cause to go with one', drawn from an Icelandic derivative *leidha* meaning the 'person in front' which referred to an individual who could guide the ships through the leads in the pack ice (Cammack, 2003).

The leader-centric perspective is associated with the qualities and characteristics of an individual, namely traits, charisma, behaviour, power and skills. These five elements will be integrated with an emerging dominant leader-centric model known as 'new leadership' (and increasingly 'authentic leadership' Avolio & Gardner, 2005).

'New leadership' – transformational leadership

Burns (1978) first coined the phrase 'transformational leadership' when he compared this phenomenon to transactional leadership. Bass (1990: 319) defined transactional leadership as:

> The marginal maintenance of performance and the substitution of one goal for another. A process of reducing resistance to particular actions.

In contrast, transformational leadership was seen as:

> Raising followers to a greater awareness about the issues of consequence requiring vision, self-confidence and inner strength to argue for what is right and good, not for what is popular or acceptable according to established wisdom of the time.

Transformational leadership is perceived to centre on personal values and beliefs where a leader operates out of a deeply held personal value system that includes justice and integrity (Burns, 1978; Bass, 1985). It is towards notions of justice and integrity that the theory has been recently elaborated to become 'authentic leadership' (Avolio & Gardner, 2005 – see the special edition of the *Leadership Quarterly* (2005, 16 (3)) for a full review). Transformational leadership is very much associated with the individual leader and follower affectation and is seen to operate at different levels in organisations (Katz & Kahn, 1978; Bass & Yokochi, 1991); although it is considered to be more prominent and effective at senior levels (Bass & Avolio, 1993; Parry & Sinha, 2005). In essence, transformational leadership is seen to be an influencing process of peers, followers and superiors, occurring in everyday acts of ordinary people to elevate people from their everyday selves to their better selves (Yukl, 1998). Transformational leadership behaviour has been grouped around four characteristics:[3]

(1) Idealised influence – charisma
(2) Inspirational motivation – vision and purpose
(3) Individualised consideration
(4) Intellectual stimulation

The four characteristics are perceived to interact jointly to influence followers (Bass & Avolio, 1990a).

In the short life of the theory, a considerable level of research attention has sought to show that transformational leadership enhances follower motivation (Hater & Bass, 1988; Bass & Avolio, 1993; Masi & Cooke, 2000), organisational productivity (Masi & Cooke, 2000) and achievement orientation (Cooke & Szumal, 1993). Conversely, transactional leadership has been found to suppress productivity and suppress follower motivations (Masi & Cooke, 2000; Parry & Sinha, 2005).[4] There is much support for, and little criticism of, the notion of transformational leadership thus far. For example, in the field of ethics the notion of transactional and transformational leadership has been used to frame interpretation of ethical leadership (see for example, Kanungo & Mendonca, 1996; Price, 2000; Kanungo, 2001; McAlister & Ferrell, 2005). The impact of transformational leadership is argued to have been responsible for a resurgence of academic interest in leadership research; so significant in fact, that these theories have become known as 'new leadership' (Parry & Sinha, 2005).

Can someone learn to become a transformational leader? Certainly the underpinning theories associated with consideration, role modelling and intellectual stimulation seek to explain what to focus on to enhance performance. The subtleties of how to perform an appropriate balance of transactional and transformational leadership in particular situations is rather complex. The method of learning aspects of each element is primarily through lived experience; it is not the norm to learn it in the formal classroom settings – chapters 3 and 4 provide the foundations to this assertion. However, Parry and Sinha (2005) argue that training can enhance capability to conduct transformational leadership, although such learning has to be highly contextualised. Their argument is that the naturalistic learning will often generate an inappropriate balance of transactional and transformational behaviours and training can bring the notion of balance into sharp focus.

The characteristics associated with transformational leadership appear to encapsulate many sub-theories of the leader-centric perspective that have been developed in isolation. Such research includes charisma, behavioural and style typologies, power, contingency approaches and leadership skills. Each of these very broad areas of research will be briefly explored. First, however, we need to address the ageless question that revolves around trait theory of leadership.

Are leaders born or made?

Chronologically, traits were the first significant area to be explored in the search for an understanding of leadership and can be defined as 'a variety of individual attributes, including aspects of personality, temperament, needs, motives and values' (Yukl, 1998: 234). An early supposition was that if leaders are endowed with superior qualities that differentiate leader from follower then it should be possible to identify these traits.

Do traits matter? On the one hand, traits reflect certain characteristics that improve leadership effectiveness and are repeated regardless of context (Van Fleet & Yukl, 1986a). On the other hand, it is argued that traits only endow people with the potential for leadership (Kirkpatrick & Locke, 1991). Criticisms of the lists approach to trait effectiveness are associated with limited explanations as to how traits are related to leadership behaviour, particularly the interrelated nature of the different traits and their combinations and trade-offs subject to contextual difference (Yukl, 1998); for example, the balance between risk and caution or toughness and compassion.[5]

Importantly though, in this equivocal debate over the importance of traits, is the notion of born or made. There appears to be considerable evidence that traits are jointly determined by learning and by an inherited capacity to gain satisfaction from particular types of experiences

(Bouchard et al., 1990). In this respect the traits that may encourage the development of a leadership orientation may be the same that encourage the development of an artist, or a musician or even an academic! The key is not so much the traits but rather the stimuli that shapes the learning towards leadership. For example, Grint (2005: 44) argues that in World War I Hitler was perceived to lack necessary leadership traits by his commanding officer. It was as a result of regaining his sight through being asked to believe in something (to address shell shock) that he felt it was his destiny to reconstruct a superior Germany. His faith in a destiny reshaped his behaviour.

Aspects of self-belief and a sense of destiny are interrelated with the notion of charisma. The emergence of charismatic theories of leadership in the last two decades have begun to make more explicit the links and outcomes between traits, behaviours and impact on follower motivations.

Charismatic leadership – 'gift of divine grace'

The concept of charisma and leadership became associated through the writings of Max Weber (1947) that identified five components (Trice & Beyer, 1986): person with extraordinary gifts; the context of a crisis; radical solution to a crisis; followers who are attracted to the exceptional person; and validation of the above through repeated experiences of success. These five elements illustrate leader, follower and situational aspects that shape the construction of leadership, and as a consequence charisma will be addressed from all three perspectives. There are three dominant theories of charismatic leadership: the first known as self-concept theory of leadership (Shamir et al., 1993), will be described under follower perspectives of leadership; the other two are associated with the leader-centric perspective – House (1977) and Conger and Kanungo (1987).

The contribution House made to leadership studies was to draw together traits, behaviour, influence and situational conditions into a comprehensive theory (Yukl, 1998). Further, he established charismatic leadership as a relational process of influence seen to have a profound effect on follower's motivations and relationship with the leader. House (1977) extended the theory beyond traits influencing follower behaviour, by identifying the significance of context and particularly the link to crisis – to be explored within situation-centric leadership.

Conger and Kanungo (1987) suggest that charisma is an attributional phenomenon, where followers observe certain behaviours of a leader and associate such behaviours with prototypical attributes of leadership, namely self-sacrifices and personal risks incurring high costs to achieve the vision; trust generated by concern for followers over self-interest; self-confidence and high self-efficacy – belief that the leader can attain the shared objective

The primary attribution process (identified later by Conger, 1989) was seen to be personal identification with the leader and, in particular, internalisation of the values and beliefs about the work that can become a source of intrinsic motivation (Yukl, 1998). Like House, Conger and Kanungo connected follower attribution with the situation and argued that additional to the above attributes, a set of conditions need to be present for charismatic attribution to occur.

The above two models of charismatic leadership catalysed interest towards a broader model of leader-centric leadership which has become the central foundation within 'new leadership'.

Can charisma be learnt? Difficult if this is a 'divine gift' as Weber (1947) described it. If charismatic leadership is seen as an attributable affect, rather than a set of qualities someone possesses then it is possible for a leader to consider how he or she may influence such attribution. Conger (1989) advocates that certain conditions need to be present for charismatic attribution to occur. These can be cultivated not just by the leader but also by the followers – such a process will be described shortly in both the follower and situational perspectives to leadership. Although Conger has identified unconventionality as an attributional dimension, caution is encouraged to leaders who suddenly decide to look different, for example, by wearing a hat, a bow tie or brightly coloured socks! The context and the relationship and expectations of leadership behaviour in particular settings must be carefully understood.

Leadership behaviour

A number of key commentators (most notably Mintzberg, 1973; and more recently Yukl, 1998) have identified a variety of behavioural tax-onomies.[6] Such taxonomies have been shown to fall within two domi-nant areas of behaviour:

- Task, production or initiating structure
- Consideration, people or relations

These two dominant behaviours of task and consideration could be seen as metalevel behaviours and the taxonomy as sub-elements of these two factors.[7] There is considerable convergence and acceptance that mana-gerial behaviours, that centre around these two metalevel behaviours, are more likely to be effective where both task and consideration are related to the needs of the situation. Adair's (1983) work in this regard has greatly popularised the importance of identifying, moderating and balancing behaviour over a period of time with the needs of achieving the task alongside the needs of the team and the individual.

Leadership skills

Building out from the trait and behavioural perspectives but still within the leader-centric theme has been a very recent conceptualisation of leadership as the notion of skills and social problem solving (Mumford et al., 2000). The key tenet of leadership skills is a movement away from behaviour patterns towards capabilities and knowledge that make leadership possible (ibid.).

The focus of leadership here is centrally on the leader and their ability to address complex organisational issues, formulate a framework for problem solving, generate ideas and develop initial solution strategies. Wisdom is a key capability within this model developed out of leadership experience (McCauley et al., 1988; Ackerman, 1992; McCall, 1998) where the leader has developed self-objectivity, self-reflection and a systemic perspective (Arlin, 1990; Orwoll & Perlmutter, 1990; Sternberg, 1985, 1990) along with social perceptiveness (Zaccaro et al., 1991). It is argued that such social skills represent an 'essential step in getting subordinates to adopt a vision or a proposed solution plan' (1991: 20). Such leadership is not seen to be the province of a few gifted individuals but instead 'leadership is held to be potential in many individuals – a potential that emerges through experience and the capability to learn' (Mumford et al., 2000: 21).

Leadership and power

Connected with behaviour, as an influence process, is the impact of power. Brown (1999) described a dimension of leadership as a 'power broker' in which a leader distributes power to influence outcomes. At the heart of leadership is the interaction of power with influence conceptualised as having three distinct types of influence outcomes (Kelman, 1958):

- *Instrumental Compliance* – an ability to control rewards or punishment.
- *Internalisation* – followers become committed to leader's espoused proposals as they appear to be intrinsically desirable and relate to the followers' values, beliefs and self-image.

- *Identification* – followers identify with the leader in order to gain approval and achieve acceptance.

A combination of these influence outcomes can be seen to occur in charismatic and transformational behaviours where both ideals and attributional identification are part of the behavioural influence on followers. Influence of instrumental compliance can be seen to be associated with transactional leadership (Bass & Avolio, 1993) and is connected with *position power* – status associated with position gives power over someone of lower status through rewards and punishments (Fiedler et al., 1976). French and Raven's (1959) seminal work viewed position power as identified with reward, coercive and legitimate power. In contrast, charismatic and transformational leadership is seen to be more closely associated with *personal power* – attribution associated with an individual's attributes (Bass 1960, 1990; Yukl, 1989b); identified as referent and expert power (French & Raven, 1959).

Personal and position power (French & Raven, 1959) are seen to overlap and the combinations in reality make it difficult to distinguish between them (Yukl & Falbe, 1991). For example, a charismatic leader with strong referent power drawn from a follower's desire to identify with the leader may be, in part, associated with the legitimacy of the leader's position. If such legitimacy declines then the leader's attractiveness may also decline, influencing the referent status.[8]

McCall (1978) extends this view by introducing a contextual dimension to suggest that it is a combination of being in the right place at the right time with the right (power) resources that gives the greatest influence. The contextual perspective links power and influence to interpersonal relations beyond personal attributes of the leader.

Leadership and relationships

The issue of identification and relationships as part of the influence process within charismatic theory (House, 1977; Conger & Kanungo, 1987) has been developed into a body of theory, known as 'leader member exchange' – often referred to as LMX (Graen & Uhl-Bien, 1991). This theory seeks to explain relationships between a leader and a follower and represent a departure from the prevailing behavioural approach that leaders treated all subordinates the same (Brower et al., 2000).

In terms of leadership as a process of achieving shared goals through collective interests, the LMX theory provides a significant contribution to extending the leadership and transactional debate into multiple dyadic perspectives of the same group.[9] There is striking similarity in the strong dyadic relationships to the attributional characteristics of charismatic transformational leadership. Equally there is similarity to the transactional nature of weak dyadic relationships.[10] It is argued by Graen and Uhl-Bien (1991) that the life cycle relationship between leader and follower dyads appears to start on a transactional basis and with deepening reciprocal trust can develop into a transformational relationship.

Such difference of perspective draws the discussion in two directions: an idiosyncratic perspective of leader behaviour influenced by their lived experience in a myriad of contexts; and a broadening view away from the dominance of leader-centric influence and extended towards a follower-centric perspective of leadership. The above theoretical discussion on relationships extends the guiding model of leadership represented in Figure 2.2, by introducing a new component – that of relationships:

The amendment of the above framework to include 'relationships' as a separate element, places emphasis on its role in the distortion of perceptions and attributions of followers and leaders to each other. Viewing leadership as a socially constructed relational process of influence further emphasises the value of relationships as an important aspect of leadership (Uhl-Bien, 2003). There is very limited specific research on this important area within the field of leadership save for the work of Uhl-Bien (2003) and colleagues described above, and Collinson and Collinson's (2005) work on leader-led relations. Additionally, Shamir, Dayan-Horesh and Adler (2005) examined the use of a leader's biography in shaping the relationship between leader and follower(s). Finally, Gardner and Avolio (1998) (and similarly with Hogg, 2001; Sparrowe, 2005) suggest that leadership theory be extended to incorporate notions of identity forged through relationships. They

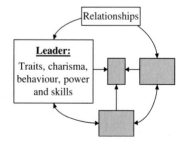

Figure 2.2   Relationships and leadership

suggest leader and follower identification encapsulate an interactive mutual process of constructing leadership in the form of a situated identity drawn, constructed and learnt in a particular context. Such processes will become most central to the findings and arguments of this book. Uhl-Bien (2003) advocates the notion of social relationships as an important aspect to be attended to in terms of leadership development.

The notion of leadership as a relationship acts as a bridge between leader-centric and follower-centric perspectives of leadership. The leader perspective is only a partial, but currently a rather dominant, view of leadership. The notion of leadership as an intentional influence process of a leader on followers does appear to integrate many sub-themes of the influence process. The notion of charismatic 'new leadership' is the most current and prevalent model of the leader perspective reflected in the dominance of published research in the *Leadership Quarterly* (Lowe & Gardner, 2000). The follower-centric perspective of leadership provides both complementary and contrasting perspectives.

The follower perspectives of leadership

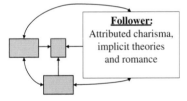

You cannot have a leader without followers.

(Anonymous)

Such a truism sits at the heart of the follower perspective of leadership, where the focus is on followers' needs for leadership. In comparison to the leader-centric perspective of leadership, there is relatively little research in this area (Graen & Uhl-Bien, 1995). Particular dimensions identified through the research of this perspective are: charismatic attribution; implicit theories of leadership; and the 'romance' of leadership. Each will be examined to create an additional perspective of leadership that reorientates the centre of gravity towards a balance of leader and follower aspects of leadership – described by Grint (2005) as putting the *ship* back into leadership. The first dimension of this orientation builds on from the charismatic literature of the leader-centric perspective and as such is a useful bridge between the two.

Charismatic attribution

The leader-centric perspective has introduced the notion of attribution associated with charismatic leadership theories. The follower-centric view orientates the attribution of charismatic qualities of the leader through comparison with themselves and their personal values, beliefs and needs. The work of Shamir, House and Arthur (1993) sought to provide a motivational explanation for the behavioural affects of charismatic leadership associated with the follower: arousal, enhancement of follower valances with respect to organisational goals, higher self-esteem, self-worth and self-efficacy and commitment. Most significant is the view of Shamir et al. (1993) that there is a reciprocal nature to charismatic leadership where followers identify a leader who is perceived to share core values and identities, with an emphasis on the construction of leadership from the group rather than a role imposed on the group (Shamir et al., 1993).

This notion of followers constructing leadership, related to their own needs, is further advanced from two perspectives: implicit theories of leadership, and the notion of the 'romance' of leadership.

Implicit theories of leadership

Implicit theories of leadership are personally learnt theories of leadership. This is most significant to an understanding of the follower-centric perspective and arguably most central to processes of leadership learning. Through interaction with leaders in particular situations, followers are seen to compare individual characteristics of leaders to their implicit leadership theories and, if the resemblance is similar, the follower then confirms leadership categorisation to the leader. (The work of Lord and colleagues is significant in this area: Phillips & Lord, 1982; Lord et al., 1984; Lord & Maher, 1990.) For example, a social role generates attribution – the greater the status, the higher perceived competence in leadership (Konst et al., 1999).

Associated research on the development of implicit theories anchors such learning about leadership as generated through early childhood experiences (Hall & Lord, 1995; Engle & Lord, 1997), particularly parental influence (Stark, 1992). For example, it has been shown that parents provide anticipatory socialisation about work and leadership, and act as the first notable leadership influence (Anderson, 1943; and later Keller, 1999). This area will be prominently developed in Chapter 4. Offerman et al. (1994) argues that implicit leadership theories can be generalised to eight dominant traits of: sensitivity, dedication, tyranny, charisma, attractiveness, masculinity, intelligence and strength.

Implicit theories of leadership can be seen to have very direct linkage to both dyadic and charismatic attributional models of leadership earlier described. But who creates leadership? Implicit leadership theories suggest that followers create the ideal leader and seek to connect an individual to this ideal. Through such connection a follower re-enforces his or her own identity and self-esteem, as the leader reflects himself/herself: in essence, the ideal leader is analogous to self (Keller, 1999). Additional to individual and dyadic relations, implicit leadership theory is also perceived to be a group phenomenon where a group can set an overall affective tone that influences the way followers process information about a leader (George, 1990; George & Brief, 1992; George & James, 1993; and related work of Hall & Lord, 1995).

The field of social cognition and its application to leadership studies is at an emergent state and Lord et al. argue that although 'the body of cognitive and social-cognitive research is quite compelling; this has not been verified in the leadership domain' (2001: 16). The potential of implicit theories of leadership to help inform on the follower-centric perspective is most useful. Additionally the role implicit theories have in understanding leadership, both from universal perspectives and local nuance understandings of specific contexts, is arguably most informative to leadership learning.

Do we all then create our own leadership? From the follower perspective of leadership, leaders are created in the minds of followers, and the individual and group affect of influencing a peer's interpretation of an individual as leader could be seen as part of the process of leadership construction. This point will be developed from the perspective of the 'romance of leadership', that perceives leadership as created by followers to meet their socially constructed expectations.

'Romance' of leadership

The romance of leadership is seen as a socially constructed desire for leadership emanating from our earliest experiences of social leadership within families (Kets de Vries, 1988; Kets de Vries & Millar, 1985; Stark, 1992; Hall & Lord, 1995). It is argued that such social construction of leadership has been shaped through generations from a biased perception that leadership, in the form of a dominant individual, shapes outcomes (Salancik & Pfeifer, 1977a; Salancik & Meindl, 1984; Meindl et al., 1985; Gemmill & Oakley, 1992; and more recently Barker, 2001).

The romance of leadership emphasises leadership as a social construction and,

> emphasises followers and their contexts for defining leadership itself and for understanding its significance. It loosens traditional assumptions about the significance of leaders to leadership phenomena.
>
> (Meindl, 1995: 330)

In essence, the relationship between leader and follower is less of a causal process of a leader influencing followers, but rather the behaviour of followers is under the influence of forces that govern the social construction of the phenomenon of leadership (Meindl, 1995). Thus leadership is revealed through the followers' interpretations of organisational reality.

Critical interpretations of the 'romantic' theory of leadership suggest very different approaches to leadership learning. Rather than focusing on leader behaviour as a process of influence (leader-centric approach), focus should be given to the manipulation of contexts; instead of the right personality, the focus is on the opportunity to create an appropriate impression; rather than leadership training, the focus would be on inculcating followers with the 'right way' to construct leadership (Meindl, 1995). This argument of follower-centric leadership can be seen to be closely associated with Smircich and Morgan's (1982) interpretation of leadership as the management of meaning.

The work by Meindl (1995) that consolidates earlier work of Pfeffer (1977), Calder (1977) and Meindl, Ehrlich and Dukerich (1985) on the follower-centric view of leadership dominates this perspective to which there is little academic criticism. However, and of significance, there is only passing reference to this perspective in, for example, two of the dominant leader-centric texts on leadership (Bass, 1990; Yukl, 1998) despite the implications that this view has on leadership learning. Perhaps this speaks to the dominance of the leader-centric view.

The 'romance of leadership', as a socially constructed phenomenon, connects closely with charismatic attribution theory (Conger & Kanungo, 1987) and self-concept theory (Shamir et al., 1993) and gives congruence and foundation to the follower-centric perspective of leadership. Further, leadership as a follower-centric phenomenon opens up critical questions around historic, cultural and socially constructed (Berger & Luckman, 1966) antecedents of the leader-centric dominant paradigm that is in everyday usage by practitioners and academics (Gemmill & Oakley, 1992; Barker, 2001).

Summary

This section has sought to make explicit the follower perspective of leadership through connecting a range of themes. The focus of the follower perspective, similar to leader-centric, is towards the universal, where notions of charismatic attribution, implicit theories and romantic ideals of leadership are seen to be generic; research has sought to demonstrate the presence of such phenomena associated with leadership. The follower perspective enriches and balances an understanding of leadership and perhaps shifts the centre of gravity away from the leader and to a more integrated understanding of how each informs on the other. The final perspective anchors the focus within the local context. Certainly both leader and follower perspectives inform on local contextualisation of leadership and the blend of the local with the universal is perhaps ever present. The final section begins to emphasise the importance of context to leadership learning through lived experience.

The situational perspective of leadership

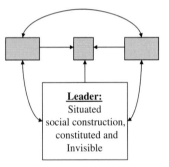

Leader:
Situated
social construction,
constituted and
Invisible

The final perspective on leadership is significantly less developed than the leader-centric view. This is particularly paradoxical as the impact of the situation on leadership is evident, albeit implicitly, in all research. A situational definition of leadership can be seen as a social process that defines reality in ways that make sense to the led, involving a dependency relationship in which individuals surrender their powers to interpret and define reality to others (Smircich & Morgan, 1982). The institutionalisation of this dependency relationship creates rights and obligations and confers roles within organisational contexts (ibid.). In essence, the situation creates leadership. This section draws together separate and disparate elements of a situational perspective of leadership as: leader-centric situational theories of leadership; contextual influence on charismatic leadership; constituted leadership – shaping followers' perspective of the environment; qualitative perspectives of situational leadership; and an exposure of 'invisible' leadership.

Situational leadership

There are a multitude of environmental elements that influence the manifestation of leadership and it is of little surprise that leadership theory of has sought universal application, regardless that the situation has repeatedly been shown to be fallible! Nevertheless, research continued in such a quest until the emergence in the late sixties and seventies of situational leadership. Numerous models have emerged that centre on the leader moderating his or her behaviour contingent to the situational circumstances and needs of followers. The following list summarises prominent explanations of situational leadership:

- *Fiedler's contingency model* (1967): A leader's impact on group performance depends on a combination of leader orientation and a set of situational contingency factors namely leader–member relations, task–structure clarification and leaders position power.
- *Path – goal theory* (House, 1971, 1977, 1996; House & Mitchell, 1974): Aspects of the situation, such as the nature of the task, work environment and subordinate attributes, determine the optimal leader behaviour for improving subordinate expectations and valances that lead to satisfaction and performance (Yukl, 1989a).
- *Situational leadership* (Hersey & Blanchard 1982): Follower performance is related to balancing the leader's task and relations behaviour according to the follower's confidence and skills – matching the leader behaviour required for the situation and according to the follower's needs.
- *Normative decision theory* (Vroom & Jago, 1988): Focus is on the level of involvement of followers in decision making appropriate to the situation, taking into account a number of variables such as technical quality, follower commitment required, level of information, clarity of problem and goal congruence with followers.

All of the above models are based on a leader-centric perspective examining appropriate behaviours to be adopted by the leader according to follower ability, confidence and motivations, and situation variables such as organisational structure and culture, position power, task complexity and technology. These various models have been drawn together into the multiple linkage model (Yukl, 1989a) advocated as an 'integrating conceptual framework that encompasses each of the important sets of variables relevant for leadership effectiveness' (1989: 274). This model is a step forward in integrating leader behaviour, traits, power and follower motivations and attributions with situational variables – albeit from a leader-centric perspective – and is a clear signal to shift attention away from a universal applicability of leader traits and behaviours. The universality of charismatic and transformational leadership theories is similarly subject to contextual influence and the extent of situational moderation is considered next.

Contextual influence on charismatic leadership

'New leadership', in the form of transformational and charismatic leadership, is argued as having universal application. The comprehensive GLOBE study (House et al., 2004) supports Bass (1997) in suggesting a tendency for transformational leadership characteristics to be applicable across cultures. However, additional research has illustrated that the transformational affect is moderated by situational variables (Bryman et al., 1996) and that there are situations more suited for charismatic leadership than others (Shamir & Howell, 1999). Specific conditions are outlined for the emergence and effectiveness of charismatic leadership and these are oriented towards macroorganisational considerations.

In the earlier discussion on charismatic leadership, the origins of the phenomenon focused on the situational catalyst of a crisis (Weber, 1947). The sense of uncertainty generated through a crisis stimulates a desire by followers for someone powerful, with clarity of direction and with high self-confidence, to provide salvation. The notion of strong and weak situations (Bell & Staw, 1988) is a useful lens through which to examine situation-centric leadership. Strong situations, on the one hand reflect a sense of environmental certainty and are perceived to enable followers to act on their own initiative (Bell & Staw, 1988). Weak situations, on the other hand, reflect conditions of ambiguity, loose structure and less clarity of appropriate behaviour. Such weak situations create a desire by followers for certainty and trigger romantic attributions towards desirable leadership to provide this certainty and direction. Hence the often heard phrase: 'the situation requires a strong leader'. Grint (2005) argues that the notion of weak environments rather reflects mythical 'God-like' notions by followers needing special people with extraordinary talents to create greater certainty – reflecting Meindl's (1995) arguments of the 'romance of leadership'. Grint (2005) advocates a case of 'wheelwrights' rather than 'white elephants', where leadership is more a sense of distributed influence – more on Grint and his notion of constituted leadership next.

The perceptions of environmental uncertainty leading to charismatic attribution by followers may be constructed through leader actions and oratorical skills (Willner, 1984; Shamir & Howell, 1999) and it is from this view of situational perception that the notion of a constituted environment of effective leadership is created.

Constituted situational leadership

A variation on the contingent perspective is the influence of a leader and others to shape the perception followers have of the situation, described by Grint (2000) as 'constituted' leadership (Grint, 2000). Rather than examining the situation objectively and discerning appropriate leadership style for the context, Grint (2000) argues that leaders, followers and other interested stakeholders shape interpretation of the context through their actions and discursive practice, resulting in subjective process indeterminacy rather than leader determinacy. For example, Parry and Hansen (2007) persuasively argues that leadership can take the form of a discourse: leadership is the message. Followers elaborate the meaning of the message that shapes ongoing sense-making and motivations. The principles of constituted leadership centre on networks and follower capability responding to the situation, rather than the leader role:

> All leaders err ... successful leadership comes from follower empowerment to recognise leader error and compensate.
>
> (Grint, 2000: 420)

Leadership from a constituted perspective is an indeterminate skill based within a process that masquerades as a determinate skill (ibid.). The emphasis on social skills of followers illustrates a complex orientation that is embedded in the nuances of local contexts. The discursive practices that masquerades the weaknesses of determinate leadership skills is often invisible to both researchers and practitioners: it is simply not recognised due to the prominence of the leader-centric paradigm and associated (and supportive) implicit theories and romantic notions from the follower-centric perspective.

To explore the invisible, socially constructed and systemic nature of leadership, there is an emerging body of research that builds understanding from the ground upwards through qualitative research of the leadership situation.

Situational leadership – a qualitative perspective

Building from this constituted perspective is a call for more situational grounded qualitative research that provides a perspective on leadership as:

> A [learnt] relationship among persons embedded in a social setting at a given historical moment. Leadership must consider the normative basis of the relationship and the setting and the distinctive performance abilities of the actors involved.
>
> (Biggart & Hamilton, 1987: 439)

Qualitative researchers in the field of leadership research have identified weaknesses with traditional leadership research that assumes a static, closed-system structure. The approach is dominated by statistical samples that are sufficiently robust to be accepted for publication as 'valid research'. Day (2000) asserts that there is a dearth of specific, contextually based research. Similarly, there has been a call for a grounded, qualitative approach into processes of leadership and its development and effectiveness within a discrete context (Bryman et al., 1996; Parry, 1998; Conger, 1998, 2004; Lowe & Gardner, 2000; Bryman 2004).

A qualitative approach seeks to illuminate the social processes that form leadership within a particular context. The complexity is not to be avoided or aggregated but rather it is to be illuminated and discussed. As such, Conger (1998) argues that qualitative research should be seen as the methodology of choice for studying leadership, as it is most adequately suited to revealing the interrelationship of context and processes of leadership influence. Through such an approach we are likely to get much closer to the reality of the world of leadership. I argue that through qualitative research we can begin to reveal how contextualised leadership practice develops and understand how individual leaders and followers learn how to enact these leadership processes. We need to make the invisible more visible.

Revealing 'invisible leadership'

Reflecting the need for situational-based qualitative research and the earlier notion of constituted leadership, 'invisible leadership' identifies socially constructed leadership that draws on both local and global institutionalised approaches (Sjostrand et al., 2001). From an examination of 11 organisations, Sjostrand et al. identified three interconnected key elements that shaped leadership that had previously been overlooked:

- *Significance of small talk* – leadership is formed through informal, innumerable, fragmented but continuous communications that socially constructs meaning about what has happened, what is happening and what will happen in the future (Sjostrand et al., 2001; and similar to Watson, 2001; Parry and Hansen, 2007).
- *Influence of unrecognised arenas* – the locations in which small talk is socially constructed (Sjostrand et al., 2001) appear to be very different from the arenas identified through traditional leadership research such as formal work group meetings or public briefings. The invisible areas associated with informal social activities such as corridors, toilets, trains or at the water coolers fuel the social exchange of small talk and the importance of this to socially constructed leadership is greatly underestimated (ibid.).
- *Institutional dynamics* – the duality of subjective and objective notions of local and global perspectives co-existing to form an idiosyncratic institutional dynamic. The 11 case studies identified that leadership can be dominated by a global leadership perspective, either in detached senior positions, or a more heavily socialised local perspective in socially interactive arenas – more typical of junior situations.

Invisible leadership can be seen to emerge from the situation, both local and global in its antecedents. The influence of idiosyncratic socially constructed leadership drawn from invisible interaction is argued to be a dynamic process of flow and flux in people's relations and interactions (Sjostrand et al., 2001). Such a focus on the situated microaspects of leadership practice reveals so much about leader-centric, follower-centric and situated-centric perspectives.

Summary

The mainstream and dominant view of situational leadership has examined the leader as responsive to variables and adjusting style and behaviour accordingly (Fiedler, 1967; House, 1977; Hersey & Blanchard, 1982b; Yukl, 1998). In contrast, the emerging qualitative constitutive perspective views the situation as subjectively interpreted by leaders and followers from which successful leadership occurs through follower responsiveness to situations (Grint, 2000). The invisible nature of constitutive leadership is created idiosyncratically through small talk in informal situations that blends global constructs of leadership with historic locally oriented perspectives (Sjostrand et al., 2001). Leadership as a socially constructed phenomenon is the nub of the situational perspective of leadership. The degree of influence which leaders or followers can have on the situation is shaped by individual learning of how to interpret and influence sense-making within particular communities of practice (Lave & Wenger, 1991 – much more on this in chapters 3 and 4). The nuances of leadership learning in particular contexts will be shown as complex and relatively idiosyncratic to organisational situations. Thus situational leadership is at the heart of leadership learning.

Conclusion: A process perspective of leadership

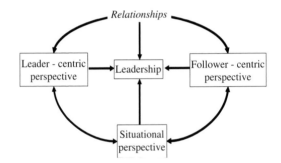

Leadership can thus be seen from three perspectives, with all three providing insights into an understanding of leadership; each perspective has significant sub-theories providing intricate deeper explanations. The dominant leader-centric perspective has had more attention and greater research examination and has begun to cohere around 'new leadership' in the form of charismatic and transformational notions of influence. The follower perspective suggests that leadership is formed from socially constructed implicit theories of a leaders role that can manifest into a dominant romantic notion of leadership and the creation of followership. Situational leadership can be seen to sit within both previous perspectives to provide insight into each, and could be argued to be a metaexplanation of leadership as an institutionalised global phenomenon and as a local socialised phenomenon, both being formed through social construction.

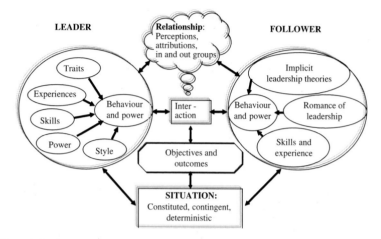

Figure 2.3   A process perspective to leadership

All three perspectives can be drawn together to reflect an underlying tenet of leadership being significantly associated with 'sense-giving': that is, influencing others sense-making. A sense-giving process of influence could be seen as an amalgam of the three perspectives into a holistic, systemic process, shaping and reshaping all constituent actors and connected stakeholders. An initial model that begins to draw this systemic process together is illustrated in Figure 2.3 and is proposed as an integrating conceptual framework that can be viewed from leader, follower or situational perspectives. In particular the model places emphasis on an idiosyncratic basis dependent on an individual's lived experience and learnt understanding of leadership: leadership as a powerful leader, or as a social myth or maybe a romantic dream.

The above systemic and processual perspective of leadership seeks to integrate the key themes examined within this chapter, and drawn in various combinations these perspectives help shape a mangers leadership practice:

- *Leader perspective* – traits, experiences, skills and style infused into leader behaviour and power.
- *Follower perspective* – implicit leadership theories and romance of leadership infused into follower behaviour.
- *Connected through relationships* – attribution and perception between leader and follower (attributed exchange relationships).

- *Situational perspective* – weak or strong environments and constituted social construction influencing leader and follower interpretations of the environment.

It is not my intention to suggest a metatheory of leadership in which all elements described from the extant literature can be seen to fit together into a comprehensive whole. Rather, a process perspective is drawn to illustrate how these perspectives can be constructed into a holistic interpretation and that many theories are complementary. Further, it is not suggested that any one perspective has greater weight or predominance than the other and certainly the model does not purport to be exhaustive in any way. Simply it is a synthesis that connects insights into the complex nature of leadership. Interventions into leadership development must recognise this complexity.

This chapter has sought to define and examine leadership from three distinctive and integrated views: leader, follower and situation. It has sought to illuminate arguments that leadership is not necessarily about the leader or the follower but rather it may be a process shaped from a number of elements that combine to influence an individual's sense-making of the situation and orientation towards an outcome. The historic focus has been overly leader-centric with limited attention to the everpresent follower- and situation-centric perspectives. Too great an emphasis has been given to survey methods that obscure important underlying contextual issues which generate the essence of leadership in particular situations. Too often this surface-level examination can only understand leadership at the highest levels of abstraction – consequently the important contextual and local detail is missed. Qualitative research would give emphasis to and begin to address the dearth of processual studies (Bryman, 1996, 2004; Hunt, 1999; Parry, 1998, 2001) and begin to reveal the socially constructed process of leadership and associated leadership practice. This book thus makes a contribution to our understanding of the social construction process by which managers develop their leadership practice at the complex nuance level of lived experience.

The development of leadership practice draws upon all three leadership centric perspectives from both general societal interpretations and from local meanings and historic embedded practices. Thus leadership is learnt through our engagement in society, through our interactions with, for example, parents, friends, teachers, sports captains, colleagues and bosses. It is learnt through media exposure, from observing politicians and other social commentators. The complexity of leadership and the source from where it is learnt are invariably too diffuse for us to recall. Leadership is, as Bennis (1989) says, like beauty. We learn to appreciate different forms of beauty and the different contexts in which something is personally beautiful. How we construct beauty, like leadership, is socially mediated. The next chapter explores the nature of social learning that enables the social construction of such leadership beauty to occur.

3
How Do We Learn?

Chapter 2 has argued that leadership is essentially a situated relational process of influence. Leadership practice must therefore be contextually learnt. Hence, the focus of this chapter is towards a social perspective of learning in order to help understand the development of leadership practice at the level of lived experience. The chapter is subdivided into key areas that will be seen to be interrelated to the process of learning a social phenomenon, such as leadership. In essence, an argument is developed that seeks to explore the notion of contextualised individual learning through an understanding of:

- *Individual learning dynamics* – a definitional outline of learning that is subsequently incorporated into an examination of individual learning through experience (Kolb, 1984).
- *Situational learning* – exploring contextualised learning that sits between and among people in communities. This perspective draws in particular on the work of Lave and Wenger (1991) and their notion of legitimate peripheral participation; embedded within such participation is shared meaning and identity.
- *Social learning theory* – providing insight into contextualised learning through an understanding of observational learning and the notion of self-efficacy. The work of Bandura (1977, 1986, 1997) is particularly insightful and central to these perspectives of learning where conception of social phenomena and social identification are interrelated to performance capability.
- *Cognition, memory and selective interpretation of experience* – examining how an individual encodes information and convert such external stimuli into knowledge-structures or schemas (Walsh, 1995), that subsequently helps to interpret events. Linked to schemas and

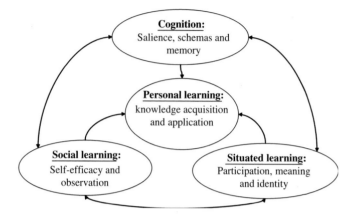

Figure 3.1   Structure of Chapter 3

interpretation of experience is the dynamics of memory (most particularly the work of Tulving, 1983; adapted by Nurius, 1993) and how memory retrieval linked to schemas is selective of lived experience and conception construction.

These combinations of extant literature are not natural bedfellows as they draw from different research traditions of psychology and sociology. However, the benefit each brings by being integrated with the others outweighs potential criticisms of mixing traditionally separate fields. These four elements are captured in Figure 3.1.

The three outer themes are interconnected and build from each other and have the effect of shaping individual learning. This framework will be used to structure the chapter and seek to represent a systemic integration of the four elements, rather than treat them as stand alone sections. The starting point of this journey is to tackle the thorny issue of defining learning.

Individual learning

Definitions of learning

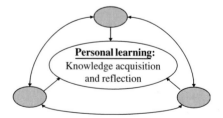

Debates on defining learning are not as numerous as with leadership but nonetheless the phenomenon is similarly equivocal in terms of definition. There are numerous perspectives of learning generating enormous complexity for assimilation (Nicolini & Mesnar, 1995). Despite such complexity there is some consensus on the meaning of learning associated with knowledge acquisition and a capacity for change:

A process by which knowledge is acquired.

(Eraut, 2000: 114)

The word learning undoubtedly denotes a change of some kind.

(Kim, 1993: 38)

A process perspective of learning is emphasised by Eraut (2000), by which knowledge is acquired, while Kim emphasises a dynamic where change of some kind is not necessarily seen as action but rather the potential or capacity to take action: 'learning can thus be defined as increasing one's capacity to take effective action' (Kim, 1993: 38). This allows both change and the potential for change to be joined together and seen within the conception of an experience leading to a transformation. In essence, learning can be seen as 'the transformation of experience into knowledge, skills and attitudes' (Jarvis, 1987a: 164). Kolb (1984) similarly linked learning with knowledge transformation and experience seeing it 'as a process whereby knowledge is created through the transformation of experience' (ibid., 1984: 38). As such, learning is seen in this study as a process of transformation through social exchange.

Learning as a social exchange

Experience is thus seen as central to learning to the extent that knowledge, skills and attitudes are being shaped and reshaped continually through social interaction (Mead, 1934); where 'meaning is not a given but evolves from the verbal and nonverbal interactions of individuals' (Ashforth & Mael, 1989: 27). Mead (1934) argued that notions of the 'self' could not be created other than through social interactions and exchanges between people. This social exchange of 'significant meanings' is, for Mead, the learning process of the development of self in the form of a social learning process. Such a view of learning and the development of the self anchors the notion of leadership learning as context-based, drawing upon social exchanges about leadership through interaction within particular communities at a particular point in time and through time.

Levels of learning through individual experience and reflection

The naturalistic process by which individuals learn (Burgoyne & Stuart, 1976, 1977) is oriented around the notion that 'the human species is born with the ability to learn. Learning is indispensable for survival' (1977: 2). Learning then has the potential to occur through all experiences. But this does not mean that we transform ourselves through every social interaction as not all experiences are of equal value.

The emphasis of reflection as a central part of the learning process focuses attention on learning as development and not simply the acquisition of information (Garrison, 1991). Reflection provides the necessary conversion of experience from uncoded data into thoughtful and productive knowledge (Usher, 1985). Reynolds (1998) draws a distinction between reflection, which is defined as making thoughtful and productive use of otherwise uncoded experience as a basis for future action; and critical reflection, as the ability of an individual to focus beyond the task or the problem to 'an analysis of power and control and an examination of the taken for granted's within which the task or the problem is situated' (1998: 189). In essence, critical reflection is concerned with questioning assumptions, pays particular attention to power relationships and is concerned with emancipation (Mezirow, 1985; Reynolds, 1998). Using Goffman's work, critical reflection is represented as an individual *outside the stage* understanding and interpreting the social construction of meaning being presented formally *front stage* and informally behind the scenes *back stage* (Goffman, 1969: 107).

The depth of conscious awareness that appears to distinguish reflection from critical reflection can be seen through Burgoyne and Hodgson's (1983) work that adapted Bateson's (1973) three levels of learning:

- *Level One* – experience and factual information that has immediate relevance but no long-term effect on a perspective of the world.
- *Level Two* – learning that is transferable from the present situation to another and is recognised by an individual as situationally transferable.
- *Level Three* – awareness of the conceptions of the world, how they were formed and how they might change. Learning that is not situation specific.

It is argued that level three learning is rare and that level two represents the dominant naturalistic learning mode, often occurring at an unconscious or tacit level of experience (Burgoyne & Hodgson, 1983), where an individual is able to draw on a background consciousness which is undergoing continual change. Learning in this respect is reconstruction, where experience enables someone to avoid solving the same problem for the second time; similar to the notion of reflection-in-action (Schon, 1983), where there is 'an on the spot (as distinct from retrospective) process of surfacing, testing and evaluating intuitive understandings which are intrinsic to experience' (Reynolds, 1998: 186). The distinction between levels two and three also reflects similarity with Argyris and Schon's (1978) earlier concept of single and double loop learning. The single loop represents habits and everyday practices connected to the background situational consciousness and deeper double loop learning related to changes affecting underlying values and general orientations (Argyris & Schon, 1978; Argyris, 1991).

What triggers level three or double loop learning? Burgoyne and Hodgson (1983) empirically identified very limited 'level three' learning yet argued that transformative change occurred gradually and imperceptibly, shaped by 'background consciousness which is dynamic rather than static in nature' (1983: 17). Further, it is argued that reflection-in-action is a very common phenomenon (Schon, 1983; Ferry & Ross-Gordon, 1998) and the process of developing deep understanding is often spontaneous, informal, implicit and outside an individual's awareness (Daudelin, 1996). However, the process of reflection and learning takes many forms and is at varying depths (Jarvis, 1987a). The ability to reflect at depth is seen to be triggered by transformative incidents or episodes that call into question a person's learning history and assumptions about the world. Mezirow (1985) argues that such transformative events lead to conscious reflection and realisation of a changed world:

> As adult learners we are caught in our own histories. However good we are at making sense of our experiences, we all have to start with what we have been given and operate within horizons set by ways of seeing and understanding that we have acquired through prior learning.
>
> (1985: 1)

The ability to be critically reflective and reflexive is seen to be a uniquely adult capacity and thus an adult learning function (ibid.; Bandura, 1986). Associated with adult perspective transformations are normative periods of heightened critical reflectivity, argued by Levinson (1978) to be between the ages of 17–22, 40–5 and 60–5 and each qualitatively different:

> The most fundamental tasks of a stable period are to make firm choices, rebuild life structures and enhances one's life within it. Those of the transitional period are to question and reappraise the existing structure, to search for new possibilities in self and the world and to modify the present structure enough so that a new one can be formed.
>
> (1978: 53)

Both Levinson and Mezirow perceive a significant trigger for such perspective transformations to be marker events or disorientating dilemmas (Mezirow, 1981). In order for an individual to question their historic interpretation of their learning biography there is the need to question taken for granted assumptions. It is events, and people within events, that force paradigmatic questioning. The notion of events centres the discussion of learning through social exchange and interpretation. It is axiomatic but worth emphasizing that an individual's leaning thus reflects knowledge, skills and attitudes that are of the social world they encounter.

Mead argued that freedom of learning and transformation is curtailed by social control (Mead, 1934), yet through critical reflexivity an individual is capable of seeing and understanding the world they are part of and constructed within (similarly developed by Reynolds, 1998). The notion of constructed knowledge through participation within particular communities reflects situated learning theories (Lave & Wenger, 1991; Fox, 1997a), which we shall come on to shortly. The importance here is to orientate our view of individual learning as contextualised experience. It is towards individual contextualised knowledge, drawn from the context of an individual's lived experience, which is both the focus of this chapter and at the heart of understanding how managers learn to lead.

Individual learning through contextualised experience

The notion of an independent learner is explored, notably by Kolb (1984), through a learning cycle of experience (Kolb & Fry, 1975; drawing on the earlier work of Dewey, 1938) where the individual is learning through experimentation on the world. The cycle of learning reflects the following: an experience stimulates reflection from which knowledge is constructed; subsequently this knowledge is applied and generates further experiences that through reflection refine, elaborate or confirm knowledge of the experience.

The learning cycle has become predominant as a development tool within management development interventions (Reynolds, 1997), where it is advocated that individuals learn within styles associated with elements constituting the cycle. The learning experience is matched to the style preference of an individual so that the learning will be strengthened (Kolb, 1984; Honey & Mumford, 1992). Very recent work by Armstrong and Mahmud (2008) confirms the continuing theoretical popularity with Kolb's (1984) notion of the learning cycle and learning styles. Incidentally their work is most interesting in the sense that they suggest that managers who have a balanced preference for all styles of learning were critical for effective experiential learning (2008: 189). They particularly examined the development of tacit knowledge in the assertion of their argument – more on tacit learning shortly. Criticism of the ubiquitous use of a cycle of learning (and associated learning styles) is associated with an oversimplification of individual learning dynamics. Reynolds (1997) argues that the pre-eminence of learning orientation based on the presumption of stability of personality characteristics has become popular with 'teachers and trainers who have hoped that the concept of learning style would contribute to the quality of education they provide' (1997: 118).

Nevertheless the cyclical process of learning through experience appears to be central to an individual's development. However, the sequential stages of the learning cycle may be more or less relevant or pronounced dependent on a variety of influences shaped by the social context and salience of the phenomenon being learnt – a point that will be expanded on shortly. Although an individuals learning from experience is highly complex and idiosyncratic, it is also fundamentally dependent on the social context in which the experience occurs.

The role of experience is thus central to individual learning but the focus needs to be broadened to a social learning perspective that sees experience as active social encounters (Burgoyne, 1995). A view of learning as an encounter or exchange within particular contexts relates to the earlier discussion with respect to the development of the individual through social exchanges (Mead, 1934), and extends the focus from notions of individual centric decontextualised learning to embedded encounters in particular situations from which meaning is generated (Fox, 1997a).

Situated learning

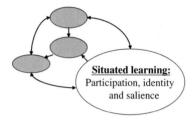

> Learning involves the whole person: it implies not only a relation to specific activities, but a relation to social communities – it implies becoming a full participant, a member, a kind of person.
>
> (Lave & Wenger, 1991: 53)

The above quote provides a central focus to situated learning and is in striking contrast to traditional learning theory (Fox, 1997a), which has an epistemology that is rooted in knowledge as an individual process of acquisition and where knowledge is free standing, decontextualised and professionally produced and disseminated. Fox comments:

> It is assumed that there is a discrete difference between profession-ally produced and lay knowledge. The former (traditional learning theory) is scientific, disciplined, theoretical, systematic and general; the latter (situated learning theory) is common-sensical but limited, undisciplined, based on narrow experience, anecdotal and ad hoc, and forever destined to be particular rather than general or law like.
>
> (1997a: 730)

Situated learning theory seeks to incorporate an alternative epis-temology that encompasses the 'mind and lived in world' (1997a: 731) where, in contrast to the mind as a container waiting to be filled (Hooks, 1994), it is the mind in action, creating knowledge and learning simultaneously in interaction with the 'lived-in-world' (Fox, 1997a: 732).

The significance of context to individual learning is central to the role of engagement and interaction in social settings, shaping what is learnt through an emphasis on what is considered important and salient to an individual within a community. The process of social phenomena being learnt through valued social exchange of meanings (Mead, 1934) reflects the centrality of shared meaning and identity within particular contexts: 'Organisations, people and groups create knowledge, negotiating meaning of words, actions, situations and material artifacts' (Gherardi, Nicolini & Odella, 1998: 274). Thus human cognition and learning are closely related to the social context in which they take place, which is a historic product of intersubjective meaning making that evolves over time (Berger & Luckmann, 1966).

Communities of practice

The notion of engagement in the 'lived-in-world' is extended by the concept of community of practice (Lave & Wenger, 1991; Eckert, 1993; Gherardi et al., 1998) and related concept of participation. Participation in practice is a method to acquire knowledge, and can be represented as practice-as-work, practice-as-language or perhaps practice-as-morality (Ehn, 1988). Through such practice, learning is less associated with knowing the world but rather more associated with becoming part of the social world (Gherardi et al., 1998). The process of communities of practice gives emphasis to the significance of relationships among persons and activities as well as illuminating the process by which the transmission of tacit knowledge (Polyani, 1966; Nonaka & Takeuchi, 1995; Eraut, 2000) and knowledge-in-action (Schon, 1983) occurs.

Knowledge within communities of practice can be related to the idea of 'habitus' or 'life-world' (Bourdieu, 1980) and reflect durable social processes and practices, emphasising a link between relationships and activities that forge individual identity and practice. Significant to the arguments of this book is the emphasis on participation and identity drawn from particular communities of practice that have shaped their situated learning about leadership. A useful framework for structuring thinking about situated learning, drawn from communities of practice, is through an understanding of processes of peripheral legitimate participation (Lave & Wenger, 1991).

Peripheral legitimate participation

Peripheral legitimate participation is seen as a pathway or trajectory (Wenger, 1998), which individuals follow to acquire knowledge, by which they become full and active participants in a particular community. The degree of legitimacy accorded to individuals through their legitimate participation affects the range of learning opportunities and knowledge in action offered to them. With respect to leadership, non-managers and managers could be seen to have different pathways and learning experiences as a result of different opportunities offered through role requirements, participation and legitimisation. Hence, access to learning opportunities may be significant to the development and practice of social roles (Lave & Wenger, 1991) such as leadership.

Prominently associated with legitimacy and learning pathways are the development and institutionalisation of multiple identities relevant and salient to different contexts. For example, Brown and Duguid (1991) argue that situated learning is 'best understood in terms of the communities being formed or joined and personal identities being changed. The central issue in learning is *becoming* a practitioner, not learning *about* practice' (1991: 48; emphasis in text).

Identity – learning to 'become'

Although there is a vast volume of literature on identity (a review of which is succinctly provided by Collinson, 2003, that builds upon Jenkins, 1996) there is limited explicit empirical research on processes shaping identity construction. Collinson (2003) argues that influences on self-identity have changed. Previous notable influences were religion and family and these have been replaced by such influences as achievement, the success ethic, materialism and career success (2003: 530). Collinson (2003) draws attention to the influence of organisations in the development of identities. Similar to Collinson, the work of Markus and Nurius (1986) explores professional socialisation processes. Their work provides an insight into identity construction where individuals, through contact with others, create 'possible-selves': temporary identities that are tried out and compared to others and used to explore and refine the identity an individual might become.

Accordingly, the focus of identity in this chapter, and throughout the study, is towards an understanding of literature associated with learning to become an identity and how such an identity is forged within particular situations as a consequence of lived experience. Processes of identity construction will be developed within Chapters 7 and 8, but the key elements examined here are the focus on 'becoming' (Tsoukas & Chia, 2002) and a sense of 'provisional-identities' (Ricoeur, 1992; Ezzy, 1998; Ibarra, 1999). Identity construction is thus seen as a fluid dynamic process that interconnects an individual's past (lived experience) with both their present identity and future aspirational identity – hence the 'provisional' notion of identities.

Lave and Wenger (1991) argue that learning involves the whole person in a relationship with activities and social communities, as 'a participant, a member, a kind of person' (1991: 53). An identity is seen as linked to social relations as well as skills and competence. It is an enactment between an individual and groups in society 'where the person is defined by, as well as defines, these relationships' (1991: 53). Social interaction, and arguably social existence, depends on people knowing who they are in order to be able to know what they should think and do. Knowing who others are allows people to anticipate and interact, enabling societal structures to develop that in turn shape identities (Hogg & Vaughnan, 2002); as for example, with the social structure of leader–follower identities and relationships within particular contexts. The concept of identity serves as a pivot between the social and the individual with the duality of self and social identities (Tajfel, 1974) acting as interplay in the process of identity creation (Mead, 1934; Blumer, 1969; Wenger, 1998).

Wenger (1998) argues that identity and practice are interconnected and inform on each other in continual reciprocity. For instance, an individual would identify themselves as a leader through their experience of leading and receiving feedback on their competence through various sources that affirms this competence and identity of this role (Hollander, 1979). Yet this experience of leading is within particular communities. Such a community has its own understanding and practice of leadership, where individuals learn certain ways of leading as well as learning what leading means in this community. A leader thus draws upon both their identity and their practice to lead in a particular community.

As an individual participates in practice and constructs an identity within that community, so meaning and practice is developed that is shared within specific communities that become part of a particular identity. For instance, a manager may hold a position of authority but the meaning and practice of that authority has been established through historic practice within a specific community. Such meaning and practice is continually under constant flux and renegotiation as a result of new membership, as well as the influence of interconnected communities in which individuals participate.

An individual is seen to participate in numerous situations and forms multiple identities and these are learnt for social use in different situations (Gergen, 1971; Srull & Wyer, 1989; Wenger, 1998). For example, an individual may identify himself as father and younger brother, where in the former he perceives a dominant identity and in the latter a submissive identity. When situations recur they act as stimuli to conceptions learnt in the past and old identities may re-emerge (Higgins, 1987) – such as with family gatherings. Tensions exist for individuals through conscious awareness of inconsistency of identity at the same time. An example of mixing contexts and identities reflects a situation of taking children to the parent's place of work where both the parent and the child experience identity confusion. The management of such multiple identities appears to be a learnt process (Wenger, 1998) where an individual recognises contexts that generate identity inconsistency and seeks to manage such inconsistency.

The temporal notion of an identity forged from past experiences and linked to future expectations fashions the respective provisional identity that is continually in flux (Markus & Nurius, 1986; Ibarra, 1999). This temporary and fluid perspective to identities is most central to this study, particularly associated with an aspired sense of becoming a leader and as such, is a foundational perspective that will be utilised in the discussion in Chapter 8. Most prominent and pertinent to this study is the empirical work of Ibarra (1999).

Ibarra (1999) undertook qualitative research in the form of interviewing 34 professional consultants and identified the dominance of observational learning and experimenting in the process of identity development. Ibarra proposed the term 'provisional-selves' to describe a process of refinement of repertoires, moving from role prototyping, through discovering what constitutes credible role performance, to identity matching with notable people who are compared to themselves in their contexts (Ibarra, 1999; similar ideas on identity and context in McGuire, 1984).

Becoming an identity

Examining the notion of 'possible-selves', Yost et al. suggested that 'we lack an understanding of how the self becomes' (1992: 110). Ibarra argues that the process of developing repertoires, through continual interaction of observation, experimentation and evaluation, both internally and externally, provide an explanation of how the self 'becomes' (1999: 110). The notion of how the self 'becomes' has recently, and influentially, been endorsed by Mischel (2004) who argues that the personality of an individual is represented as a set of 'behavioural signatories' that have tendencies to shape behaviour to suit recognised environmental situations. These 'signatories' are representations of the self as an identity, drawn from memory recall of feelings, expectations, beliefs associated with people and past events.

Ibarra (1999) connects observation and experimentation as key processes of identity construction and that exposure to a broad range of notables in a variety of contexts extends the richness of repertoires. This point will be significantly developed under contextual comparisons between owner-managers and the employed managers in Chapter 7 and in Chapter 8 exploring contextual variation.[1]

The work of Hill (2003) examined processes of becoming a manager.[2] She identified that junior managers moved towards a new identity as a generalist manager and 'changed their perception of themselves and the world around them. They began to act like a manager; they began to become a manager' (2003: 84). The notion of becoming (Tsoukas & Chia, 2002) and aspiring to become the social identity of a leader is similarly addressed by Wenger (1998). Wenger sees identity as a central feature of situated learning, where individuals invest themselves in a community's activities and mutual relationships, through legitimate participation that generates meaning and an embedded identity recognised by themselves and others (1998: 97). Wenger describes modes of belonging that encompass the process of identity formation through: involvement and engagement; imagination connecting experience with expectation; and alignment of activities to 'become part of something' (1998: 179). The trajectory and legitimacy of career pathways provide opportunities for individuals to belong and become identities that are supported by others in the particular communities in which they participate (Lave & Wenger, 1991).

The notion of plurality of identities implies a need for an individual to make sense of a number of possible leader identities that they could become. The transition from one identity to another has been argued to be an evolutionary process of integrating lived experience with prospective anticipations within current situations (Ezzy, 1998). Ezzy utilised the work of Paul Ricoeur (1992) to persuasively argue that identity is constructed by an individual reflecting on themselves and others, where the individual sees themselves as an 'imaginary other emplotted in a situation with others' (1998: 245).

Identity is a not a fixed phenomenon or one that is acquired and then perhaps discarded. Rather identities emerge in response to the situation in which someone is 'emplotted' and, through interaction, become developed. Further, people have multiple identities that come to the fore in response to circumstances, and an individual learns how to manage such identities. The learning process to become is thus centrally affected by the situation, and interactions with people. The potential number of identities we could become is vast. However, this is not the case as, from the countless social interactions in our daily lives, certain phenomena become more salient and such salience directs our attention towards particular identities.

Salience of identities

There are potentially too many multiple identities 'and man is simply not capable of mentally juggling his entire repertoire of concepts at any one instant' (Gergen, 1971: 31). Gergen (1971) suggests that the salience of an identity relates to:

- The amount of learning and association with an identity: such an example is gender classification to a person.
- Identity association with situations acts as stimuli to recall learning and become that identity; different identities related to specific contexts. Using my-self as an example: a father with my children, a son at my parents' home, a partner at my own home and a lecturer at work.
- The value of an identity to an individual.

The degree to which identities become highly salient is seen to be associated with situational accessibility where an identity is highly valued and occurs frequently (Hogg & Terry, 2000): 'Individuals tend to choose activities congruent with salient aspects of their identities' (Ashforth & Mael, 1989: 25). The dominance of motivation to the salience of an identity can create self-identities that become the person in situations where the identity is not salient. For example, a teacher may continue to see himself/herself as a teacher in other social settings as the salience of the identity is so strong to the person. In essence, the salience of an identity may become the person as a result of intense belonging and identification (Wenger, 1998). Such intense belonging and investment into becoming an identity is wonderfully encapsulated within the following:

> That stiff and formal manner into which the young teacher compresses himself every morning when he puts on his collar ... The didactic manner, the authoritative manner, the flat assured tones of voice that go with them, are bred in the teacher by his dealings in the classroom ... and these traits are carried over by the teacher into his personal relations.
>
> (Waller, 1932; in Gergen, 1971: 55)

The strength and salience of identities within particular ongoing contexts can appear to dominate an individual's personal and social identity and create stable selves. However, identity is seen to be highly malleable and dynamic (Markus & Nurius, 1986; Ezzy, 1998; Ibarra, 1999) and attention needs to be focused on context specific selves and the maturity or trajectory (Lave & Wenger, 1991) of identity construction in particular situations (Linville, 1987).

The notion of salience of identity shaped through concepts of situated learning and an individual's pathway of participation will be argued to be most significant to leadership learning. Salience of particular identities and processes shaping both identity construction and conceived approaches to leading are embedded in lived experience. Yet lived experience is itself subject to cognitive processes that distort and bias interpretation of such experience, to affirm identification and self-efficacy of leading.

Knowledge construction through processes of social cognition

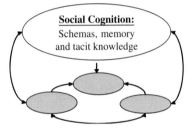

In this section I will briefly touch on aspects of knowledge construction to help inform the examination of the lived experience of leadership learning. The application of aspects of social cognition in the field of leadership studies is limited, and severely limited in understanding leadership learning. (Useful in this respect is the work of Lord and colleagues: Engle & Lord, 1997; Hanges et al., 2000; Lord & Emrich, 2001; Lord et al., 2001.) Lord et al. argue that although 'the body of cognitive and social-cognitive research is quite compelling this has not been verified in the leadership domain' (2001: 16).[3] The aspects considered useful to aid this study are: knowledge structures, memory and tacit knowledge.

Schemas – knowledge structures

In order to sustain rapid information processing, perceptions of the world are categorised and generalised as prototypical for a particular phenomenon. Subsequent contact with the same phenomenon is interpreted in light of earlier information processing (Mischel, 1973; Walsh, 1995; Hogg & Vaughan, 2002). However, for a phenomenon of greater salience or familiarity shaped by numerous experiences, understanding is reinterpreted creating nuances of interpretation (Smith & Zarate, 1992). For example, the greater the salience of leadership linked to numerous experiences, a greater depth of understanding and interpretation is argued to develop – this issue will become a significant aspect when employed and self-employed manager's conceptions of leadership and their respective lived experiences of leadership are compared in Chapter 7. When a phenomenon is categorised, a schema or knowledge structure is created that 'represents organised knowledge about a given concept' (Fiske & Taylor, 1991: 149). Such interpretation is processed from the knowledge structure in one of the two ways:

- *'Top-down'* or theory driven, where past experiences in similar circumstances guide information processing and affects encoding and inferences about new information (Walsh, 1995). For example, a follower may interpret a leaders behaviour through the assumption 'that all leaders are the same'.
- *'Bottom-up'* or data driven, where the current information and the context guides and shapes interpretation, and is likely to reconfigure the schematic structure to be available for later top-down information processing (Walsh, 1995).

The need for efficiency and limited individual capacity to attend to the array of phenomena requiring information processing, leads invariably to the dominance of the top-down theory driven process in all but the most novel situations (Louis & Sutton, 1991). Schemas are argued to enable interpretation of a phenomenon beyond the information presented (Catrambone & Markus, 1987). Although such interpretation is efficient and often highly effective, there is also the significant danger that schemas can limit an individual's ability to understand situations through inferring data by 'filling in the gaps' (Gioia, 1986: 346) and can lead to 'impoverished views of the world' (Weick, 1979: 68): 'The paradox, then, is that schematic information processing can be at once enabling and crippling' (Walsh, 1995: 282).

A cautionary comment is to stress that understanding of knowledge development is incomplete and it is argued that few theorists understand how such structures are formed, other than to suggest that:

- Schemas are formed by experience (Neisser, 1976, 1982).
- Developed through continual exposure to information about a particular phenomenon (Neisser, 1976, 1982; Lurgio & Carroll, 1985).

- Individuals who have well-developed schema are able to assess particular situations more reliably and predictably (Neisser, 1976, 1982; Smither & Reilly, 1989).
- Greater self-awareness and self-induced reflection is seen to be associated with schema change (Neisser, 1976, 1982; Millar & Tesser, 1986; Walsh, 1995).

Of particular interest for this study is the development of schema knowledge structures related to managers' categorisation and perception of learning stimuli, which has led to their understanding of leadership. There is a distinct and interrelated relationship between social identity (Tajfel, 1974) and social cognition (Turner, 1985) through self-categorisation where an individual develops 'prototypical' generalisation of himself/herself related to others (Hogg & Terry, 2000: 123): 'I'm a leader by comparison to others in particular situations.' Self-categorisation suggests that people generate identity prototypes, rather than seeking to recall people as individuals. They then categorise themselves against these prototypes (ibid.). For example, leadership could be seen by an individual as a depersonalised symbolic prototype formed from memories and experiences of a range of significant people.

Such self-categorisation and schema development of leadership are argued to be stored in the memory and are constructed, maintained and modified by contact with the immediate or more enduring social context (Fiske & Taylor, 1991; Hogg & Terry, 2000). This suggests that knowledge development is greatly enhanced by contextual variety of learning stimuli, such as a bad boss or working in a new organisation.

Dynamism of memory

The interactive functioning of memory is seen, from the perspective of social cognition, to be sensitised to the external environment through sensory perception, which brings into focus information that requires purposeful attention. As individuals we 'must be parsimonious about what we see and hear ... or risk being quickly overwhelmed by the flood of inputs' (Wofford & Goodwin, 1994: 263). It is thus argued that information is sought that is consistent with what 'we know' and what 'we expect' and therefore we tend to,

> neglect information for which we have no experience or that is contradictory to our beliefs ... what we already know exerts a strong influence on what we take in and remember. In short, memory is a

constantly integrative and reconstructive process ... our past is not maintained as a historical record but undergoes change as we do.[4]

(1994: 266)

Memory appears to most readily recall episodes or events which reflect the following criteria (drawn from the work of: White, 1982; Neisser, 1982; Stewart et al., 1982; Pillemer et al., 1986; Srull & Wyer, 1989):

- Events are more readily recalled if they are novel and rare.
- There is some form of emotional significance to the event.
- Life transitions as novel, emotional and relatively unique events causing major adaptations to cognitive structures (Levinson, 1978; Mezirow, 1985).
- Nouns (particularly people) are recalled more readily than verb-oriented descriptive events.

The above characteristics identify critical incidents as being central to memory and the recall capability of critical incidents can be seen to be associated with the significance of the event to an individual. In the context of this study, a manager's understanding of how to lead would be oriented to events and people, early career experiences, good and bad bosses, emotionally significant hardships and successes. It will be argued in the book that these aspects have a disproportionate influence on formative leadership learning.

An aspect of the memory known as 'procedural' memory relates to 'knowing how' to do something (Srull & Wyer, 1989; Walsh, 1995; Hogg & Terry, 2000) and can be seen to closely relate to notions of apprenticeship and the development of practice. The development of procedural memory also gives an insight into the development of tacit knowledge – that which we know but cannot tell (Polyani, 1966). In a sense the increasing depth of procedural memory through continual participative interaction increases unconscious know-how that becomes increasingly difficult to communicate with the depth and complexity of procedural experience. Our ability to draw out procedural memory and describe this to someone is very limited.

Tacit knowledge

In Chapter 4 on leadership development, it will be argued that accidental and informal learning about leadership occurs predominately unconsciously (Burgoyne & Hodgson, 1983; Marserick, 1988; Marserick & Watkins, 1990); such learning and knowledge acquisition can be seen as procedural absorption of everyday activities. A person may have been socialised into the norms of an organisation without being aware of either learning or the norms that have been learnt. An individual is thus unaware until, through some form of intervention they are made aware (Raelin, 1997; Eraut, 2000), 'people may not know that they have knowledge on a particular phenomenon as it resists articulation' (Armstrong & Mahmud, 2008: 189).[5] In this sense, it is most understandable that managers in this study, at the beginning of the interview, repeatedly said that they must be born with leadership skills. By the end of the interview they were surprised at how much they had learnt but had not been aware.

Armstrong and Mahmud persuasively argue that tacit knowledge can be studied but 'the relationship between experience and the acquisition of tacit knowledge has never been fully established' (2008: 201). Their study shows the importance of context and roles, and not the duration of experience. They go on to assert:

> Most learning to manage occurs on the job in tacit, culturally embedded ways through peoples work practices within organizations. How then can management educators substitute for such learning when formal education programs continue to separate learning from practice? ... On the basis that the present study confirmed the context-dependent nature of tacit knowledge these approaches [learning through participation in social practice] may benefit from more deliberate attempts to closely match learning experiences with situations that are consonant with the specific management context.
>
> (2008: 201)

Of importance to this study is the significance of tacit knowledge to the development of leadership practice and as a corollary that such learnt practice is not likely to be capable of immediate recall.

Summary

This section has provided an argument and justification for a focus on events to help elucidate learning of leadership practices due to the anticipated way the memory functions: managers would be more likely to recall significant, novel and emotional formative events of leadership learning than routinised and socialised learning episodes. Nevertheless the routine and socialised aspects of lived experience, captured in the procedural memory, greatly informs on tacit knowledge and subsequent shaping of leadership practice. However, managers are not likely to be able to recount and evidence such learning. The notion of situated learning very much encapsulates tacit absorption of learning and provides a useful framework to help reveal the tacit knowledge of leadership practice. The final lenses through which such tacit knowledge of leadership practice has been acquired, and thus can be partially revealed, are through processes of 'social learning'.

Social learning theory

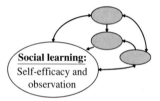

The notion of social learning theory is drawn from the field of social psychology and in particular social cognition. Social learning theory is seen to be associated with 'how thoughts, feelings and behaviour of individuals are influenced by others' (Hogg & Vaughan, 2002: 2) and how cognitive processes construct their subjective reality of social phenomena (Fiedler & Bless, 2002). Social learning theory (Bandura, 1977, 1986, 1997) not only draws from, and connects with, key principles of social cognition but also can be seen to engage with situated learning as follows:

- The focus is on social phenomena and the nature (process) of the relationship of social phenomena to the perceiver.
- The roles of self and social identity are formed in relationship to social phenomena in particular contexts.
- Individuals construct social phenomena from direct experience, indirect from observation or inferred symbolic cues drawn from memory.
- The above characteristics create a bias in social phenomena conception.

In many respects Bandura's work is most informative to the purpose of this study seeking to reveal underlying influences on leadership learning. Two salient elements of social learning theory will be examined: self-efficacy and observational learning.

Self-efficacy – expected performance outcome

Social learning theory (Bandura, 1977, 1986, 1997) is argued to be centred on a fundamental triadic reciprocity and exchange between behaviour, cognition and environmental events:

> The relative influence exerted by the three sets of interacting factors will vary for different activities, different individuals and different circumstances.
>
> (1986: 24)

This triadic interrelationship of cognition, behaviour and environment generates, for an individual, the notion of self-efficacy (Bandura, 1977, 1986, 1997; Wood & Bandura, 1989), described as 'people's judgments of their capabilities to organise and execute courses of action required to attain designated types of performances' (1989: 391).

Self-efficacy is a significant link between thought and action. In the context of this study it provides a link between lived experience and the interpretation a manager makes of experience to form judgments, or beliefs or expectations in his or her capability to accomplish a certain level of performance of leading in a particular context. An individual manager's self-efficacy of leading might be seen to be shaped by both pre-organisational experiences and notably their organisational career. Chapters 7 and 8 will explore, in detail, the impact of the variety of lived experiences of leadership and consequential self-efficacy beliefs of leading. Here I will describe the mechanics by which self-efficacy operates and the implications of self-efficacy on leadership learning.

Individual self-efficacy arises from direct and mediated experiences (Bandura, 1977) and has the effect of shaping behaviour by anticipated performance capability; associated with such performance capability is the value of the outcomes sought. Activities that are valued and desired are weighed against the person's ability to achieve them. If perceived as important, the person may invest effort to improve capability and thus enhance self-efficacy, and continue to invest himself/herself to this valued outcome. If the outcome of say, becoming a leader, is of low value or the cost is too high, there is limited investment to raising self-efficacy expectations of learning how to lead in an organisational context.

It has been argued earlier in this chapter that through situated learning and participation of practice, both salience of leadership and identification with leadership could distort encoding and interpretation of the environment by a manager's focus on learning leadership over and above other phenomena. As a consequence of the perceived value of leadership, their capability of performance at leading becomes significant. Thus an interpretation of Bandura's concept of self-efficacy (1977, later expanded in 1986 and 1997) is that the valued activities are those that we seek to improve our capability at performing. Equally activities which we are good at, and which we attribute value to, we may identify with. Those activities which we do not value and identify with may, as a consequence, have low self-efficacy. A personal example is given to help illustrate this important point. I play tennis but my value on tennis is low, although I enjoy playing at a club level. My self-efficacy is limited and I identify myself as an 'average club player' with many weaknesses. However, as a lecturer and researcher on leadership the role is most salient and it is not personally acceptable to have low self-efficacy; as a consequence I'm most conscious towards responding to direct and observed experiences to enhance capability in the desire to become a 'better teacher'. The notion of an interrelationship between salience, identity and self-efficacy is significant to this study and is prominently developed in Chapter 8.

Societal influence can create a distortion to self-efficacy beliefs. For example, Betz and Voyten (1997) argued that self-efficacy of career expectations and gender is interrelated. For example, young women were seen to have low self-efficacy expectations of non-standard careers in such fields as management – the work of Betz and Voyten (1997) is developed in Chapter 8 through an examination of gender influences on leadership learning of women managers.

Bandura (1986) argues that self-efficacy can greatly influence the way an individual interprets situations and anticipated outcomes based on their lived experience. However, such interpretation is anchored in contextualised social learning where past experiences and current conceptions shape the ongoing interpretation of situations and performance expectations.

Baudura (1986) constructs self-efficacy from four sources:

- *Direct experience* – personal enactment of leading reflected as learning by doing.
- *Vicarious, observed experience* – comparison through modelling of others performance.
- *Verbal persuasion* – examples of which are instructions, coaching or feedback.
- *Emotional arousal* – hardships and low confidence have the effect of lowering self-efficacy.

The dominant sources of self-efficacy are direct experience and obser-vation and, as a result of experience, are relatively inflexible over the short-term. If self-efficacy is central to leadership learning then there is the potential for significant policy issues associated with modifying self-efficacy expectations over the short-term – developed in Chapter 9. Seeking to modify the above sources and enhance self-efficacy is argu-ably problematic due to the triadic nature of self-efficacy formed around environment, cognition and behaviour. For example:

> To succeed at easy tasks provides no new information for altering ones sense of self-efficacy, whereas mastery of challenging tasks conveys salient evidence of enhanced competence.
>
> (Bandura, 1977: 201)

Using an example from leadership development, an easy task might reflect an intervention in the form of experiential exercises of leading a group through a 'spiders web'. The context may be considered too simplistic to provide evidence for altering a manager's self-efficacy. However, if the exercise is utilised as a vehicle for reflection to draw out fundamental issues of behaviour based on lived experience, this may be considered by the manager as a metaphor and enable learning and possible enhanced self-efficacy. Belling, James and Ladkin (2004) have developed arguments for such use of experiential exercises in such a manner, although they do not relate this explicitly to self-efficacy.

In many ways the issues of challenge and the development of self-efficacy relates to the work of Davies and Easterby-Smith (1984) who illustrated that managers learnt how to manage and lead through a variety of experiences and responsibilities from a number of varying contexts: the greater the authentic challenges to leadership learning, the greater the likelihood of a manager enhancing self-efficacy.

In a similar way, the greater the variety of notable people encountered in a manager's lived experience the greater the likelihood of enhanc-ing self-efficacy. The final part of this chapter on learning focuses on observational learning as it draws together many aspects of the chapter and will become most central to the arguments of this study on how managers learn how to lead.

Observational learning

Bandura (1986) argues that one of the key cognitive capabilities of individuals is their ability to learn vicariously. Unlike learning through experience of action, which has been described earlier, there is a dearth of research specifically oriented towards observational learning (Anderson & Cole, 1990):

> Even though virtually no research has examined the possible role of significant other representations in general social perception, many theories of personality and behaviour have long proposed that mental representations of significant others influence the ways in which people conceptualise.
>
> (1990: 385)

Through an understanding of observational learning an argument can be made that this is a central learning process that integrates many of the themes examined in this chapter, most prominently the symbolical nature of represented images of knowledge from notable people that shape social identity in the form of self-categorisation (Turner, 1985; Hogg, 2001). Salience of leadership identity is greatly influenced by notable people (Fiske & Taylor, 1984; Higgins & Bargh, 1987; Ibarra, 1999) and depth of memory recall is significantly biased towards people (Ganellen & Carver, 1985). Observations of others are a central feature of participation within situated learning (Lave & Wenger, 1991).

Bandura (1986) posits that observational learning lays down the fundamental building blocks of knowledge refined through enactment in the world. It is a form of approximate learning, oriented around the generation of symbolic models and acts as 'one of the most powerful means of transmitting values, attitudes and patterns of thought and behaviour' (1986: 47). Of importance to observational learning is not imitation, but rather,

> in cultivating human competencies modeling imparts conceptions and rules for generating variant forms of behaviour to suit different purposes and circumstances.
>
> (Bandura, 1986: 48)

Additional to generating symbolised broad patterns of social knowledge, observational learning can serve as social prompts to individuals to enact previous learning that may have been previously inhibited or is being induced to enact through salience (Anderson & Cole, 1990). A process of observational learning outlined by Bandura (1986) suggests four constituent processes:

- *Attention* – what is being observed in the social world is influenced by conspicuousness and attractiveness, salience and perceived value, preconceptions and prior knowledge. For example, 'experienced people within a particular domain recognize fine differences that are indistinguishable to the untutored' (1986: 53).

- *Retention* – observed activities are recalled in memory as 'abstract symbols that act as representative guides' (1986: 59). These appear to be most predominant in early formative learning from which learning becomes refined and contextually more specific. In particular, notable people are recalled for their difference in particular contexts, and such differences enable deepening self-categorisation to a particular identity (Anderson & Cole, 1990).

- *Production* – converting the symbolic conceptions into appropriate actions that match the circumstances. Formative observation leads to generative schemas applicable in a range of contexts (Bandura, 1986; additionally argued in Medin, 1989; and amplified in Idson & Mischel, 2001) that become contextually refined through participation and identification (similarly argued (from a very different perspective) by Wenger, 1998 within notions of communities of practice).

- *Motivation* – people do not enact everything they observe, but rather recall and act upon observed learning when there are incentives to do so. In essence, people are more likely to attend to particular observed behaviour if it results in valued outcomes (Slife & Rychlak, 1982). This motivational bias in attention and encoding is shaped through salience of observed people in particular contexts.

These four attributes of attention, retention, production and motivation seem a useful framework for guiding the sense-making of observational leadership learning from notable people. Additionally, this framework can be extended by examining temporal and contextual perspectives using the work of Gibson (2003).

Gibson argues that there is little attention towards understanding the impact of notable others beyond childhood, adolescents and early stages of organisational socialisation (Gibson, 2003: 591). Gibson's (2003) work (see also Gibson, 2004) has identified that the development of self-concept and social identity is malleable through adulthood and continues to be shaped by social comparison through a variety of notable others. (Similar to the earlier work of Ibarra, 1999 as 'provisional-selves'.) Through studying how people select notable others in their organisational context, and attach meaning to these people through different points in their organisational careers, Gibson (2003) suggests that people construe their notable others from a number of dimensions: positive and negative; global and specific; close and distant; hierarchically superior, peer or subordinate. These dimensions vary between career stages. In early career, people were found to focus on notables to create their self-concept; in mid-career they seek models to refine their self-concept; while in later stages they seek out notables who affirm particular identities.

Linking Gibson's (2003) typology with Bandura's (1986) four attributes provides two useful lenses through which to examine observational leadership learning. In essence, Gibson's observations about learning through time or career can be seen to draw upon a number of dimensions shaping observational learning. The work of Bandura (1986) has the potential to explore these temporal aspects and related dimensions in greater depth.

Bandura (1977) returns time and again to the role of observational learning in generating representational symbols. He argues that human survival and change is partly the result of the human capability to learn vicariously through such symbolic generalised patterns. Observational learning, particularly of notable people, will become most central to the explanation of how managers learn to lead.

Conclusion

> The way in which a man conceives of himself will influence both what he chooses to do and what he expects from life.
>
> (Gergen, 1971: 2)

This statement captures the essence of their arguments within this chapter, which has sought to cohere broad areas of learning theory to be able to provide foundational insights into the process of leadership learning. From the orientation of social interaction, the concept of self is seen to be a major interdisciplinary link between the fields of sociology and psychology (Gergen, 1971). This is of pivotal significance to the construction of this chapter on learning. It has been shown that rather than taking an individual or social perspective to learning, both fields of knowledge have been utilised to illustrate an integrative perspective.

For example, situated learning (Lave & Wenger, 1991; Fox, 1997a) provides a glimpse towards an understanding of how tacit learning occurs and is shared between communities through participation. Within such participation an individual manager enacts activities reflecting experiential learning (Kolb & Fry, 1975; Kolb, 1984) and through legitimised role enactment is able to observe and learn vicariously from others' behaviour (Bandura, 1986). Identities are fashioned out from such participation that is continually elaborated through social comparison and personal investment. Such investment of themselves into particular roles and identities can be similarly associated with salient oriented activities that are valued by both the individual and the community in which the role is enacted. Further, salience has been argued to shape perception and encoding of experience, and memory has been described as a malleable process reconfiguring experience to fit conceptualisation of phenomenon such as leadership and identity. The emphasis in this chapter has been on integrating learning literature to create an interdisciplinary perspective of learning in the social context, captured by Burgoyne as 'a collective entity of individual–in–environment which adapts and develops as a mutuality, by a process of meaningful participation' (1995: 63). Thus an integrative view of an individual-centric psychological perspective and a sociological perspective will provide a central foundation to be applied to the case studies of Chapter 7 in order to provide insight to the explanation of how managers learn to lead.

4
What Is Understood about Leadership Learning and Development?

The leadership development phenomenon

Many organisations view leadership as a source of competitive advantage and have been investing in developing both the human and the social capital within their organisations (Conger, 1996; Drath, 1998; Moxley, 1998; Day, 2000). Leadership is seen as a key ingredient for future success, with e-business and capacity for change ranking lower (CIMA, 2000). The scale of investment into activities loosely described as leadership development has been highlighted in Chapter 1, and is estimated to be in the many billions of pounds.

Yet there is a striking paradox to this growth in development training of leaders. Through the eighties and nineties, researchers (Davies & Easterby-Smith, 1984; Bennis & Nanus, 1985; McCall et al., 1988; Marserick, 1988; Cox, 1989; McCall, 1998) argued that the predominant development arena was informal, and accidental learning in action; the key development areas were seen to be stretching project assignments, notable people and hardships (McCall et al., 1988). Processes of leadership learning and development appear to be through informal and unintended learning as part of the milieu of general societal and specific organisational experience; yet formal development programmes continue to be dominant in practice. Equally, there is another paradox in that while so much research has been undertaken in understanding the phenomenon and characteristics of leadership, there has been a relative dearth of explicit research into leadership development (Day, 2000) and in particular whether these billions of pounds spent make any difference – what is the efficacy of leadership development?

Associated with these equivocal issues and potentially magnifying confusion is the question as to whether management development is different from leadership development, and whether leader development should be distinguished from leadership development (Day, 2000).

In order to address these issues, this chapter is structured around the following themes:

- Management, leader or leadership development? Defining and distinguishing between these three phenomena.
- Formal leadership development: An exploration of literature that has shaped the dominant focus of activity on formal leadership development.
- Informal leadership learning: Illustrating the prominence of naturalistic processes of leadership learning including childhood and organisational experiences.
- Emergent issues for understanding leadership learning and development: Act of faith? Contextualisation? Education or training? Or perhaps simply a 'gift of divine grace'?
- Conclusion: Sense of agreement towards the informal naturalistic processes shaping leadership learning and development.

Progression through these themes creates a movement from explicit formal organised development interventions to implicit accidental learning and development through everyday experiences. The chapter concludes with the current emergent themes drawn from the discussion that particularly highlight a dearth of discrete research on leadership learning – hence the need for this study.

Management, leader or leadership development?

> Despite considerable recent attention to the topic, management development may still be one of the most ill-defined and variously interpreted concepts in the management literature.
>
> (Wexley & Baldwin, 1986: 277)

Such ill-definition reflects the relative dearth of literature on leadership learning and development compared to other management subjects (Hall & Seibert, 1992; Yukl, 2001). The field of research, examined in this chapter, evolves around an acceptance that management and leadership development are seen to be synonymous. This conflation of management and leadership development will be shown to be prevalent and reflects a broad definition, for example, 'as the whole complex process by which individuals learn, grow and improve their abilities to perform professional management tasks' (Wexley & Baldwin, 1986: 277).

The focus of organisational interventions for management development typically centres on the individual, in the form of human capital, rather than seeking a broader development of social capital. Day (2000) explores this distinction and suggests that greater definitional clarity is required between leader development programmes as human capital and leadership development as social capital, and comments on current leader development as,

> occurring primarily through training individual, intrapersonal skills and abilities ... these kinds of training approaches, however, ignore almost fifty years of research showing leadership to be a complex interaction between designated leader and the social and organisational environment.
>
> (2000: 583)

The view of leadership development as social capital is very much at the periphery of research activity and practitioner intervention. The overwhelming dominant model of leadership development assumes individual centrality and a desire to develop skills across a broad range of functional areas, such as budget management, planning systems, technical training, or strategic management. Much of this perspective accords with a transactional orientation to management and have only a limited focus on transformational leadership (Russell & Kuhnert, 1990; Lowe & Gardner, 2000). Leadership learning and development research follows and interprets management development practice and reflects an ambiguous understanding of the nature of leadership, resulting in breadth, diversity and generality of foundations (Barker, 2001).

For purposes of clarity the differences between leader, leadership and management development need to be made explicit. I wish to argue that:

- Management development – aims at broad interventions to develop management and leadership approaches.
- Leader development – focuses on interventions to develop interpersonal leadership skills.
- Leadership development – explores the systemic context in which leaders and followers operate and seeks to intervene to enhance effectiveness.

- Leadership learning – examines how an individual has learnt leadership; it may include interventions from the above activities and/or be naturalistic influences gained through lived experience, such as observing others or enacting leadership roles.

However, the literature on leadership development does not fit neatly into the above definitions. For example, informal interventions such as mentor–mentee relationships are described as leadership development; similarly, accidental learning through hardships is also labelled leadership development, even though no designed intervention occurred.

This study on leadership learning specifically relates to the individual perspective, explicitly focusing on how a manager who is working in a large or a small organisation, relates to leadership and how or what influences have shaped his or her leadership practice. These may be formal or informal interventions (leadership development), or naturalistic and emerging as unplanned influences occurring as part of everyday activities.

The term leadership learning will be used throughout the book, but both leadership learning and leadership development will be used in this chapter to reflect the broad field in which the literature is located. Hence, the headings will use those meanings from where the research originates rather than transpose the working notion of leadership learning onto extant theory.

The key point to emphasise is that there is much confusion and lack of clarity around leadership development, leader development and management development. I argue that we need to become much clearer. It is an explicit intention of this book to develop a clear argument and explanation of leadership learning that may give greater clarity to these equivocal issues.

Formal leadership development

It was argued by Schriesheim and Neider (1989) that leadership development activity has become overly focused on two areas, and this remains similar today, namely: behavioural skills and awareness training that often incorporates behavioural psychology; and broad education on management development that seeks development implicitly and in rather an emergent and anticipatory fashion, often incorporating functional skills. If we use these two areas as two dimensions we can illustrate the variety of leadership development activities available in organisations:

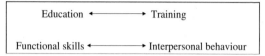

By combining these two continua, the following segmentation grid is proposed reflecting the dominant formal leadership development interventions, as shown in Figure 4.1.

Yukl (1989a) separates development from training; the former being embedded in organisational activities and the latter conducted during a defined time separate from organisational activity. However, such a distinction has become significantly blurred through experiential and action learning projects that interact with and within an organisational context. The elements shown in the grid have been identified to be predominant in usage (Saari et al., 1988; Rothwell & Kanzanas, 1994; Fulmer and Wagner, 1999; James & Burgoyne, 2001). Early management development interventions were accentuated towards functional education and training (Wexley & Baldwin, 1986). For example, Wexley and Baldwin (1986) suggested that 85 per cent of American companies that engaged in leadership development activities used formal classroom programmes, and this remains similar ten years on (American Society for Training and Development, 1995). However, in the UK over the last decade a shift has occurred from formal to informal development (Burgoyne et al., 2004).

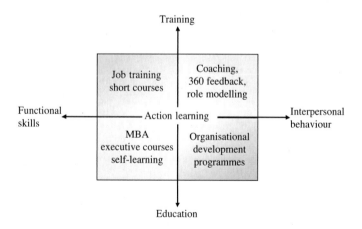

Figure 4.1   Leadership development grid

Criticism of broad education has centred on teaching individual managers about management, rather than how to manage and that there is too little opportunity to learn about practice and become competent in behavioural skills (Pfeffer, 1977; Waters, 1980). Further, there are concerns about educational competency programmes being able to replicate the competence of effective managers (Vaill, 1983); in particular whether trainers and educationalists can design and deliver competence training that replicates, and can be migrated into, the idiosyncratic context of organisations (Bradford, 1983).

A shift of foci has occurred that has seen a movement towards interpersonal behaviour within organisational contexts and particularly within the context of daily activity and interaction (Day, 2000; Burgoyne et al., 2004). Such a movement has given greater emphasis to coaching, mentoring and role modelling behaviour. The current pattern of best practice development has extenuated this shift from taught classroom-based activities to action learning, coaching and mentoring with an ever-increasing focus on competencies and 'anywhere any time' (James & Burgoyne, 2001: 9) organisationally focused learning, oriented towards and aligned with corporate strategy (Fulmer & Wagner, 1999; Burgoyne et al., 2004).

In a review of corporate 'best practice' within management development programmes, James and Burgoyne (2001) identified a range of published case examples of organisations that concentrated less on formal training and significantly more towards the development of the next generation of leaders through action learning projects and senior leaders teaching and mentoring (similarly echoed by Fulmer & Wagner, 1999; Burgoyne et al., 2004). The effectiveness of these activities to the development of leadership is equivocal (Burgoyne et al., 2004). Burgoyne et al. comment that:

> [t]he large proportion of the literature and reports on management and leadership development is not, to any significant degree, evidence based. Where it is, it is so in a relatively weak form ... that which is done within organizations driven by their own policies and plans ... gives us confidence to say that management and leadership development can have beneficial effects.
>
> (2004: 78–9)

In essence, Burgoyne et al. reflect the discussion of best practice intervention that seeks to anchor effectiveness not necessarily into return on investment measures, but rather into measurement oriented towards organisational needs, most prominently that associated with an organi-sation's strategy (Fulmer & Wagner, 1999; James & Burgoyne, 2001; Ready & Conger, 2003). In contrast, an emphasis that formal manage-ment development is a good thing is argued by Watson and Wyatt (2000):

> Establishing formal programmes to develop leadership at all levels is a priority ... the more companies do to develop leaders, the greater their financial success on shareholder return, growth in net income, growth in market sales and return on sales.
>
> (Watson & Wyatt, 2000 in James & Burgoyne, 2001: 16)

Bass (1990) expressed an unequivocal view that effectiveness has been shown through citing a comprehensive review of published research on leadership training (Latham, 1988) and argues that Latham's review substantiates the efficacy of leadership training. Support for effective-ness of leadership training is associated with particular theories of lead-ership where training evaluation is measured against specific criteria of the respective theory (for example, Blake & Mouton, 1982; Bass & Avolio, 1989).

However, each of these approaches represents a rather narrow com-ponent of the phenomenon of leadership (Wexley & Baldwin, 1986) and improved managerial effectiveness may relate to improved inter-personal skills rather than the use of the respective leadership model (Yukl, 1998). For example, Ready and Conger (2003) cite an organisa-tion that:

> offers a new leadership training program approximately every two years based on a current best-selling book. The programs to date include training experiences designed on the basis of well-known books by respected researchers, such as Stephen Covey's 'The Seven Habits of Highly Effective People', Peter Senge's 'The Fifth Discipline' ... and Daniel Goleman's 'Emotional Intelligence'.
>
> (2003: 85)

Overgeneralisation of perceived successful leadership development reci-pes to complex local contexts calls into question the efficacy of such formal training interventions. Hoffman commented that:

> [g]iven the value and costs of management development activities it is unsettling that so little evaluative evidence exists and that so many

people question whether these efforts do anything to upgrade actual managerial performance.

(1985: 34)

Over a decade later Yukl (1998) also questions the efficacy of training approaches to developing leadership:

Despite the massive volume of leadership training that occurs there has been relatively little research on its effectiveness ... More research is required of different training techniques for different types of leadership skills and behaviour.

(1998: 490)

Day (2000) goes further and argues that leadership development practice, including both training and education foci on skills and behaviours, has failed to recognise research that shows leadership to be 'a complex interaction between designated leader and the social and organisational environment' (2000: 583). Over the last 20 years, the process perspective of leadership has led to a reconceptualisation of leadership development. From this perspective, Day (2000) suggests that leadership development should be seen from the two interconnected perspectives of human capital and social capital. Day advocates that the traditional formal models of coaching, mentoring, 360-degree feedback and role modelling need to be moved from a perspective that:

development occurs through specifically designed programmes. ... Instead it is a continuous process that can take place anywhere. ... It means helping people to learn from their work rather than taking them away from their work to learn.

(2000: 586)

Barker (1997) suggests that formal leadership development should focus significantly less on training and more on development and education. He advocates that development is a blend of cognitive and emotional integration that influences self-motivation, self-direction and self-identity. Formal development activity should draw these out of individuals in order to develop self-control through integration with their motivations and the wants and needs of the group. Education places emphasis towards conscious awareness of social patterns that produce insights into knowledge, ideals and experiences that shape individual and group beliefs and values, to enable collective integration into collective goals.

It is to this last point that the central focus of this chapter is oriented. Leadership learning and development is much more than the development of individual skills through training and education – described in Chapter 3 by Fox (1997a) as decontextualised knowledge. It is prominently an emergent and socially developed understanding that an individual acquires within a context or system (in the form of contextualised learning as advocated by Lave & Wenger, 1991). Chapter 3 described such learning as situated and naturalistic. The next section clarifies what is known about such naturalistic influences on leadership learning and development.

Informal leadership learning

Informal leadership learning can be described as development through experiences where managers learn, grow and undergo personal change as a result of the roles, responsibilities and tasks encountered in their jobs (McCauley & Brutus, 1998), and so reflect emergent and accidental events rather than a deliberate and consciously planned approach to development. A significant group of researchers have identified that leadership and management development occur primarily through developmental experiences and relationships. These researchers have not sought to distinguish between leadership and management. As a consequence the review of extant informal management development literature will draw insights interpreted to be related to leadership learning.

Formative childhood development

The impact of relationships and experiences occur at a very young age, shaped by parents and teachers. From a relational perspective, parents act as role models (Anderson, 1943) providing value standards, such as work ethic (Bass, 1990) or the value of education (Gibbons, 1986). The influence of, and relationship with, a strong maternal authority was seen to be influential (Bass, 1990). For example, research on 30 CEOs, selected because of their business success, were found to have strong parental role models; again in most instances these role models were their mothers (Piotrowski & Armstrong, 1987). Children who were in leadership roles in teams appeared to be associated with parents who set high standards and had achievement expectations linked to discipline accompanied with parental warmth (Klonsky, 1983). Within the family environment, children's participation in decisions has been seen to stimulate a child to be more active, socially outgoing, intelligent, curious, original and constructive; in larger families social cooperativeness is developed along with an ability to work towards a group goal (Bass, 1990).

Cox and Cooper (1989) identified, in their study of 45 chief executives in the UK, that a common feature of their sample was the affect of childhood experiences on the level of independence and an ability to rely on one's own resources. A similar and related earlier finding of ambition and social direction was seen to be significant to leaders who had experienced high quality family relationships (Bass, 1960). In a study by Jennings (1943) it was identified that people in leadership roles identified themselves with a member of their family whom they described as sociable, reliable and encouraging. Non-leaders identified themselves with family members who expressed discouragement, anxiety and worry. Childhood and adolescent experiences, represented as favourable family conditions, were also seen to be significant in the Piotrowski and Armstrong (1987) study and a link has been suggested between childhood responsibility and respect from elders with the notion of charismatic leadership (Hall, 1983). Leadership is more likely to be displayed by 'school-boys' in which the parental environment grants high levels of responsibility and independence (Hoffman et al., 1960), often illustrated by the eldest sibling given responsibility for younger siblings. A family environment which is risk adverse and which restricts opportunities to experiment commensurate with a child's maturity, can restrict development and may be exhibited in adults as carelessness, overconfidence and limited social skills that would have otherwise been learnt through experimenting in social situations (Bass, 1990). Jones, quoting Freud, sums up the relational role model thus:

> A man who has been the indisputable favourite of his mother keeps for life the feeling of conqueror, that confidence of success that often induces real success.
>
> (1953: 5)

The influence of parents as role models and the environmental experiences shaping a child's development appear to provide interesting clues to the early development of leaders' attitudes and skills within social situations. Certainly the leadership development process may begin at a very early age and the pattern and ability to learn from both relationships and developmental experiences is forged at a time when the effects cannot be easily traced to the causes.

What is perhaps most striking is the role of parents in socially constructing implicit theories of leadership in terms of traits, values, skills and attitudes that reflect broad cultural, as well as idiosyncratic, family-oriented features – see Chapter 2 for a discussion on 'implicit theories' of leadership.

Educational context of informal leadership learning

The impact of relationships and developmental experiences can be seen to be continued from the parental context into the educational environment, in the form of teachers extending the development process as well as reinforcing children and adolescents' understanding of the leadership phenomenon. Bass (1990) identified the above socially constructed development process as being explicit in the system of public schools in producing leaders for the British Empire. However, the focus by Bass understates the cultural continuation of advantaged socio-economic groups to create and sustain a leadership cadre and instead focuses on the formal development process. Gronn, for example, links education with 'family socialisation of status, hierarchy and authority norms through intense peer socialization in boarding houses' (1997: 4). Lapping (1985) describes an instilled class-conscious socialisation from family and schooling: 'They were Plato's guardians – a caste apart, bred and trained to be superior' (1985: 811).

This naturalistic development process arguably occurs in school contexts where teachers can be seen as 'leaders', establishing societal role model characteristics that embody notions of authority, power, discipline and morality. The continuation of the development of implicit theories of leadership (Phillips & Lord, 1982) is first started with parents and arguably subsequently developed within the educational arena. There is very little published research on informal leadership learning and development through the education process. Literature on the parental development phenomenon may be extrapolated to the educational arena where teachers and notable head teachers may act as a surrogate parent that reinforces both 'implicit theories' and the 'romantic' perspectives of leadership (Pfeifer, 1977b; Calder, 1977; Meindl et al., 1985).

Organisational context of informal leadership development

Significantly greater research focus has been placed on informal management development within an organisational context, particularly towards relationships and developmental experiences. However, such focus is relative to the volume of research on parental and educational informal leadership development. If compared to general leadership research, attention has been limited in terms of numbers of researchers and publications (McCauley & Brutus, 1998). Most notably there is a particular dearth of research examining informal developmental processes within an organisational context that is explicit to learning leadership practice.

As introduced in Chapter 1, research into understanding informal management development in organisational contexts came to prominence in the late seventies and early eighties through the related literature of a group of researchers (Burgoyne & Stuart, 1976; Burgoyne, 1977; Burgoyne & Hodgson, 1983; and in particular Davies & Easterby-Smith, 1984). The work of these researchers helped to establish interest in management and leadership learning experiences. Interestingly, at the same time descriptive studies seeking to understand the nature of management and leadership were being undertaken – such as the work of Mintzberg (1973), Kotter (1982, 1988), Bennis (1989) and latterly Watson (2001).

Burgoyne and Stewart (1976) identified the significance of learning through experience and examined the learning and development processes of managers within the context of their normal work and suggested processes associated with self-development that were anchored in experience. The contribution of Davies and Easterby-Smith (1984) was to identify differential learning and development between managers drawn from their everyday work, and this differentiation could be seen to be associated with organisational context. For example, managers reported greater development and learning in turbulent environments or in situations of establishing new roles with greater freedom of operation. Development was stronger for individuals who chose to move into areas that faced issues that could not be resolved from previous practices. Additionally, Cox and Cooper (1989) illustrated that experience of a wide range of situations associated with high mobility, early in a manager's career, appeared to contribute significantly towards development. Similar interpretations of individual development and learning from experiences beyond previous learnt routines were identified by Burgoyne and Hodgson (1983) and Davies and Easterby-Smith (1984). Of particular significance were the implications that managers learnt through greater risk and responsibility for a discrete area (usually self-induced), through addressing something very new (rather than a career move that was more of the same) through having freedom to act (even non-standard behaviour) and by shaping role definition according to changing situations (Davies &

Easterby-Smith, 1984). A useful synthesis of the developmental role of experience is summarised thus:

> So it appears that experience – as we have all known for a long time – is the key to development of managers: but some kinds of experiences provide more effective development than others.
>
> (1984: 180)

Building from Davies and Easterby-Smith (1984), McCall et al. (1988), within the notable text *Lessons of Experience*,[1] synthesised the field of study into informal development through experience that has since become a central citation for many subsequent commentaries on informal leadership development.

Key lessons of experience

Research undertaken in the Honeywell organisation (Zemke, 1985) identified similar dominance of on-the-job experiences as the primary source of development, as well as the primacy of two key developmental processes. It was identified that approximately 80 per cent of reported learning came from contact with key people in the workplace and on-the-job experiences. These two clear initial findings have framed the field of management learning through experience and particularly influenced the work of McCall at al. (1988) that synthesised research developed over a six-year period (McCall & McCauley, 1986; Lindsey et al., 1987; Morrison et al., 1987).[2] They identified three major themes:

- *Job assignments* (60 per cent of lessons) – challenging due to inexperienced circumstances, requiring skills not used before, under significant pressure and usually associated with interpersonal conflict.
- *Notable people* (20 per cent of lessons) – provoked learning about values and politics 'and understanding how to direct and motivate others as a complement to the power of the managerial role' (1988: 82; similar point emphasised by Bass et al., 1987).
- *Hardships* (20 per cent of lessons) – significant reflection and 'heightened awareness of own shortcomings, a clearer view of themselves … and compassion and tolerance for the foibles of others' (1988: 119).

Although the findings of McCall et al. are seen to be a significant contribution to learning through experience, there are a number of issues to be explored with respect to the specificity of leadership learning.

Rather than a discrete focus on leadership, McCall et al. focused on management, as illustrated by their opening research question: 'When you think about your career as a manager ... '(1988: 5). This suggested a broad direction of thinking that allowed respondents to interpret the role of manager from an undefined perspective. Within the text, *Lessons of Experience* (McCall et al., 1988), the terms management and leadership are intertwined and used liberally, leading to ambiguity of interpretation as to whether the lessons relate to management or leadership, but presumably both. From an examination of the contents of the lessons, there is a greater association of management with assignments – being particularly task-focused; while the lessons of hardships and notable people could be seen to be more prototypically associated with learning about leadership. The authors do not seek to make a distinction between management and leadership and there are no critiques of the research available in this respect.

An issue of significance, commented on by McCall et al. (1988) (and similarly echoed in Davies & Easterby-Smith, 1984, as well as Broderick, 1983 and Zemke, 1985), was a link between the success of interventions and the context of the individual. It has been identified that the relevance of intervention and its impact was greater when it occurred at, or near the time of a significant learning episode. Burgoyne and Stewart (1976), Davies and Easterby-Smith (1984) and McCall et al. (1988) and later McCall (1998) placed emphasis towards greater salience of leadership learning as a consequence of contextualisation through hardships, notable people, change of environment or difficult role assignments, rather than general decontextualised learning through information transfer in classroom settings. This important assertion has been affirmed through very recent research by Armstrong and Mahmud (2008).

The notion of organisational context influencing learning and development also shapes socialised learning and leads to lessons that are relevant to managing and leading in specific contexts. The importance of contextual influence on learning has been emphasised in Chapter 3 with particular areas of learning theory, namely situated learning and community of practice, identity construction and social learning.

Learning from others in developmental relationships has been highlighted (Morrison et al., 1987; McCall et al., 1988; McCauley & Douglas, 1998) as both deliberate (as with mentors) and accidental (through daily contact with good or bad role models). The significance of observational learning to leadership development is rather understated (Kempster, 2006, 2007, 2008). There is no specific focus on a deeper understanding of the processes of influence relating to these notables, good or bad or a temporal perspective as to when notables had influence: for example, earlier or later in people's careers. There was only a limited discussion on processes of observational learning with no great weight of attention to its significance and prominence to the development of leadership practice.

It should be noted that research by McCall et al. (1988) did not seek to understand processes by which the lessons shaped learning and development of individual managers. In no sense have the researchers claimed to understand the individual process of leadership learning as distinct from management learning.

However, the research does highlight an issue that learning and development through experience predominantly occurs when a manager realises that their previous experience is not sufficient for the situation at hand (Beck, 1988), or that the way the manager previously anticipated enacting skills for the situation is no longer appropriate (Kelly, 1955). Such realisation often occurs inaction (Schon, 1983; Ferry & Ross-Gordon, 1998) or reflection-on-action (Schon, 1983), but can be seen to be catalysed through key events that disrupt routines and allow new behaviours to be learnt for new situations (Brett, 1983; a similar argument was suggested by the formative work of Whitehead, 1933).

Linked to Davies and Easterby-Smith (1984), Brett (1983) suggests that such routines are broken and development results as a consequence of an individual's perception of uncertainty and expectation; in a sense, an emotional and anxious episode. Associated with routine breaking and subsequent development, is the notion of mid-career change causing individuals to trial activity in new areas leading to greater adaptation that is often associated with changes in personal and social identity (Gergen, 1971; similar arguments in Ezzy, 1998; Ibarra, 1999). Such explicit triggers for reappraisal of values, identity, self-efficacy and behaviour have been associated with hardships (McCall et al., 1988) and, in particular, executive derailment (McCall, 1998).

Developmental relationships, through observational learning, appear to be much more emergent and subliminal (Bandura, 1986) and may only be recognised through the identification of particular formative incidents recalled through episodic memory (Srull & Wyer, 1989; Walsh, 1995). For example, work by Avolio and Luthans (2006) identified the importance of 'trigger moments', Bennis and Thomas (2002) highlighted 'tranformative experiences' that shifted an individual's identity, and Janson (2008) identified the significance of 'leadership formative experiences' – often attached to emotional incidents. All three studies anchor leadership learning to events and all three are aware that such events are only part of the story – difficulty lies in seeking to explore the gradual and imperceptible learning that occurs through the routine and mundane activities of everyday leadership acts – see Chapter 3 and the discussion on tacit knowledge.

McCauley, Moxley and Van Velsor (1998) synthesised their understanding of prominent processes of leadership learning and suggested that developmental experience is shaped by three elements:

- Assessment – understanding the need to change and how this can occur.
- Challenge – an opportunity that is perceived to be developmental.
- Support – an environment that encourages development.

The authors suggest that within the framework of assessment, challenge and support, learning through experience can be organised and enhanced by creating a variety of rich developmental experiences that are further heightened through developing an individual's ability to learn within an organisational context. Further, Conger (1993) argues for an organised approach and believes that too much leadership development has occurred in a 'haphazard process' (1993: 46), with little intentionality, accountability or evaluation (ibid.). Drawing these notions of development together, an equation is offered (McCauley et al., 1998: 223):

Feedback intensive programme + skill-based training + 360-degree feedback + developmental relationships + hardships = Leadership development.

(1998: 223)

In summary, the equation completes the circle of the literature review by paradoxically returning us back to organised formal leadership development where McCauley et al. (1998) argue that intervention is enhanced through embracing naturalistic experiences within a formal process. Yet there is also a paradox to this simple (perhaps simplistic) equation: the lessons that are developmental are those which often occur when least expected, but are highly relevant to the context and are idiosyncratically interpreted by an individual as additional to previous experience. Can the unexpected and the idiosyncratic be planned as part of a formal development programme? Can interventions span sufficient time to allow naturalistic experiences to take effect? In terms of efficacy, can outcomes be measured in relation to designed inputs?

In essence, can naturalistic development be controlled and accelerated if a significant part of leadership learning occurs through repeating routines and socialisation over extended periods? This range of questions set the scene for the next section that addresses emerging issues for leadership learning and development.

Emergent issues for understanding leadership learning and development

The final theme explores four interrelated issues. The first examines whether leadership development can be measured or whether it is simply best understood as an act of faith. The second theme explores the essential need to contextualise any form of intervention if any progress is to go beyond the act of faith. The third distinguishes between training and reflection, building on the assertion within this chapter that naturalistic learning predominates in generating complex situated practice, and perhaps reflection on individual practice is preferable to training solutions. The final theme returns full circle to the born-versus-made-debate. Can transformational leadership be taught or is it a 'gift from god'.

Leadership development – an act of faith?

The research base of both informal and formal leadership development has been deleteriously affected by the historic conflation of management and leadership. Only a few commentators – notably Messrs Day (2000), Barker (2001), Burgoyne et al. (2004) and Conger (2004) – argue the case for greater differentiation and understanding of the process by which managers learn how to lead, as distinct from how managers learn how to manage. Their arguments build from Baldwin and Wexley who, in 1986, had identified,

> several fundamental concerns regarding research and practice ... The body of literature is descriptive, anecdotal, non-empirical and faddish often emerging as lists of requirements; traditional formal development follows particular theories resulting in a narrow focus to a broad concept which arguably results in simplistic interventions.
>
> (1986: 286)

These concerns remain relevant today as leadership learning and development is, for the most part, an act of faith (Burgoyne, 2001). Programmes developed out of the practice of one organisational context are assumed to be generalisable across the leadership and management development industry without empirical evidence (argued by Burgoyne et al., 2004; repeating earlier concerns of Freedman & Stumpf, 1982; Hoffman, 1985; Huber, 1985). The lack of empirical evidence on leadership development emphasises significant question marks on the efficacy of interventions and the return on the organisational investment (Moxley, 1998; and more recently by Burgoyne et al., 2004). Is it more of an act of faith to continue to invest in organised formal interventions despite the prominence of research suggesting that informal, naturalistic influences appear to be predominant? Further, the focus on the individual, as the measure of the return on the investment, is also problematic. For example, Drath (1998) advocates that leadership development will move towards team development in the form of distributed leadership. Day (2000) argues for leadership development as the development of social capital, and an investment into developing social systems as vehicles of leadership influence may have greater longevity than an investment in human capital in the form of leader development. Difficulties may then become associated with seeking to measure the efficacy of interventions to develop a broader social group; such difficulties emerge as a consequence of potentially numerous unintended social interactions that may stimulate or limit development processes. This notion of interaction within an 'open-system' has been an argument limiting an ability to understand the efficacy of investment in leadership development (Burgoyne et al., 2004): hence the continuance of a 'blind faith' supported by equivocal metrics. Often such faith is reassured by drawing upon others 'best' practice. Two questions emerge: how transferable are 'best' practices? Can recipes drawn from best practice be applicable regardless of contexts? The next section examines the issue of contextualised intervention.

Need for contextualisation

Various reviews of leadership best practice (James & Burgoyne, 2001; Fulmer & Wagner, 1999; Conger, 2004) have highlighted that although there are a number of dominant themes common to organisations perceived as offering best practice, the emphasis is towards contextualisation. Implicit in the best practice recommendations (notably of James & Burgoyne, 2001) is a connection with informal, naturalistic experiences, such as assignments, hardships and bosses (McCall, 1988). These implicit systemic influences within complex situations have not been explored in depth and within particular contexts – hence the need for this study. For example, the development of leadership practice appears to draw on societal interpretations of leadership but is significantly shaped by local meanings and historic embedded practices – the central argument of Chapter 2. If such practice is required to change then interventions would need to recognise the local influences and historic practices to enhance intervention success.

Further, both best practice recommendations and extant theory on informal experience are also content to conflate leader and manager concepts rather than isolate these two particular phenomena. Certainly there was no research available, at the time of writing, which was explicit about revealing underlying influences within organisations that are perceived as specific to learning leadership.

In a paper entitled 'The brave new world of leadership training' Conger (1996) argues that the old models of leadership are no longer appropriate for coping with the consequences of the magnitude of change which is facing organisations. He argues that leadership development must change and become contextualised, yet his research has identified that organisations are turning, more than ever before, to outdated 'off the shelf' interventions that have questionable efficacy in terms of applicability to local situations. The thrust of his vision for leadership development is towards an acceptance that:

> in many organisations leadership training is merely a deceptive play with words. They say they are concerned about developing leaders, when in reality they feel more secure with managers. The art of leadership development is still in its infancy.
>
> (Conger, 1996: 57)

Leadership development – reflection rather than training?

Drawing on Conger's (1996) and Burgoyne et al.'s (2004) concerns about the efficacy of leadership training, and linked to Day (2000) and Drath's (1998) argument for leadership development to be oriented towards social systems, should formal leadership development emphasise education more than training? The complexity and idiosyncratic nature of contextual learning limits the appropriateness of 'how to' training methods of leadership (Barker, 2001). Rather, a reflective and educational accent might enable managers to understand their social phenomenological relationship with leadership and compare this to other models of leadership from which they can make relevant connections to their specific context. Such a reflective pedagogy may give greater emphasis to learning how to lead through making sense of self, related to situated experience. Enabling an individual to surface, make sense and differentiate the quality of the informal experiences occurring in the context of their everyday activities, appears to be a critical catalyst to individual leadership development (Cunliffe, 2001). Such a capability may greatly increase individual recognition of developmental environments and developmental experiences (Davies & Easterby-Smith, 1984) – recommendations for the development of educative practice are elaborated in Chapter 9.

A key development issue appears to be helping people to learn from experience (Day, 2000; Velsor & Guthrie, 1998; McCall, 1998; Conger, 2004). With respect to 'high-flyers', McCall (1998) argues that the most significant common attribute of these people was the talent that they had for learning from their experiences. He argues that just because someone goes through an experience, it does not mean that they have learnt from that experience. For example, it was shown that most managers were not active and continuous learners (Bunker & Webb, 1992). The point is amplified by Velsor and Guthrie:

> To learn, managers needed to let go of their current strengths long enough to acquire new ones. They must be strong and secure enough to make themselves vulnerable to the stresses and setbacks in the learning process.
>
> (1998: 242)

Despite the criticisms of formal intervention in comparison to the emerging consensus toward naturalistic informal experiences, ironically (and echoing McCauley et al., 1998) formal education may be a key catalyst for enhancing the dominant arena of informal leadership development: 'It means helping people to learn from their work rather than taking them away from their work to learn' (Day, 2000: 586). The notion of learning from *their work* anchors learning and development to situations. The final issue explored in this section examines how the situation and *the work* may shape a shared understanding of leadership within leader–follower relationships, allowing some leaders to be perceived as transformational and others as transactional: A 'gift of God' (Weber, 1947) or perhaps a gift generated through the situation?

Transformational leadership – can it be developed?

Chapter 2 has identified the prominence of 'new leadership' in the form of transformational and authentic leadership. Exponents of this model of leadership advocate its potential significance to organisational performance (Parry, 2001). The work of Parry and Sinha (2005) suggests that transformational leadership can be developed through training interventions and Parry has pioneered such interventions through classroom settings. Others, most notably Conger (1996), have taken an alternative perspective and argue that it is very unclear how, for example, individuals develop charisma and vision, and certainly how to formally develop charismatic leadership? These issues remain understandably elusive. Conger questions whether,

> training can develop such skills as vision as it is a by-product of experience and an openness to ideas and trends ... can we teach it? Not likely.
>
> (1996: 56)

If vision or charisma cannot be taught, how do some leaders become charismatic and transformational? If it is not through training then is it, perhaps, simply as Weber (1947) argued, a 'gift of divine grace'? The argument of Chapter 2 outlines a case of leadership (including transformational, authentic and charismatic modes) being formed through a constructed process of both universal aspects (traits/behavioural norms and implicit/romantic theories) and local contextualised approaches.

Learning about both these elements appears to be anchored in naturalistic experience. The contextualised *by-product* (Conger, 1996: 56) of organisational experience reflects an acquisition of meanings and practices (Lave & Wenger, 1991) shaped among a particular community. The attribution of qualities of leadership, such as charisma, to a manager may reflect a shared understanding of leadership that could be symbolically represented through (and perhaps embodied in) the manager. The leader's behaviour may be attributed as charismatic, as a consequence of being in resonance with the meanings and practices that followers hold, and such attribution may reinforce a sense of the manager believing they can lead: in essence, there has been no training of the manager ... rather the manager has 'become' charismatic in a particular content.

Summary

The preceding discussion on informal development has outlined and substantiated the strong presence and influence of informal experiences in shaping leadership learning and development. There is thus an essential need to focus on leadership (as distinct from broad-based management) and understand the underlying influences that shape an individual manager's understanding of leadership and related leadership practice. This requires an examination at the level of lived experience. Whether such an understanding can be utilised within formal leadership training is uncertain especially if it is essentially an idiosyncratic, experiential process developed over a significant period of time: unless such formal intervention reflects a form of apprenticeship where the quality of long-term naturalistic experience is enhanced (Kempster, 2006) – a point to be returned to in Chapter 9.

Conclusion

The role of formal leadership development has been shown to be efficaciously limited in developing leaders compared to the naturalistic (Burgoyne & Stuart, 1977), accidental and informal process of development. However, the popularity of management development training and consequently the funding that is invested in it, has probably not reached its zenith (James & Burgoyne, 2001). The recent work by CEML and work for the Cabinet Office (Cabinet Office, 2000) and more recently affirmed in the Leitch report on UK skills development (Leitch Report, 2006) illustrates the significance of leadership development both to the government in the UK and to organisations. The anticipation of performance returns as a result of investing in leadership development is almost palpable.

Research is encouraged to explore and illuminate systemic processes of how leaders develop, in order to strengthen the link between leadership development systems and required leadership practice (Lowe & Gardner, 2000). The predominant influences on leadership learning and development appear to be through informal interaction within particular contexts and are generated by dual processes of socialisation and idiosyncratic experiences. However, it has been argued that little is known at the level of lived experience of these processes and how they may differ in particular contexts.

The chapter has outlined the significance of early developments in the making of a leader, in particular the role of parents and teachers with respect to values and behaviours. Further, the role of organisational experience appears to have significant impact on management leadership learning and development through: relationships with key people in the workplace; and on-the-job experiences.

For the most part researchers have not explicitly sought to distinguish management from leadership development. There is considerable need and scope to examine such influences on learning and reveal whether assignments, notable people or hardships are prevalent, as has been suggested (McCall et al., 1988), or whether other influences, alone or in various combinations, are prevalent in shaping leadership learning and development. Further, the literature has not sought to distinguish between types of organisations or sectors in which underlying influences operate: does the public or private sector have the same influences? Are these different between men and women, or the employed managers and owner-managers? There is simply too little empirical research that seeks to isolate and examine influences on leadership learning within an organisational context, and this is the specific emphasis of this book.

A ten-year review of the *Leadership Quarterly* (Lowe & Gardner, 2000) summarised the situation on leadership development research by citing Conger (1998): 'we do not know enough about how organisational systems develop leaders' (1998: 495). They emphasised the need to understand how organisational systems enhance the efficiency of leadership development efforts (Lowe & Gardner, 2000). Yukl succinctly summarises the situation thus:

> Despite the massive volume of leadership training that occurs there has been relatively little research on its effectiveness.
>
> (2001: 490)

The enormous investment into leadership development also reflects 'that there is considerably greater interest among leadership development practitioners but surprisingly little scholarly interest in the topic' (Lowe & Gardner, 2001: 495). This book seeks to make a contribution in this regard. The argument for the need to dig deeper at the level of lived experience and explore underlying influences on leadership learning has been made. The next chapter draws together the key aspects covered in Chapters 2, 3 and 4 and outlines a summary, encapsulated within a model of what we know about leadership learning and the development of leadership practice, and argues for what we still need to know.

5
So What Do We Know So Far about Leadership Learning?

Chapter 4 has illustrated how an understanding of informal leadership development has begun to cohere towards an emphasis on the variability of contexts and the breadth of individual experience that shapes leadership learning. For example, greater variety of contexts and roles were seen to be associated with an enriched appreciation of leadership and approaches to leading (Davies & Easterby-Smith, 1984). Similarly, task assignments in a range of contexts with associated hardships and modelled opportunities for observation were common broad themes shaping leadership learning (McCall et al., 1988; McCall, 2004).

Chapter 3 provided an understanding of learning processes, particularly emphasising the social and relational nature of learning. The notions of both social learning, in the form of observation and enactment, and situated learning through participation and acquisition of practice, meaning and identity, established the importance of contextual interaction in developing context specific learning and practice.

Chapter 2 established a systemic view of leadership as a constructed relational process of social influence between leader(s) and follower(s). The review of extant literature demonstrated that leadership can be seen through the three perspectives of leader, follower and the situation. The leader perspective suggested a more universal orientation of leadership, with an emphasis towards a learnt attribution of traits and behaviours which are seen to be more favourable in influencing followers. The followers' perspective outlined how followers learn to construct romantic and implicit theories of leadership that have a sense of universal application, but are often learnt and applied to the local context. The situational perspective anchors leadership into a locally developed relationship of intricate nuances of contextually constructed meanings

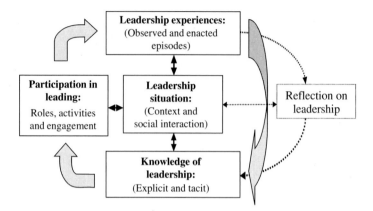

Figure 5.1 Leadership learning through lived experience (adapted from Kempster, 2006)

and practices of leadership. Both the high level universal and detailed local perspectives are learnt through relational experience.

Taken together, these three chapters outline foundational insights on the notion of leadership learning. At the very broadest level, Figure 5.1 (adapted from Kempster, 2006) seeks to diagrammatically represent the extant understanding of leadership learning by drawing upon the experiential learning cycle (Kolb & Fry, 1975; Kolb, 1984) and in particular the notion of learning about a phenomenon as a deepening cycle of experience.

The model of leadership learning through lived experience draws upon the work of Bennis and Thomas (2002) examining the 'crucibles' in which learning occurs, as well as reflecting on the recent the work of Janson (2008) examining leadership formative experiences. The cyclical model commences (if a starting point could be identified) with reflection-on-action (Schon, 1983) which makes sense of an experience from which knowledge conceptualisation (Neisser, 1976; Walsh, 1995) follows. Experiences of leadership generate knowledge and understanding of leadership. Such understanding (and of course connected experience) relates to the situation from which it is drawn. The personalised understanding of leadership is subsequently operationalised for application in further and similar experiences through participation. In a sense this is a movement from understanding leadership to participating in leading. Yet participation is itself an element in which learning is absorbed tacitly through situated learning. Through such participation the notion of practice and identity is developed.

The five elements of this framework of leadership learning through lived experience are suggested to capture the reviewed theory and inter-relate them as follows:

- *Leadership situation* – the context of lived experience is placed centrally, as both a catalyst of available learning opportunities and as a filter shaping processes of social (Bandura, 1986) and situated learning (Lave & Wenger, 1991).
- *Leadership experiences* – the variety and qualitative difference of experiences of leading drawn from situations enable greater development to occur (Davies & Easterby-Smith, 1984; McCall et al., 1988; McCall, 2004).
- *Knowledge of leadership* – understanding of leadership becomes interrelated with the situation and subsequently interprets the situation (Neisser, 1976; Walsh, 1995) to provide guidance or prompts to leadership approaches. I am not suggesting that someone's intention to act is unmediated from a variety of possible interactions and stimuli. Rather, the outlined framework of lived experience suggests conceptions simply provide prompts or guidelines. However, there is a growing argument that schemas and self-concepts have a significant role in shaping behaviour (Markus & Wurf, 1987; Mischel, 2004).
- *Participation in leading* – engagement with leadership is within situations. Participation through roles and associated activities creates opportunities for experiences of leading. Through participation, knowledge of detailed nuances of leading in a particular context is absorbed, mostly tacitly by processes of situated learning (Lave & Wenger, 1991). Arguably it is through participation that leadership practice is developed.
- *Reflections on leadership* – Burgoyne and Hodgson (1983) argue that reflection in managerial learning is limited in daily practice. Additionally reflective recall is argued to be more closely associated with transformative learning (Mezirow, 1981, 1985), triggered by critical incidents (Cope & Watts, 2000; Avolio and Luthans, 2006; Janson, 2008). Empirical research to date is limited in terms of exploring routine, everyday events that imperceptibly influence leadership learning and the development of leadership practice.

The above framework is sufficiently broad and inclusive to integrate theory of informal leadership development and principles of experiential learning. This framework enables a simple argument to be put forward outlining how lived experience is central to leadership learning. It also illustrates the integration of learning literature to provide a systemic social perspective and in some way alludes to the difficulties of intervening into leadership development. However, such a broad and simple explanation of leadership learning through lived experience would fail to explain the underlying influences on lived experience that lie behind the generic headings shown in Figure 5.1. The detailed nuances of influences and their interactions in particular contexts need to be understood if intervention is to avoid the efficacy question mark that has challenged researchers and practitioners alike – outlined in Chapter 4 (notably: Wexley & Baldwin, 1986; later built upon by Conger, 1998; Day, 2000; Lowe & Gardner, 2001; Burgoyne et al., 2004).

The case for the centrality of leadership learning through lived experience has been outlined and the case is strong. Gaps in knowledge lie towards revealing underlying influences and their systemic integration and contextual detail. It is the need for identification and explanation of such influences of leadership learning lying within lived experience that the third part of this book addresses. Part III has a change of focus and style. The focus is on the real world of lived experience and leadership learning. Chapter 6 will outline a method of digging deep into such experiences to reveal influences on leadership learning. It has been structured to enable (and encourage) someone to apply the process to themselves and compare their learning to the insights that are revealed in the four case studies of Chapter 7; perhaps looking at all four cases or selecting the case that resonates most to personal experience. The four cases are: male perspectives in the public and the private sectors; female perspectives from both the sectors; and perspectives from owner-mangers. In Chapter 8, the underlying themes from these cases are drawn together to provide an explanation of how managers learn to lead. The final chapter presents conclusions and provides suggestions for action. An example is provided of an intervention with owner-managers that applies the underlying influences of leadership learning to enhance leadership practice.

Part III

6
Revealing Leadership Learning From Lived Experience

This chapter will outline the method used to reveal leadership learning. The chapter has been written to enable someone to primarily allow themselves the opportunity to undertake the process to discern their own leadership learning through lived experience. This may also be useful for critical comparison when reading the cases in Chapter 7 and interpreting the explanation of leadership learning in Chapter 8.

It has been shown in Chapter 4 that leadership learning is overwhelmingly naturalistic, often occurring through daily interactions that go unnoticed. Thus the difficult issue is how to reveal the everyday routines and events that make up the milieu of our lives. This point struck home to me through the failure of my first two pilot interviews.

A problematic beginning

The first pilot interview occurred with a colleague, John, at the University and this was significantly unsuccessful. Not because of the interviewee but because of the nature of the subject I wanted to explore and the way I constructed the interview process. I wanted to limit bias to the discussion and sought to enact an informant-led interview. Such an interview is characterised by limited intervention. As a consequence there were only three questions:

- How would you define leadership and describe your leadership practice?
- What are the key incidents that have influenced your thinking about leadership?
- What rules of thumb guide your leadership practice?

I expected these questions would allow expansive discussion. This was far from the case. The comments on the first and last question were lucid but seemed disconnected. The middle question was very difficult for John and the discussion lacked depth. He could not clearly recall much that had influenced his thinking.

In light of this disappointing interview, the second interview with a senior colleague, was much more structured with many more questions to provoke discussion in the areas I wanted to explore, that is, how have you learnt to lead? The second interviewee described a feeling of frustration that he was inhibited in discussing his experience in a more integrated manner and he felt that the structured set of questions did not enable exploration.

Reflecting on a *Michael Parkinson'* television interview, it struck me that the interview was structured chronologically; Parkinson worked his way through the person's life relating the discussion to pre-interview chronological notes. In the spirit of good science I experimented on myself. I created a timeline starting from my earliest memories to current influences, as shown below:

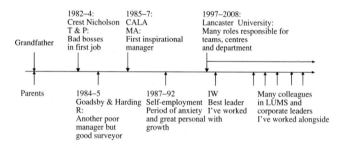

It seemed useful – I discovered some interesting insights that I had not reflected on previously. The process seemed to order and structure my thinking. It put together my experiences into a holistic story. I read work on narrative methodologies and found that I had hit on a rich vein of knowledge that would guide the development of my naive embryonic timeline process. Particularly useful was the work of Kuhnert and Russell (1990) and Wengraf (2001).

Narrative and storytelling

By accidentally bumping into the narrative approach I discovered a potential solution to the problem of making explicit the imperceptible leadership learning that occurs through our lived experience. Narrative is argued to be most appropriate for exploring tacit knowledge (Wengraf, 2001) for the following reasons:

- Embedded socialised use of narratives – adults have a socially constructed understanding of what is required of a narrative (Goffman, 1969) and this operates at low consciousness and therefore is subject to less censoring control (Wengraf, 2001).
- Structure – Labov and Waletsky (1967) identified a normative pattern of narrative used in every day conversation.
- Rich expressive tapestry – narrative is able to blend a mix of lived experience with cultural norms and assumptions that flow out of the respondent to reveal detailed information that would be difficult to access through structured questions.
- Triangulation – such expressive and enriched narrative is held together as a complete story. Cultural norms compel the narrator to tell the complete story (Alheit, 1994). In essence, censorship within the narrative begins to undermine the completeness and naturalness of the account and it becomes obvious to the listener (ibid.) and difficult for the narrator to hold the themes together.

So the narrative timeline approach provided a number of benefits. It enabled the managers in the interviews to follow a well-practiced structure, that of telling a story – particularly one that they are familiar with. Issues of truthfulness were addressed through the managers seeking to tell their story, as they understood it. It needed to primarily make sense to them. The depth of the conversation yielded insights that are of significance to the managers – the process needed to be of value to them as much as it was for me. Finally, the structured narrative would lead to a glimpse of tacit knowledge – a major stumbling block for previous researchers in exploring naturalistic leadership learning.

Third and fourth pilot interviews

The timeline was subsequently used with an MBA alumnus who was keen to assist. The timeline created both depth and holistic meaning to the interviewee that enabled her to make sense of the phenomenon of leadership learning in a manner that appeared to elicit an appreciation of knowledge that had not been considered before, or capable of being expressed. Further, and of significance, the three questions were addressed in a manner that illustrated coherence and integration – viewing the phenomenology from a number of perspectives or dimensions that gave a strong sense of reliability and more importantly respondent triangu-lation (Janesick, 1998). The fourth pilot interview with another MBA alumnus further helped refine the narrative method for illuminating lived experience of leadership learning and led to the development of the structured framework.

A structured framework

The experience of the pilot interviews clarified issues of interview style. The desire was certainly to create a process that would focus the interview onto experiences of leadership learning and be able to draw out from the interviewees' salient memories. Such memories would enable the inter-viewees to surface experience, and illustrate data related to underlying influences shaping their leadership learning. To assist each respondent's articulation, greater structure was required and the following stages were piloted with the third manager and refined with the final pilot interview:

- *Pre-interview:* Interviewees asked to prepare a timeline diagram identi-fying influences that have shaped their leadership learning from the youngest age to the present.
- *Stage One:* Interviewees asked to describe their view of leadership.
- *Stage Two*: Biographical data on leadership learning – interviewees asked to talk through their timelines from the earliest influence to the present date. Reflections were given on experiences and learning both during and at the end of the interview.
- *Stage Three:* Identify interviewees' heuristics of leadership – inter-viewees were asked to think of rules of thumb that they use in action or would describe to someone else which illustrate their approach to leadership. These rules of thumb are then discussed and compared to the biographical data.
- *Stage Four:* Final reflections on the definition of leadership given at the outset in light of the discussion through the interview.

The four stages of the interview are diagrammatically outlined in Figure 6.1 and illustrate the holistic triangulation process.

In light of the need to adopt active interviewing to unearth tacit knowledge, yet limit the distortions of the conversation, the focus of each interview was to arrive at a triangulated understanding for the interviewees (Janesick, 1998) of how their lived experience shaped lead-ership learning. The four explicit stages of the conversation (described above) and use of the timeline helped to sustain the flow of the

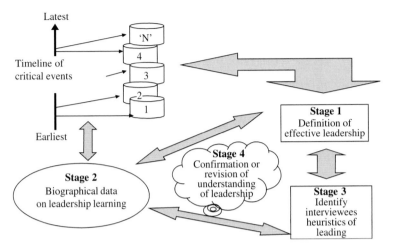

Figure 6.1 Structure of interviews (from Kempster, 2006)

interview. I wished to avoid seeking to answer my own research questions about underlying influences of leadership learning. These would come out of a free-flowing, in-depth interview. Of importance was that the interview would be insightful to the interviewee. Thus a fundamental assumption of the interview process was that the research questions would be implicitly addressed if the interviewees had a successful conversation in terms of understanding their lived experience.

Social situation – research relationships

It needs to be stressed that part of the success of the process was due to the relationship I had with the respondents. A successful interview, in terms of in-depth interviewee triangulated understanding of leadership and their lived experience, did not occur by accident. Key principles shaping such an output appeared to centre on:

- Trust – interviewees were known to me. This requirement enabled openness and the ability of the interviewer to cross-question and challenge as appropriate on very sensitive reflections.
- Empathy – needed to illustrate a sense of understanding and appreciation of the interviewee's experiences of leadership and contexts in which leading was described.
- Time – the four stages of the interview process had an average duration of between 120 and 140 minutes. For the senior managers to

give up such relatively considerable time required both interest and commitment to undertake the interview and a desire to have a meaningful outcome from the process.

- Relevance and experience – the salience of leadership to the interviewees greatly influenced the interview process and had a marked impact on the depth of discussion. This was illustrated by the owner-manager group that had a distinct a-schematic perspective on leadership and limited identity with the role of leadership.
- Location – although all but three of the 40 interviews were at their place of work, the interviewees invariably organised privacy, dedicated time and limited interruptions.

These five aspects are important for someone if they wish to participate in developing their own narrative of leadership learning. The next section uses an approach I had developed that builds direct from the above methodology. I used this with four groups of 20 senior managers, and has subsequently been used by colleagues with a further ten cohorts. The structure of the process relies on implementing the above five principles. For someone considering examining their lived experience the following has been found to be additionally useful:

- Select someone with whom you can have an open and trusting discussion – consider undertaking the interview with a colleague, friend or partner.
- Consider both of you undertaking the exercise – this will generate greater trust and empathy to your insights and reflections.
- Select someone who has interest in you, or similar depth of leadership experience – otherwise you may find that the conversation will be cut short due competing distractions.
- Find a quiet place and give at least an hour to the process.

I recall being persuaded by a group of senior managers that instead of carrying out the activity in tents (which I had provided) they would sit in the 4 star hotel bar. The result was a lot of merry people, good networking ... but very little useful insight on leadership learning!

The 'tents'

The tents exercise was utilised within a leadership development programme designed for the development of senior managers to become Principals of Further Education Colleges. The programme ran over a twelve-month period and was constituted mainly of action learning projects instigating change in the FE Colleges. Thematic modules were interspersed throughout the programme and the tents were part of a module on 'learning and leadership'.

The purpose of the tents was to deepen reflections of a manager's lived experience on leadership by isolating them from competing distractions. We used a nearby outdoor centre that was mostly fellside. This had plenty of space so that each manager could only see one other tent – the person with whom they would share their insights. It is not necessary to buy a tent and persuade a local farmer to use his fields; but I would encourage metaphorically finding a tent and field – the outcome is worth the effort.

Below is the brief as it was given to the delegates.

LEADERSHIP LEARNING

You are in a field, in a tent with a bottle of water and some chocolate and hopefully alone! What I would like you to do is concentrate only on leadership and address these three questions:

- What do you think leadership is?
- How do you approach leading?
- What has shaped your thinking and approach to leadership?

To address these questions please do the following:

Think about how you would define leadership and write this down. Draw a line and create a timeline which you will populate with memories on leadership. These could go as far back as childhood and probably would incorporate organisational experiences. As you recall these memories try to capture them onto the timeline and then go back and work your way through the details and clarify what these memories mean to you. Don't rush this – you have 90 minutes. Conclude with listing how your thinking shapes your approach to leading. The list might reflect advice you would give about leading in your organisation or another context. For example, 'be in control and be seen to be in control'. Look at the list and see if you can determine whether the points can be connected to your memories.

You should be able to see only two other people and they will be your interviewer and your interviewee. Please do not contact them until you have been alone for 90 minutes. After 90 minutes make contact and meet with them at one of your tents. Interview each other in detail for at least 45 minutes each.

Start with the person's definition of leadership and then work your way through the timeline, in detail exploring what the person means – ask questions and ensure you clarify things as you proceed. At the end, talk through the rules of thumb on how to lead and see how they relate to the experiences. Then switch roles and repeat the above process – make sure you capture critical issues emerging from both interviews, as this will be useful in the afternoon's discussion.

Enjoy and soak up the sun!! I hope you can take advantage of this rare quiet time to concentrate on just one issue. As with everything – the more you put in to this the more you will get out of it. Good luck.

STEVE

When someone has undertaken this exercise the outputs are typically: a detailed timeline of incidents, people and situations; connections between an understanding of leadership and the experiences that have shaped this understanding; connections between experiences and rules of thumb that guide leadership practice – an integrated appreciation of lived experience shaping leadership perception and practice. Feedback from running these sessions has repeatedly shown that the process generated new insights and a clearer understanding of an individual's picture of leadership and importantly a glimpse of how this picture has been crafted.

Chapter 7 allows comparisons of self-experience to that of others. If someone has undertaken this exercise they will be able to compare themselves to similar contexts as their own, in terms of public or private sectors; and be able to compare themselves to male and/or female experiences of leadership learning; and between the employed and the self-employed. Chapter 7 seeks to reveal prominent themes that emerge between the different groups and enables someone to critique self-experience and reflective insight against these themes. Such comparative critique can be further developed and deepened through Chapter 8: an explanation of leadership learning.

Summary

In this chapter the method utilised to explore lived experience has been outlined. The importance of this method is its potential to contribute to revealing part of the complex process of leadership learning and provide a glimpse of the situated and tacit nature of leadership practice.

The narrative approach has allowed the 40 interviewed managers to gain a greater understanding of their previously unstructured experiences and make sense of the prominent features that have shaped their learning. It is hoped that not only is the method understood but also that it is possible for someone to apply the process to themselves. The rewards for investing experientially in this method will hopefully be obtained when the four cases are described in Chapter 7. It is intended that someone would be able to vicariously learn from these cases as well as critique my themes against their interpretative themes drawn out from their own lived experience.

The final section of the chapter is a critique of the methodology and could be skipped over for the gripping exploration of the four cases in the next chapter.

Critique of the approach

The context of this study is a limited understanding of underlying influences on leadership learning, and the research approach sought to map out influences shaping leadership learning at the level of lived experience. This section will briefly critique the methodology that has clearly shaped the arguments of the book.

Developing themes from the interviews

I will briefly outline the approach used to analyse the data from the transcribed interviews. The approach used in this study is drawn from Grounded Theory (Glaser & Strauss, 1967) which seeks to identify themes influencing the manifestation of social processes – in this case the social process is leadership learning. A particular technique developed by Hycner (1985) is applied to the data that seeks to move from bits of data (units), to clustering these units and then to seeing themes that emerge drawn from the clusters. A passage of transcript (adapted from Kempster, 2006) from one of the interviewed managers has been outlined below to show this movement:

- *Units of meaning*

An extract from Joe talking about someone he worked with is given below:

He was a very **HARD** task**MASTER***. He* USED TO REDUCE HALF THE STAFF, AND PARTICULARLY *his* SECRETARY, INTO SHIVERING WRECKS. *I often found myself in a **position of translating** what he meant into **something slightly***

more palatable ... *he just had a very* **HARD VIEW ON LIFE** *and was* **very driven.** *Not surprisingly he was a* PROJECT DIRECTOR *by achieving goals and milestones.*

The above example highlights units of meaning, coded by different fonts to match the clusters below. The actual transcripts were colour-coded and were assimilated through constant comparison with emerging clusters of meaning evolving out of the whole transcript.

- *Clusters of meaning:* Drawn from the above text, and reinforced in the remainder of the transcript, the following clusters of meaning emerged that became significant to the interviewee:

  1. Notable people – impact of behaviour
  2. Task-driven – a primary focus on production rather than consideration
  3. ABUSE OF POWER – BULLYING
  4. **Supportive/CONSIDERATE – an appreciation of the needs of individuals**
  5. SOCIAL IDENTITY – IDENTIFIACTION WITH LEADERSHIP

This list of five clusters of meaning expanded to 15 clusters of meaning for the whole transcribed interview with Joe.

- *Themes:* Working iteratively between the clusters and the transcribed interview, a set of dominant themes emerged as central features shaping the lived experience of leadership learning. These themes began to emerge and cohere towards underlying influences on learning. For this interviewee they were:

  1. Clarity of beliefs about effective leadership driven from experience
  2. Impact of notable people and critical episodes on understanding of leadership
  3. Social context shaping leadership perspectives
  4. Abuse of power – bullying
  5. Value of task-driven behaviour
  6. Importance of teamwork

The themes highlighted are subsequently compared to managers within the same group and then compared between the groups to develop insights into leadership learning. The themes illustrated in Chapter 7 provide the foundations for an explanation of underlying influences on leadership learning outlined in Chapter 8.

Sample characteristics

Although a purposive sample strategy (Ritchie & Lewis, 2003) was adopted, the breadth of characteristics of the sample requires discussion. Many respondents within the sample were identified through a convenience sample of prior personal networks with the author and this may have had a distorting influence on the interview process. If any sample distortion did exist, the strategy of hiding the research questions limited potential for respondent bias. The size of the sample in each sector reflected my judgement on a variety of respondents required to explore dimensions of leadership learning. It was considered that about ten managers were sufficient to reveal common and distinctive characteristics of influences present in respective populations at a cross-sectoral perspective. Criticism of the representative nature of the samples is acknowledged, most particularly with owner-managers, where ten managers have been examined out of a population in the UK of some 3.5 million. However, a strong justification lies with the practical limitations of the volume of transcribed qualitative data that can be interpreted without losing sight of the context from which it was derived, and not overlooking the nuance detail contained therein. Finally, it needs to be emphasised that the sample constitutes white men and women resident in the UK. An ethnic or non-UK sample of managers could well produce very different influences or different emphases of suggested causes shaping leadership learning.

Generalisation

Can 40 interviews provide the basis for generalisation on leadership learning? It would be an appropriate criticism of this study if claims were being made that the explanation of underlying influences on leadership learning were representational to all situations. To no extent is it being claimed in this book that the explanations can be inferred as representational across the sectors – rather that explanations reveal influences of what appear to be common in some situations examined, but not in others (notably in owner-manager contexts). Thus explanation and theoretical propositions in this book are, at best, only a suggestion of tendencies for influences to shape leadership learning. Further research on explanations in alternative contexts would enable such tendencies to be explored and give, perhaps, more insight into underlying influences.

Leadership learning of women

Emphasis needs to be made to a specific weakness in this study related to stumbling onto the influence of gender. It was not the intention to explore such differences; rather the differences emerged through the grounded research. In hindsight, this perhaps was most obvious, particularly after reading part of the abundant literature on gender and its impact within organisations on careers and career expectations of women. It now seems inevitable that the lived experience of women, and associated influences on leadership learning, would be notably different.

Criticisms could be made regarding the research strategy, for example, in terms of sample size and sample heterogeneity, or for the relatively limited literature reviewed used to interpret the data from the lived experiences of the women sample. In essence, the interpretations may be severely restricted in regard to the explanations explicated. I decided that despite such potential criticisms, the importance of the emergent findings and explanations should be discussed with a clear caveat recognising the limitations and the need for further research.

Phenomenological analysis

Of great significance to the process of data analysis has been the use of phenomenological analysis (Hycner, 1985). Judgement has been used to create the clusters of meaning and associated themes that have been central to the substantive thesis of leadership learning. But not all the steps advocated by Hycner (1985) in phenomenological analysis were followed. Specifically, Hycner recommends that independent verification should be utilised to check that the clusters and themes could be found independent to the researcher. I decided that it would be more relevant to the focus of the study to check that the emergent clusters and themes had resonance with the interviewees – did the themes and associated explanations make sense to them?

Summary

The above criticisms need to be seen in the context of the overall aim that the explanations and arguments of leadership learning need to have resonance with experiences of managers. To date the themes and explanations of Chapters 7 and 8 have been discussed both with the interviewees and with many managers subsequently in leadership development programmes. Although aspects and emphasis of the explanations vary, from manager to manager there appears to be the resonance I was seeking. Resonance is the key word. The themes and explanations do not in any way purport to be truths. The explanation is 'an' explanation; there are many possible explanations. The importance is in the extent that the ideas are helpful to managers and researchers to understand the complex and contextualised process of leadership learning and the development of leadership practice.

7
Exploring Leadership Learning: Four Case Profiles

This chapter seeks to explore how contextualised leadership learning occurs. The structure of the chapter will first examine leadership learning in the public sector, and then compare these insights to the private sector, to women's leadership learning and finally to owner-managers. Although the insights are drawn from a sample of managers in each of these groups, the chapter will highlight one individual per group. This is to enable someone who wishes to compare their experiences to those of another individual from a similar context. Accordingly each case profile will be established. A narrative is outlined of the story of their lived experience from which themes are drawn out. Finally comparisons are made between the groups to identify similarities and differences.

This chapter will separate each of these groups into Parts A, B, C and D.

Part A: Influences on leadership learning in the public sector

The prominent themes identified in the public sector were the salience of leadership and associated identity construction as a leader forged through career pathways. These pathways enabled role experiences and most significantly provided access to, and participation with, notable people. These elements will be shown to dominate leadership learning in the public group. For these managers, processes of formal learning were considered low in significance compared to informal naturalistic learning. The public group constitutes ten managers. Daniel's story usefully represents the other nine managers.

Daniels's Story

Daniel, Director of Education for a county council was in his late fifties at the time of the interview. His entire career was within the field of education. He initially was a teacher but then moved into educational administration for the vast majority of his employed experiences. Daniel has been employed in locations throughout the UK. His story captures the public sector ethos of service and as such he is a most suitable representative of the public group.

Aspirational identity – a desire to become

For the managers in the public group leadership was a most prominent aspect of their lives – it was highly salient. The salience had increased through their career pathways but invariably there was a trigger or catalyst that brought the importance of leadership to the fore. Daniel commented on the significance of leadership to himself in carrying out his role:

> It's at the heart of what I do. You wade through great piles of paper and then you stop and you read something, or you hear something, or you pick up something in the business and you say 'just a minute, clear the paper away, this has now got to preoccupy me. This is what I'm here to do.

The association of personal salience and identification with leadership and how that leadership is practiced was closely associated with organisational purpose and role identification; Daniel continued:

> I have got a lot of managerial skills but I think leadership is what I'm about. Some times I feel almost like a spare part, things are going on and people are leading different aspects. I use to think 'what on earths going on', my Protestant work ethic would force me to get in there. But I've come to understand in this role that sometimes I have to be strategic, set the climate and other times I need to address small things and be visible. I like to think people would say of me that he doesn't interfere when he's not needed but if you need him he's there. One of the strengths of this department is our response to crises and I think it's true of a lot of public service that they pull every single stop out. We've had bus crashes, with school children on board, with the roof being ripped off under a low bridge, or schools being burnt down – 4 schools destroyed by fire in two and half years.

I would go out cos I thought that was important for the head to be seen and active with the governors, head-teachers, parents, children the community; intervention is invert to success, if the schools or my team are successful then [I] tend to stand well back. It's too easy to roll up your sleeves and interfere.

The essence of Daniel's orientation and practice of leading and sense of identity as a leader in his context of a local authority reflects the history and antecedents of leadership practice anticipated in this situation. Additionally there is a sense of uniqueness that Daniel brings to his practice as a result of his lived experience in terms of values, skills and behaviours associated with leadership. The idiosyncratic and highly personal nature of leadership learning through lived experience is captured in Daniel's timeline.

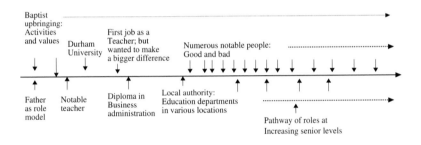

What cannot be illustrated through timelines is the complexity of influences that occur as continual routines of experiential impact. The importance of these 'headline' notations is akin to memory stores of someone's tacit knowledge of leadership shaping their leadership practice. By identifying and exploring these 'memory stores' Daniel was able to recall and draw together insight into his sense of 'becoming' a leader. Of greatest significance to Daniel and the other managers, both in the public and private sectors (and of similar note in the extant literature) was the influence of organisational contexts. However, prior formative experiences are important as initial foundations or catalysts for leadership learning. For example, the Christian upbringing as a Baptist and his father's role as a Deacon were expressed as continuing values that shaped Daniel's sense of purpose and have influenced his practice: 'a sense of security and deep trust and rootedness, the importance of vocation and the notion of personal relationships'. The Baptist church provided Daniel with opportunities to observe people (elders of the church) in prominent leadership positions and role enactments:

> When I was with youth teams I used to lead groups. When I went to university I used to take the services at the age of 18! There were two of us and we would take it in turns to do the leading and the other the sermon bit in small village communities.

What is most difficult to explicitly draw out in Daniel's story, and echoed with all of the managers interviewed, is a sense of what Lave and Wenger (1991) describe as situated learning – a process of learning akin to an apprenticeship (see also Kempster, 2006). Within such apprenticeships Lave and Wenger identified the gradual process of 'becoming' associated with engagement and participation with others in particular contexts. Daniel's story reflected a process of 'becoming' a leader; this process was catalysed in his formative youth through involvement with the Baptist church, and notably his father. This was different for the other managers in the public group; leadership was not salient until the commencement of their employed experiences and even then much later dependent on how quickly they joined the career pathway to leadership apprenticeship. The catalyst for all the managers appeared to be through observing at close hand notable people in particular circumstances: for Daniel in his formative years but for the remainder within their organisational careers.

Impact of notable people

The impact of notable people, both positive and negative, arguably has had a greater impact than other aspects of these managers' learning of leadership. In particular, notable people within an employed situation at the formative career stage of becoming associated with leadership appeared to be most dominant. Daniel's journey to leadership in the public sector commenced as a schoolteacher, teaching A-level French, then he met a key person:

> I wasn't sure how long I would do this, or where it would lead. I remember thinking would I be satisfied being a head-teacher and filling in forms. Then I met the Deputy Director of Education for Newcastle, through my wife, and spent an hour with him. I remember he said 'don't stay too long in teaching otherwise you won't get the range of experience you need'. This was most formative really. I planned my career a bit like a military exercise. I did a range of different teaching at different places. I felt I needed formal management

qualifications, perhaps it was a lack of confidence, anyway I did a Diploma in Public Administration for two years at Newcastle Polytechnic, and then I went into Warwickshire to my first post in administration as Deputy Area Education Officer.

In this post Daniel spoke of being 'immediately thrown into things that made a difference'. He spoke with passion about working on children's training centres for children with learning difficulties. Daniel connected his aspirations to make a difference with a clear vocational purpose associated with education. He recognised that being in a leadership role was the key for him to make this difference. This aspiration to make a difference through leadership drove Daniel to continue to advance his career. The following extract from Daniels's interview illustrates the unfolding of his career pathway towards this aspirant goal. He described numerous roles and even more numerous formative influences of notable people:

And I went from Warwick to Leeds and Leeds just blew my mind. From L [name removed] ... he was an appalling man, Machiavelli would have felt at home. C [name removed], who became Director in Northumberland, he was a very good role model for me, and I learnt a tremendous amount from that. Then there was S [name removed], who became the Director at Leeds he was much more staid but he was very stubborn. In Warwickshire I worked with B [name removed] who became Director in Solihull and he was energetic but he wasn't in the same league really, I would say, as a leader as S. S was 6'4" and I only saw him lose his temper once and that was with the NUT and there was stunned silence. The job I had in Leeds as Research and Planning Officer was fortuitous in a way as I got to work closely with the deputy and director. S was always very supportive. The role gave me a national profile and as a result of this I became elected to the National Council of the Society of Education Officers. I worked with some impressive people. The President J [name removed] was brilliant, he was Director of Education at Cheshire. I remember a meeting he was chairing and he let me lead, 'my colleague Daniel will now take it up'.

Daniel continued to talk of numerous other key people he worked with both in his role in Leeds and in the Society. The prominence and dominance of influence from notable people was common to the other managers in the public group. Of importance for these mangers was the early formative influence related to leadership practices and identities of the contexts they operated in: for Daniel this was the Education

Department of a County Council. This association of people with current identities and contexts was common in the entire sample. The fluency and richness of descriptions of notables, both good and bad, was most striking as a common and distinctive process shaping conceptions of leadership and the importance of observational learning from notable people seems to be most significant. The occurrence and prominence of notable people was invariably through role enactments. These allowed Daniel and the other mangers to not only come in contact, but also participate with these notables.

Role enactment

Of surprise in the analysis of the public sector managers was the relatively limited emphasis on the process of learning through enactment or learning by doing. The surprise is associated with a difference from the extant literature which has identified that learning by doing dominates learning of management. Perhaps in part this finding illustrates the difference in learning processes that managers within this study associated with leadership. Within each interview there was an explicit focus on 'how have you learnt how to lead'. The orientation of the response was towards learning from others and incidents, or episodes of learning, in which notable others dominated. The managers did not recall the numerous episodes and incidents of their leadership. This might reflect a sense of modesty and humility, although I did encourage them to tell more. For example, Daniel's story continued with his next career move:

> So I applied for the Deputy's job in East Sussex and was appointed. The deputy's job was interesting. T [name removed] was a very experienced, soon to retire Chief Education Officer, and he was a gentleman. He had a wonderful turn of phrase, he was very good at final speeches and farewells. And I picked up a lot from him. One of the attractions to the job was that he let you get on with it. He should have managed more, but he had been there for a long time and I was relatively young and energetic and we changed a lot of things. It was the first time that I was actually aware of the need for structural change. I was a leader at East Sussex and a lot of people knew me and we went through some interesting and challenging times.

This form of description without detail of the experiential learning from the role enactments was most typical. The managers struggled to describe the specifics of the enactments and how these shaped their learning and their practice. The nearest Daniel came to reflective exploration of a learning incident was the following:

> We closed a special school and that put me on television and in conflict with Mr Baker (Secretary of State for Education) ... and we introduced GCSEs and I had two complete loonies ... who said we aren't going to teach GCSEs, we are historians. I like history but crying out loud ... so I was on television for that. I sacked both of them eventually. But it was really interesting just to work your way through that.

This was a typical illustration of descriptions of learning through enactment. There is very little reference to specifics on leading people but rather more to do with events. This may reflect the repetitive nature of personal leading that is difficult to recall in memory, unlike major and discrete non-recurring emotionally charged events – explored in Chapter 3 reviewing memory recall from repetitive activities. However, all of the interviewees provided a chronology of roles with increasing levels of responsibility. The enactment of such roles within career pathways provides an implicit development process of learning towards becoming the aspired identity as leader. Nevertheless it needs to be stressed, even if this is axiomatic, that roles and their enactment are prevalent to the group and undoubtedly most central to learning how to lead.

Situated learning

Daniel's interview echoes that of the other managers. He described learning in participation with notable people within discrete communities. His practice of leadership was embedded in the roles, skills, values and assumptions of these contexts. His identity and sense of purpose was anchored within the broader community of local authority education, this being, in a sense, a form of learning of a practice that reflects an apprenticeship. Not an apprenticeship in a formal organised sense, but rather informal that occurs through the enactment opportunities provided through a career pathway. In essence these elements form the learning process known as situated learning (Lave & Wenger, 1991 – described in Chapter 3).

None of the managers provided details of this form of learning but it was unquestionably implicit in their stories. It is perhaps inevitable that there is minimal reflection towards recall of the detailed aspects of situated learning as it generates tacit knowledge – that knowledge and learning about something that you know and understand but cannot express. It reflects a sense of becoming without knowing how you have become. It is shared knowledge within a community that exists between people which enables them to behave as a community. It provides the subtle cues of what it is to be a leader in the Education Department of a Local Authority as understood by Daniel and by the community. This form of learning seems most significant as it connects together many aspects overtly described by the managers in their reviews of their lived experience, however, it is imperceptible to the managers, thereby limiting immediate recall. The importance of situated learning of leadership practice did not become salient until processes of data analysis and examining the transcripts in detail. As a consequence the interview process did not seek to explore such learning during the interviews. With hindsight aspects that might have been explored with the managers reflect the following:

- How particular meeting agendas are organised and conducted
- The values and beliefs that underpin discourse
- The accessibility of leaders
- The clothes leaders wear
- Forms of power used by leaders

If as a consequence of undertaking the process outlined in Chapter 6 someone has examined their leadership learning they might want to go back over their experience and distil such aspects. These aspects of situated learning are described by Gherhardi et al. (1998) as situated curriculum and occur along pathways of participative practice. Such situated curricula are naturalistic occurring through the activities of undertaking roles. The nature and specificity of these curricula is bespoke to the organisational practices required to undertake the roles. Through this process of situated learning, practices become learnt and subtly specialised to a particular context. For example, how meetings are run in Lancaster University Management School will be different to other University Management Schools if an examination is undertaken of the fine detail of the practice. During these participative apprenticed pathways a manager's sense of identity and confidence in their capability to enact the role and practice of a leader in a particular context becomes tested. In part these tests are akin to assessments in an apprenticed curriculum.

Confidence and capability to lead

Through all cases there are a number of key incidents or episodes that have caused the managers to re-evaluate their perspective and practice of leadership and their self-efficacy of leading. Daniel outlined a most 'brutal learning incident' when he sought to become promoted from a Deputy to Director of Education:

> I didn't get East Sussex. I felt absolutely gutted when they appointed an experienced director who had been there as a professional assistant many years before. He was fine, a very able and professional person. But I was really gutted by that. Appointments are made by members with a Chief Executive to steer them. The Chief Executive is often looking for people in their own image. It sort of took me quite a while to regain my confidence. For example, I applied for five jobs as Director of Education over six months before I got this one. I remember going to Devon and the leader of the council said to me, quite appalling when you look back on it; he said "how would you manage in a big public meeting trying to close a school? You're a bit of a poofta really!"

Daniel continued to explain that the members were seeking people like his earlier 'bad' role models up in Leeds. He chose then to connect this bad experience to a feminine approach to leading and commented:

> What I haven't said as well is the impact of women leaders. In this job I have appointed more women leaders because they were the best people and I actively try and distance from the macho male leadership models.

The emerging shift in values and styles of leadership oriented around masculine and feminine leadership within Daniel's context will be developed shortly within the women managers group. However, it should be noted that this was significant to Daniel and despite the incident affecting his confidence it reaffirmed his desire to become a director and change the system and attitudes towards leadership from a position of influence. He was appointed as the Director of Education of a major authority in the Northwest in 1991 and remained in post until he retired recently. The authority is highly regarded in no small part due to his leadership capability and practice leading the largest department in this Council. Daniel has been recognised for the leadership he provided signalled by his becoming an honoree lifetime President of the Society of Education Officers.

It is interesting to note that Daniel described in detail many leadership issues that have faced him and ongoing issues that are part of the flux of his everyday leadership role. Undoubtedly Daniel is learning from these but his story of learning reflects his formative experiences. In a sense his practice and identity have been formed, and the everyday enactments are further refinements. This refinement of practice and identity is within a community. Daniel is being shaped by his ongoing interactions with others in this community. Equally, and of importance to Chapters 8 and 9, Daniel is shaping and elaborating the next generation of apprentice leaders through enactments in roles, through himself as a notable person and through the complex nuances of situated learning.

Formal learning

It is unsurprising to note that Daniel, as Director of Education, greatly values the formal role of education. However, it is also interesting to note that he didn't place prominence on formal learning in his development. The only connection in his formative development was the Diploma in Public Administration he undertook to enable him to switch from being a teacher to commencing the pathway to becoming a Director of Education. This would appear on first glance to be central to the development of leadership practice. Not the case. The value here was in regard to confidence. It may also be associated with the beginning of the informal apprenticeship and signalled a change in aspirant identity from being a teacher to a manager or leader. This perspective on formal learning was continually reflected with all managers in the public sector group.

This is not a surprising finding. The extant leadership – outlined in Chapter 4 – confirms that we learn how to lead not in the classroom but through our lived experience; particularly our experiences within organisational contexts. Daniel's story affirms this point.

Summary of themes

The dominant process shaping leadership learning in this group of public sector managers was notable people. The impact of notables appeared to create a stimulus for identification and salience of leadership to the individual, and notable people stimulated an example for role enactment. The context of leadership had significant impact on the behaviour of notable people and the variety of notable people available to observe. The context provided the structural and cultural background to processes of situated learning that has a subsequent impact on role enactment and the development of leadership practice.

The limited explicit mention of learning within role enactments does not mean that learning has not occurred. Rather, like 'black-matter' in the universe, its presence seems ubiquitous. In essence, imperceptible learning from daily routines through participation enabled the nuance meanings and practices of leadership to be learnt. This argument reflects the emergence of leadership learning as an informal, naturalistic apprenticeship with a situated curriculum bespoken at each context. In a paradoxical way the identification that formal learning had limited impact on the lived experience of these managers confirms that learning to lead must occur through other sources – such as those identified. Nevertheless for a number of public sector managers' formal learning was a context catalytic in its impact on identity, self-efficacy, affirmation and reflection.

The next case profile of Ian will compare these dominant themes from the public sector with managers from the private sector.

Part B: Influences on leadership learning in the private sector

The private sector group constituted 12 managers. There was strong similarity of influences on leadership learning between the public and private sector groups. Embedded practices learnt through participation were similarly present in the private sector as with the public sector. Role enactment had limited discussion, with a comparable low value placed on formal learning. Perhaps the largest difference between the groups was that identity and salience of leadership were arguably stronger in private sector, along with a clearer and more valued career pathway to becoming a leader that started much earlier in a manager's career. The most striking similarity was the dominance of notable people formatively influencing leadership learning.

Ian's Story

Ian was in his mid-fifties at the time of the interview. He was the Managing Director of a manufacturing company in the ceramics industry, but his career had predominately been in vehicle manufacture until his current post. Employed by six organisations he had experienced a wide spectrum of situations and circumstances. His breadth of experience in a range of contexts makes him an interesting window through which to capture the private sector managers.

Within the public sector group most of the managers built up their story of leadership learning from their early family experiences. Daniel, for example, continued to anchor his sense of identity and practice as a leader with values learnt from a young age. This was much less common with the private sector managers in terms of significance placed on formative involvement. For example, Ian did not anchor his experiences to his upbringing other than with teachers. For Ian the crucibles of his development were the variety of organisational contexts. These were dominated by notable people, good, but mostly bad captured in his timeline.

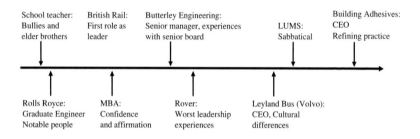

The story behind the prominent headings is the dominance of contextual variety and the ever presence of notable people. A theme that continues to recur throughout Ian's discussion on leadership is the notion of a leader as a 'bully' or an 'elder brother'. These two characters emerged in Ian's earliest recollections of leadership – schoolteachers:

> I guess my very earliest influence were schoolteachers where again every teacher had their own different style. Some were bullies – there was no question about that, motivating by fear. But there was one, Mr S [name deleted] who particularly influenced me. He did have a reputation at school for being an absolute tyrant. In reality he was nothing of the sort. He was firm and stood no nonsense but equally if you had a problem he was more than happy to sit and talk it through with you. I always felt that was probably the most formative style. There was no question about his being in control of the classroom. He led the agenda. He moved the pace. He censured those who were out of line; but would occasionally ask 'can you come and see me sometime? I think we need to chat about a few things'. You would go and see him in his room and he was helpful, supportive, questioning. Almost like a big brother in a sense. But he could be a bit of a bully as well; he could be a bit of a tyrant. But equally he was a friend. I think that is probably the earliest influence I had, being able to fill those two roles. This has stayed with me through my career.

This dominant dichotomy of bully and elder brother will be shown to be most central to Ian's experiences in the variety of employed contexts. Ian began his career as an engineer, after graduating from university. Through his career a shift of identity occurred moving away from engineering to leadership. However, through all his experiences, as an engineer or as a leader, notable people were the most prominent and formative influence on the development of his leadership practice.

Notable people

The influence of notable people was the most dominant and common influence for all of the private-sector interviewees. Frequent mention was made of numerous people, conceived and differentiated between good and bad leadership behaviour, experienced predominantly in organisational contexts. The interviews identified the generative impact of notable people on leadership conceptions and practice in a manner that was strikingly similar to the public sector group:

> My first work place experience was as an engineer for Rolls Royce. After graduation I went back to Rolls Royce and completed the fifth year of the five-year apprenticeship and then took up my first placement. The guy that recruited me into the department I have to say fell into the big brother category and he was a very positive influence. There was never any question that he was in control. He would come out and say 'do this for me and I need it by three o'clock' and you did it because you knew that if he said he wanted it by three o'clock he needed it by three o'clock and his ass would be on the line if it wasn't ready. He just had this aura about him. He never conned you. He never tricked you. He never asked you for things that weren't necessary. He was always there to provide advice if you asked him. You could always go into his office and say 'I've got a problem can you help me?' Monday to Thursday he was completely in control. He was like a big brother. Then on Fridays the work pattern at Rolls Royce was that we finished at lunchtime so it was a half-day. And it became a tradition that we all went to the pub on Friday lunchtimes and of course he was there and he always bought the first round. In one sense, he was clearly in control but at the same time he had the ability to be one of the team. To say he was the first among equals would be totally wrong because he was clearly and unquestionably in control. But had the ability to be part of the team but not surrender his status.

As Ian progressed through his timeline he illustrated more and more examples of notable people – both good and bad. Ian moved from Rolls Royce to British Rail where he described bad notable people leading his group of engineering researchers. The situation got so bad that Ian was asked by his boss's boss to step in and lead the team. This would lead to his first enactment of leading; but first the description of his boss:

> I left Roll Royce and went to work for British Rail Research in the research centre. And I guess that was when I first came across what I would call a disastrous manager. The guy was political. He was looking to position himself in the eyes of collective superiors. This guy just didn't have the ability to relate; to get engaged; to communicate and all we saw was the positioning and political maneuvering. And he just lost the respect of people. There was no respect for him at all and eventually it ended in disaster.

Situated and enacted learning

Through Ian's story he described a series of roles rather than enactments. This was similar for all the mangers both private and public sectors, male and female. The same argument described in Daniel's story applies similarly to the private-sector interviewees. There was limited discussion of enactments and a dearth of insights into situated learning. These were clearly occurring but not readily accessible. Discussions in Chapter 3 on the functioning of memory highlighted that events are more easily recalled if they are novel, the first experience or an emotional episode. Ian illustrated this point in his ability to recall his first moment of leading in an organisational context:

> In the British Rail role I did get thrust into leadership. I mean in a small way. I was about 25 at the time. We had a small department. The head of that department was the guy described earlier. We were a sub-contract group. The relationship between the head of our group and the head of the client group broke down to the point that it actually became quite personal. Quite nasty. The head of our group was moved to one side and his line manager asked me to lead the work. I had to do a lot of bridge building to try to re-build the relationship with the client group. Sometimes it was a bit like dancing on eggshells. Being very careful, trying always to stress that we were not trying to undermine their position or criticise them but there were issues we needed to discuss. That was I guess the first time I had ever been asked to take responsibility for a group of people directly.

What I learnt very quickly and have followed since is that people have got justifiable sensitivities and you try not to ruffle them up, or to upset them or to antagonise them. So you do go carefully. You go round them, you are reassuring. Other times you just want to jump on them. I think one thing I did learn in those early stages it is always wrong to try to ignore that those sensitivities exist. I think they always have to be put on the table. To indicate that you recognise them.

The frequency and variety of roles and critical incidents described in each respective interview implied enactment and the potential of learning through doing. However, and most similar to the public sector group, the interviewees did not describe how they learnt from their own enactment, but rather linked learning to other people through role participation along their career pathways.

Career pathway enabling leadership learning

What became striking to Ian from this episode of leading was the increased salience of leadership. At the time of the incident Ian saw himself as an engineer. This enactment of leading acted as a catalyst. He saw the value placed on leadership and the career opportunities. The career pathway to becoming a leader became very explicit:

I basically ran with that project for about a year and a half. As an individual I was now becoming more interested in the organisation/ managerial aspects of industry rather than purely technical matters. I was very heavily technically oriented. In fact at one point I was considered an expert on the lubrication of high-speed taper rolling bearings in railway applications! I guess it was managing these sensitive relationships that awoke me to the fact that I quite enjoyed it. And it was also quite clear that within the research division of a nationalised industry, as it was then, the opportunity to develop a career in that direction would be limited. I actually took two years leave of absence from British Rail and went to Manchester Business School. That was 1977–1979 so I would be 27 when I made that decision.

After the MBA Ian's pathway to leadership became more explicit. He joined (UK PLC) a company he would rejoin, and was with them at the time of the interview:

I was dispatched to one of their engineering companies in Derbyshire. My boss in that situation was the MD and he was ex

MBS – some five years ahead of me. And we got a great team going. We were early to mid 30s and we turned the business round as simple as that. Great camaraderie, great team spirit. A lot of mutual respect. We had our disagreements but there was a lot of mutual respect and we were not treading on each other's toes in our areas of expertise. And we changed the company from the roots upwards. It was evident that one of the characteristics of the company was that there was a high level of status awareness. Individuals carried their perceived status in symbols, their car, their class of travel by air or rail or the convenience of their allocated parking space. This status carried over into the decision making processes which in turn meant that the evolution of the business was severely hampered due to the dominant influence of seniority and hence tradition.

The next part of the pathway was to Rover:

I was head-hunted. Probably extremely flattered to be head-hunted and I accepted the job to head up the computer engineering group in Rover. And I guess I'm now moving into the most formative period of my career. We had everybody in Rover – from the guy you could work with to the guys you would willingly take into a corner and put a bullet between their eyes. Rover at that time was in absolute and utter chaos. It was in the downslide from management styles and stupid decisions were being made all over the place. A lot of the decisions were being made by people who were blatantly incapable or inappropriate to make those decisions. And a lot of the decision-making was politically based. So it was absolute and utter chaos. And I worked with – or came across people who were just blatant bullies. Anybody who had any lack of backbone was just sort of rolled over. And I think that quite clearly demonstrated to me what was bad about management. How not to manage, how not to deal with people and the kind of environment in which people do not perform. Fortunately I got out of it when I was offered a role with Leyland Bus, part of the group which had recently been taken over by the Volvo Corporation. They were looking to re-build their management team and I was offered the job of Operations Director with responsibility for manufacturing, assembly, logistics, purchasing and that sort of thing – operational activities. And to me it was a god-send it was an opportunity to get out. I'm richer for the experience but for me the scars lived long.

The pathway of enactments continued with the 'Volvo experience'. Ian moved from Operations Director to Managing Director with the departure of the MD in the space of a few months. He commented on this leadership career progression:

> So I suddenly had responsibility for 1500 people in two factories. And working on integrating the business into the Volvo Bus Corporation. I guess going back, the thought of suddenly being responsible for a company of 1500 people is quite daunting. In my British Leyland career I started off heading up a small computer group which was responsible for about four people. Then I was given responsibility for technical development, which gave me a team of about 50 people. And then I was moved to run production in the pressing division with responsibility for two factories: Swindon, and Llanelli in South Wales with responsibility for about 3000 people. Around my career I had this responsibility for large numbers of people and so picking up responsibility for a company and 1500 – it wasn't the size of the job that was new, it was in terms of the legalities of being a company director that was quite a sharp learning experience.

Although Ian had two more posts in his career, he did not consider them to be formative to his leadership practice:

> These last two posts refine what I know. Its not that I'm not seeking to be better, but I think I am the leader I'm going to be.

The leader career pathway appears to be highly valued within the private sector. The valued goal of becoming a leader itself perhaps raises the salience and aspirational identity at an earlier stage than in the public sector group. This may be through the greater visibility of the career pathway to leadership at a much earlier stage; perhaps reflecting the prominence of teams and the team leader role at all levels in the private sector. The pathway as an influence on leadership learning not only appears to enhance salience and identification, it also provides legitimised arenas to observe notable people and enact leadership through successively more significant and demanding roles.

   The leadership pathway implicitly affirmed a leader identity and increasing notions of self-efficacy of performing this valued identity through the role enactments and confirming process by the institution. Hence there is a sense of apprenticeship and acceptance of becoming a leader by both themselves and by others in the organisation.[1]

Aspired identity and salience of leadership

The career pathway travelled by these managers appeared to have greatly influenced their recognition both explicitly and implicitly of an identity as a general manager and as a leader. However, it should be noted that for some, professional identities such as an engineer, marketing manager or accountant, affected their timing for entering the career pathway and shifting orientation away from their professional identity and towards that of a leader. Interestingly, two of the group who described themselves as middle managers identified much less with being a leader and were much more comfortable with being associated with their professional expertise. In a sense they were part-way along their apprenticed journey – leadership was becoming more salient. It would be most interesting to return to these managers as they progressed along their pathways to explore degrees of salience and identity of leadership and self-efficacy expectations of leading – more on this in Chapter 8.

A metaphor to describe what may be occurring would be like a brightness switch: for the middle managers the light was dim but increasing; for the late identity switchers, the accountants and engineers such as Ian, the light had become stronger midway through their careers. For the managers who commenced their careers as generalists the light become bright early on – they strongly valued and identified with leadership and aspired to become such a valued identity at a very earlier stage in their careers.

For all the managers in this group, like with the public sector group, the importance and high personal salience with leadership and the role of the leader was triggered by a critical incident involving a notable person. Such participative engagement with notables, can also be seen as an unintended outcome of formal learning through peer comparison.

Formal learning

Formally organised development, in the form of education and development training, was seen to be of low significance to leadership practice of the private-sector interviewees in terms of designed curriculum. All of the group had experienced some type of formal development and were generally jaundiced about the value of the training in terms of learning about leadership. Rather it acted for some as a catalyst to reflect over their experiences, often eliciting comments of affirming understanding and providing assuring confidence. For some, formal training was an opportunity to network and benchmark themselves against their peers. Ian commented on the value of his MBA:

> I learnt a lot of technical skills, accounting and so on. I felt it was the accounting and finance that I thought was the one bit of my portfolio that I needed to build up from scratch. Quite a lot of the

other stuff was useful and I enjoyed it but the over-riding conclusion I reached and it sounds a bit arrogant is that it was legitimising the instincts that I had developed. So it was not changing the way I behaved or the way that I thought about it. What it did actually do was to give legitimacy or under-pinning credibility to some of the intuitive or instinctive views that I had formed about dealing with people and working with people and being motivated. I think it also gave me the confidence to come out and jump into situations which previously I might have backed off from because I thought it was out of my depth.

The intended impact of formally organised development is suggested to have been very limited. However, it does appear to have other unintended outcomes, in particular a sense of shaping and affirming identity and the opening up of career pathways. For example, being chosen to attend a formal development programme was a sense of recognition by the organisation that the delegate was seen to have potential worth investing in – for some this recognition was the first time they saw themselves having leadership potential. As such, formal programmes have the potential to be the start of an apprenticeship by making leadership salient and stimulating identity association with this role.

Comparing influences between the public and private groups

The comparison between the public and private sector groups illustrates striking similarities of influences on leadership learning. Table 7.1 provides a summary of commonality and areas of contrast.

Table 7.1 Comparing influences on leadership learning: Public and private sector groups

Public sector managers	Private sector managers
High identity and salience of leadership	Very similar, but functional distortions
Less explicit career pathways	Career pathways very explicit
Observational learning (notable people)	Similar as public sector
Situated learning of structures and practices	Similar as public sector
Limited discussion on enacted learning	Similar as public sector
Low significance of formal training	Similar as public sector
Critical incidents most prevalent	Similar as public sector

The similarity appears to centre on situated learning that arguably enables, through career pathways of participation, access to observe and interact with notable people. Further, such situated pathways of participation take the form of role enactments that appear to have an associated influence on increasing salience and identification with leadership. In essence, these influences appear to work together, reinforcing leadership learning.

Most striking is the dominance of observational learning, particularly catalysed by notable people. The opportunity to observe a range of people is provided through career pathways, as well as initiating learning through role enactment. Additionally, the pathways appear to enhance the salience of leadership and the value of the identity that the pathway is leading to.

For both groups, formal development was prevalent in occurrence, but considered of low value in terms of efficacy, shaping understanding and approach to leading. Rather, the impact of formal development was associated with the unintended process of being selected for courses – affirming identity, networking and assistance in pathway trajectory.

Seniority, roles and responsibility as development themes

There are a number of common themes between the public and private sector groups that relate to seniority and the interrelated issues of responsibility and the variety of roles. The more senior the individual, the greater the:

- Identification with and salience of leadership
- Number of notable people in similar role situations to their own
- Emphasis on teams and the development of team leadership – particularly with the private sector group

For example, very few of the directors of both groups commented on parents as formatively influential in their development. Rather their lived experience predominantly commenced within their organisational careers – thereby closely associating the development of their leadership practice to an organisational context. The more junior the individual, the greater the emphasis on:

- Pre-organisational role models
- Pre-organisational experiences
- Professional identities such as accountants or engineers

It was much more common for the junior managers to anchor their development experiences with both domestic and school experiences. The greater the breadth and depth of experiences along the leadership pathway, the greater the association of learning from within the organisational context shaping leadership practice and sense of 'becoming' a leader. At a more junior level leadership practice appears to draw more prominently on formative family and pre-organisational experience. The significance of these contrasting issues is linked to key themes identified within the data of the owner-manager group to be described further on.

Differentiation of leadership learning

Although there are striking similarities of influences on leadership learning, two aspects stand out as being different. Table 7.1 has identified that salience and career pathways have a different emphasis and orientation between the two groups. The private sector group had a much greater emphasis towards the prominence of career pathways that appeared to structure and enable learning of leadership. It appeared that the end goal of being a leader was highly valued in the private sector. As a consequence the salience of leadership and corresponding aspirational identity to become a leader was much more visible. The public sector group did not have such a clear picture of a career pathway structuring and shaping leadership learning. For sure there was a pathway, and Daniel's story illustrated a career trajectory towards becoming the Director of Education, but this appeared to be much more subtle than explicit, and more initiated by the individual and their aspirations to lead.

Thus contextual structures can be seen to influence the prominence and diversity of influences along career pathways and the strength of salience and identification with leadership. The influence of context on leadership learning is much more prominent with the women managers and creates additional influences not present within the groups examined thus far.

Part C: Influences on women managers' leadership learning

As with the previous two male groups there is a degree of similarity of underlying influences on leadership learning, reconfirming an emergence of common themes. However, these common influences are greatly shaped by structural conditioning within contexts and such structural conditioning has arguably a greater impact on women than for men. For example, women managers appeared to be greatly influenced by aspects of social marginality and gender. The previous outlined influences of identity, career pathways, notable people, critical incidents, enacted learning and even formal learning have to be interpreted through such lenses of marginality and gender. The ten women managers that constitute this group will be represented by Catherine.

Catherine's Story

Catherine (mid-fifties) is a Chief Medical Director. She qualified as a general practice doctor, but it was not until she commenced a family that she joined the Civil Service within an Agency that supports benefit provision. She became managing director of this service until it was outsourced. In the private sector Catherine became chief medical officer for an organisation that has since been acquired twice – she has remained a senior leader through all this change. Her experience in both the private and public sectors allows her case to illustrate issues from both sectors and connects many arguments of the women managers group.

Aspirations to become a leader?

What was most striking from the interviews with the women managers was their relationship with leadership: this was different to the men in terms of identity equivocation. Some of the women strongly saw themselves as leaders and had aspired to such a position. In contrast, a few members of the group were uncomfortable to be associated with a leadership identity. As a qualified doctor Catherine's first identity was most explicit and arguably it has persisted through her career. Her second and third identities, which she commented on in detail, were that of a wife and a mother. It was only in the latter stages of her career that the identity of a leader emerged as significant but in balance with these other identities. Catherine commented on a particular stage after qualifying as a doctor and in the early days of being married:

> My husband at that stage was an Able-chaplain so he was attached to a variety of ships, so I thought that looks like quite good fun really and so for the next few years, during the child rearing years, I was really engaged in hanging on to my career. I knew that, having moved off the developmental ladder that was in place in Newcastle – there were certain jobs you did, in a certain order. So I chose jobs with certain must-haves; working with people I respected because of their

ability to be good doctors – the sort of doctor I wish to be and learn the variety of skills needed.

Catherine linked this discussion on juggling the development of her practice and identity of being a doctor, with being a mother, in a non-structured career path and the impact this had on confidence:

> I observed other women doctors losing confidence having to deal with emergency calls and night visits. With the real coalface stuff you can quite quickly lose confidence in managing those situations particularly if you move away from a structured environment for any length of time. Well I recognised that the loss of confidence wasn't just a personal thing; it also actually makes you move away from any sort of career ladder that you might want to get back on to because a number of people who did it, and they usually were women who had the main child-care responsibilities, were always drifting further and further away from the hard-edged, fun end of medicine that I would regard it as. A lot of them ended up as people like school doctors or in child health clinics which has its place, certainly has its place but as a career it wasn't what I personally wanted to do.

This discussion from Catherine highlights a number of most significant and distinguishing aspects from the two previous male groups. Firstly, the type of narrative here reflected multiple identities being 'juggled'. It described structural gendered orientated expectations of family and a mother. It emphasises questions of confidence and importantly how these elements impact on being able to engage with career pathways. None of the conversations with the 30 plus male leaders spoke in these terms on such issues as disruption to career pathways, paternal identity, lack of confidence or multiple balancing of identities and expectations.

Although many of the women managers have aspired to lead, and saw the impact leadership can make, they often expressed concerns with connotations associated with the gendered noun of '*leader*'. As a consequence, the influence of identity aspiration shaping leadership learning was more opaque and significantly more complicated in terms of many identities than was illustrated with their male counterparts.

Career pathways and situated learning

All of the women in the group had rich and involved careers, but the pathways towards becoming a leader were mostly described in a less clear and less overtly structured manner, certainly less overtly structured than the private sample. The extract from Catherine above amplified this point. Catherine's timeline illustrates the variety of experiences, identities and roles.

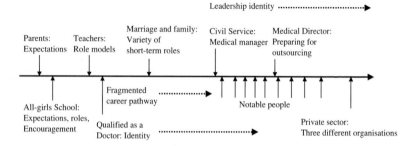

With regard to the above timeline and that of the other women, there were a number of connected structural issues surrounding career pathways that appeared to have been heavily influential within their lived experience as leaders:

- Professional backgrounds – all but one of the sample had professional qualifications providing a foundation of peer credibility through professional skill and experience.
- Access to a managerial career pathway through professional success in early careers.
- Glass ceiling – gender expectations shaped the trajectory, terrain and speed of the women's career paths.
- Networks and sponsors (mentors) – sought out or purposively created female networks to counter perceived male structures.
- Marginality – being outside male in-groups appeared to be both problematic in terms of access and participation; but also an advantage in terms of providing a sense of independence of mind, and freedom from being embedded in the organisational practices.
- Extramural expectations and commitments – competing role as mother and a break in the career path created associated issues of confidence and doubts of self-efficacy – expressed more explicitly than with the men.

The above six influences identified in the interviews have greatly shaped these women's experience of leadership learning through career pathways. Such influences were not overtly prevalent and salient to the preceding male managers and have had a marked effect on the career pathways of these women. Recognition was given to these aspects and personal interventions were made to purposively address these perceived differences. For example, professional status allowed credibility and access to networks; women support groups were formed or found to overcome issues such as a lack of confidence.

Career pathways have been shown to be significant to both men and women learning leadership, but from an examination of the different groups, influences and opportunities along career pathways are qualitatively different between men and women. Nevertheless these career pathways did provide access to notable people, although the manifestation of the influence was different.

Observational learning from men and women

As with the two previous groups, observational learning from notable people was a most dominant influence on women managers' leadership learning. However, the women managers placed greater emphasis on the positive influence of notable women rather than men, and there was greater connectivity and association (as well as passion and emotion) when the women described notable women than when describing notable men. That is not to say that men were not influential on their learning, but rather that emphasis in terms of role models was given to women notables.

Emphasis needs to be made of this finding. With so few women leaders in organisational contexts, their prominence in the lived experience of the women managers is important. For example, there are estimated to be only 24 per cent of women in management roles reducing to 9.9 per cent at director level (Davidson & Burke, 2004: 101). Within the organisational context the women did cite numerous examples of both men and women shaping leadership understanding in similar numeric balance. However, the positive emphasis tended towards notable women; frequently these were drawn from outside the employed context and often from formative pre-organisational contexts such as family and school. Catherine provided such an example when she commented on the expectations of her father and influence of her mother:

> He [her father] died when I was 18, just as I was about to go to University but he was very strong in saying 'ok well girls can do anything boys can do'. He always very strongly held that women could do whatever men could do. I have to say that when I decided I wanted to do medicine he was pretty horrified because I don't think he quite expected it but I think that came from his own background.

> She [her mother] was straight forward, supportive, meals on the table, uniforms sorted, a little bit doubting of what's going on here and I think she'd still say 'why don't you get a proper job and look after your family properly'. Very intelligent, articulate woman who had made choices that were down to society at the time really. She became pregnant and gave up work. Bit like me in some ways. But things were different then. I was encouraged and supported, I guess, to expect more.

This encouragement to follow an unconventional pathway was bounded within the structural expectations of being a mother and placing priority on family over work. Building on expectations of women, Catherine spoke of the influence of women schoolteachers she experienced at the Girls Grammar School she attended:

> I think yes, the teachers at that time given that, goodness this is making me sound terrible, there were an awful lot of them who were probably the first group of women who did an academic sort of education, a number of them for all sorts of reasons had absolutely a career focus, and had no family commitments or anything else. Many of those women were inspirational in giving girls confidence and expectations. Really excellent teachers.

Drawing out from these comments on the influence of people is a broader set of contexts, not singularly towards organisations, as was predominant with men, but a broader inclusion of formative family and educational influences additional to organisational contexts. This is expanded within 'female contexts', further on, in which notable women act as role models shaping career expectations in non-traditional female careers – historically associated with management.

Enacted and situated learning

Most similar to the male groups was the limited discussion, or cited examples, of learning through enactment. Replicating the experience of the men, the women described roles rather than their learning from roles: a strong and similar sense of 'becoming' a leader through situated participation. However, the women experienced different influences during enactment and participation that will be expanded on shortly under the structural influence of gender.

Catherine's pathway towards becoming a leader emerged in response to her husband becoming a vicar in a parish in the Northwest of England in 1985:

I thought I'd work for the civil service for a bit. We have five children and they were quite small at that stage and I thought I'll do a job where I don't have to do nights or weekends and I joined the civil service as a sort of temporary basis; flexi time, just amazing. Then I found out I really enjoyed certain aspects of what I was doing. I also liked the stability of management within that environment. There were management opportunities for doctors, which are actually pretty rare in the NHS or anywhere else. I moved through increasingly senior management posts over the next seven years or so. Then all changed with the roller coaster of government outsourcing. We were part of the first wave in 1992. This took five or six years where there was a move from market testing through to privatisation and I became the Medical Director. I had responsibility for all of the operational aspects of the delivery of the medical service so I was responsible for the administrations, for the quality, for the management of the doctors and the 2000 sessional doctors and all the rest of it so by that stage it was a very meaty role. I felt rather vulnerable at this stage in terms of the outsourcing and during this period I decided now I was a manager that I needed an MBA. So in 1995–96 I did my MBA.

During these intense ten years Catherine moved from a technical role to a managerial role. Her leadership learning apprenticeship and her development of leadership practice was oriented to primarily leading doctors. Her approach, which I have observed over an extended period of time, is a unique mix of the professional with the managerial, with an absorbed appreciation of the values, assumptions and practices of working within the civil-service environment.

Catherine, along with all the others interviewed, had limited recall of enactments that have been part of her everyday interactions and the situated learning that has occurred through the multiplicity of enactments. However, the pathways that provide participative access are constructed with situated curricula. As outlined in Daniel's story, the notion of situated curricula reflects aspects of how practice is enacted; examples of which might be the way people dress, the conduct of meetings, or where conversations occur or perhaps the types of discourse used related to leadership practice of a particular context. Such aspects of situated curricula that help constitute the mechanisms influencing situated learning of leadership practice may be problematic for women to assimilate and utilise in the development of their practice. In a sense the awkwardness of the pathway and issues of marginalisation, confidence and gender that the women managers have described, speak of the presence of a situated curricula that is perhaps structured to favour men over women. The presence of situated learning, the earlier described 'black-matter' of leadership learning, has been evidenced through the consequences of its affects on the women.

The issue of differential experiences of situated learning between men and women needs to be stressed. There are clearly aspects of imperceptible situated learning that enable men to engage and participate in the practice and enactment of leadership that are problematic for women. It is perhaps simplistic to capture this issue within the common notion of a 'glass ceiling'. The commonality of discussion from the women associated with overcoming obstacles, is dealing with the unobserved processes of situated learning that have been constructed within particular contexts by historic male practices – hence the notion of management as a non-traditional career for women.

Catherine's apprenticeship, like that of the other women managers, is qualitatively different from the men. Unlike the men, the dominance of organisational learning within an organisational context was balanced through learning drawn from pre-organisational contexts, such as family and school, as well as parallel responsibilities and identities outside of the working environment. In essence, the women appear to draw on a number of contexts of participation that have shaped identity and practice of leadership. One of these contexts was the formal learning environment; but again for some this was a gendered and problematic experience.

Organised formal learning

The women group strongly reflected the same theme as the men: the low value placed on formal leadership development activities. Catherine's context in 1995 was that she had become Medical Director with considerable leadership responsibility and expectation. She perceived that an MBA would greatly assist in developing leadership skills suitable for her role; she described what she learnt from her MBA:

> I learnt that there wasn't a single way of doing it; there wasn't a truth. Which I knew but it confirmed this. For example different leadership styles are OK, and that people didn't need to be either incredibly organised or charismatic in order to be a leader. I think one of the other things I learnt was to observe leaders and what resonated with my experience was that those traits that are constant are generally to do with trust; and people who are excellent leaders

engender trust in other people. So I think that added an awful lot in terms of confidence for the next stage of my career which I knew would be very different moving from a public sector environment to the private sector.

For the women group of managers, the key themes drawn from formal learning, similar to the men were a sense of affirming knowledge and skills previously learnt; observing and comparing with colleagues on the programme; and enhancing confidence through comparison with other delegates. Additionally there was a point of concern expressed by a few women, related to gender issues within formal learning contexts connected to delegates, trainers and, more generally, the male dominance of the educational process. Examples of leaders were overwhelmingly of men (including guest speakers), teaching faculty were predominantly men, the cohort was mostly men (two or three women in a class of 30) and the consequence was often a masculine oriented conversation in the class. One of the women managers described the use of experiential learning as 'an echo of the masculine workplace'. The classroom inadvertently reflected the gendered structural issues that the women faced in the workplace – such issues will be examined shortly.

Contextual variety – public sector versus the private sector

The outsourcing of her organisation into the private sector extended the development of Catherine's leadership practice. She had become a director on the board of an organisation with a very different ethos and style of working – different practices of leadership. The outsourcing was not the end of the journey:

We've been acquired twice, we started off as [name of organisation], we were then acquired by [name of organisation], an American company. Then we were sold off again to the present company. It's all been very different to the civil service, the level of change I think for me as a leader has been difficult, because we've now had three different companies with very different cultures and requirements of people and the other thing's that speed of change but also speed of our ability to acquire other companies, we've grown tremendously in the last four or five years. The civil service moves very slowly for a while you know it sits around and thinks a lot, quite rightly, and then it implements quickly so whatever's implemented next year will have been cooking for the past five or six years. In the private sector your cooking period becomes short as well as your implementation.

And what else did I learn? I learnt that it's quite an unforgiving environment, not just this actual company, but all the others as well.

The cultural differences have also generated changes to her practice
through her latest and current role as Medical Director:

> But it has extended my ability to lead. I think what I've learnt in
> this one is a degree of tolerance that I probably didn't have in the
> others, didn't need to develop particularly in the other roles. Also an
> appreciation of the way that different personalities can actually add
> to your ability to lead. I've learnt to have much more contact with
> people who would violently disagree with me rather than those who
> perhaps would say, 'yeah, you're doing a great job, that's fine'. And
> I've also learnt, which is something I didn't particularly recognise in
> the past that you can actually be a leader without necessarily being
> the expert in the field so working in a matrix sort of structure. I know
> that sounds a bit odd, something you should have learnt very early
> on really I suppose, but it's been reinforced and highlighted in this
> job, tremendously reinforced.

The variety of contexts Catherine has experienced has been most catalytic in her development. What is most striking is the sense that even
later in her career she has significantly advanced her practice. This is
different to nearly all the other stories – both men and women. For the
other managers, different contexts or new roles were more of a stimulant to refine their practice. For Catherine her leadership pathway of
learning has been later than the others. Leadership has become salient
in the last 12 years. The period of outsourcing and the variety of private
sector organisations has been a period of exposed risk and change running in parallel with heightened attention and salience to becoming
and surviving as a leader in a very different context. In many ways
Catherine has 'become' the leader she wishes to be in the context in
which she works, captured in the following comment:

> There have been times when I suppose, in the job that I do, the
> concepts can sometimes be in-between the ethical questions and the
> profit questions in the private sector. This is similar in the public sec-
> tor but to do with politics and ethics – the pressures have been there,
> the same way within the commercial environment. I decided that
> you have to actually come down on one side of the fence or the other
> and I decided that my line would be that I will always take the ethical

argument. The commercial people may disagree with me but it's the leadership role I take I suppose. If I say I think this is what's required, the organisation know the side of executive boundary I lie and I know I'm going to be listened to. You have to make that decision at one stage or another as a leader in the sort of work that I do.

The sense of independence of mind that comes through with this comment was common with the women managers. One of the women interviewed described this independence arising from a sense of marginalisation and a consequential sense of freedom:

I feel sorry for my male counterparts who have no freedom to speak up. They see themselves as wedded to the organisation, often as the main income and have to go along with what's happening.

The context of the women's lived experience is qualitatively different from that of the men and social structures have greatly influenced how women have experienced leadership learning – described earlier under situated learning. Related to the effects of the context and differential situated learning four areas have been highlighted as distinctive to the women 'group' that need to be emphasised: women-only contexts, gender, social marginalisation and managing confidence.

Formative influence of female contexts

Of the women managers interviewed eight of the ten referred to female contexts where women were dominant in prevailing structural relationships. Interestingly all the women interviewed went to all-girls schools. This educational environment appeared to be most formative in shaping role aspirations. Associated and reinforcing a belief in female expectations was the role modelling influence of women teachers and in particular women head teachers. The opportunities provided within these structural conditions of an all-girls school necessitated that females occupied leadership roles. These situational examples illustrated the influence of the context shaping the interviewees' expectations, confidence and self-efficacy of performance – a point that will be returned to later.

There is a strong sense from the interviews that such opportunities became manifest due to limited male competition for leadership roles and explicit encouragement by notable people, particularly teachers and/or parents, to shape expectations. Further, the experiences offered up in these environments were more salient to the women than for the men. For the most part the men described such early formative experiences in an anecdotal manner. In contrast the women managers placed greater weight and significance on the value of these early experiences. There is a strong similarity of this finding with that of the owner-managers – described in the final section.

Early formative contexts that enabled these women to enact leadership roles, experience notables exhibiting leadership and to be encouraged to expect and aspire to non-traditional careers, were prevalent and appear to be significant.

Contextual issues affecting confidence

A key theme evident from the interviews with the women managers was the maintenance of confidence in their ability to lead. All were conscious of it and actively sought to maintain such self-belief. The necessity of maintaining confidence was triggered, for most, by breaks in their careers for bringing up children – described earlier by Catherine.

The significance of career pathways and the learning opportunities, generated on the trajectory of organisational careers, has been identified with both the men and women groups. Yet breaks in this trajectory have an impact on the process of leadership learning in a way that greatly differentiated women's leadership learning from men. The necessity and importance of sustaining confidence was also raised by women who juggled career with raising a family; Catherine illustrated this issue:

> Well I recognised that the loss of confidence wasn't just a result in a personal thing it also actually makes you move away from any sort of career ladder that you might want to get back on to because a number of people who did it, and they usually were women who had the main child care responsibilities, a number of them just never did it. They were always drifting back and further and further away from the hard-edged, fun end of medicine. A lot of them ended up as school doctors or in a child health clinic which has its place, certainly has its place, but as a career it wasn't what I personally wanted to do.

This example from Catherine illustrates a most central issue. The pathway that enables leadership learning through participative engagement has to be managed in a way that is very different from the men. The men did not describe the necessity of maintaining confidence and consciously managing this process. The men did not mention 'career pathway'; rather they described a relatively linear movement from one role or situation to another. The women were aware of a 'pathway' as it was a visible issue for them prominently expressed through the notion of sustaining confidence. Only the women made explicit the connection of the role of confidence and activities to maintain confidence. This does not mean that the men were never unconfident – simply that they did not emphasise or highlight this issue. The women did, and they did something about it. They sought out all-women support groups or created support groups from within an organisational context, and outside the working context. Thus the women proactively developed informal networks – as individual agency action – to create local support structures to counter the perceived impact of underlying social structures.

For women managers issues of confidence and self-efficacy expectations of leading may be more pronounced as a consequence of embedded practices which favour men and perhaps are problematic for women. Catherine provided a clear example of such underlying social practices:

> I think there's an element where men bond differently from women, so if you're working in a heavily male environment then you need to make some choices about how you're going to interact with the men. This in itself isn't an issue but sometimes if you're the only one out of ten then you think, 'what do I do now?' but I wouldn't particularly regard that as an adverse thing it's just a social thing that you have to deal with. In the early stages yes, there were some distinct gender issues because I was a young married woman, bound to have children and therefore expectations of people are that you don't really want a job that will interfere.

This last point emphasises a sense of being marginalised through male expectations of women's potentially limited career commitment to the organisation. Such collective expectations manifest into social structures that appeared to create a contextual issue for the women, perceiving a sense of social marginality within organisations.

Social marginality and leadership

The competing demands described above by the women managers appear to lessen their perceived identification with their respective organisations and often placed themselves more at the margins of organisational culture. Such marginalisation was reinforced through antecedent structural role expectations of a male leader reinforced with limited number of women in senior leadership roles. This sense of marginality is perhaps further extended by perceived unconventional behaviour associated with a need to demonstrate capability to lead and not to be marginalised by social expectations described by one of the women as dealing with the issue of 'a woman's role'. Marginality was also described by a number of the women as providing an advantage. The ability to provoke, be unconventional and to be on the margins of organisational norms appeared to provide freedom to a number of these women leaders.

The social marginality and scarceness of women as leaders in organisational contexts appears to provide conditions for an attribution of a woman's leadership behaviour as unconventional. (The in-depth discussion in Chapter 2 examining charismatic influence of leadership identified unconventionality to be an important attribute.) There is a sense of paradox that the social marginalisation itself creates an opportunity for women to be perceived as providing leadership by 'not being men' and thereby being unconventional to the leader social norm.

The antecedent structural conditions shaping lived experience illustrated a final major difference between the women's group and both men groups: the prevalence and dominance of the issue of gender.

Gender and leadership

The issue of gender was ever present in the discussions; many of the previous quotes from Catherine explicitly or implicitly touch on gender. There is a strong conscious awareness of gender and structural powers that women needed to address or exploit to progress into organisational leadership. The continuing dominance in numerical terms of men in senior positions has the potential for the continuance of such structures. Interestingly research by Parry and Fischer (2003) examined gender prevalence within industries and the extent that gender influenced leadership style. It was shown that where women were more dominant in numeric numbers there was a greater prevalence of social processes of transformational leadership. In contexts dominated by men there was a tendency for a more transactional style to be prevalent. This is an important issue. Historic male dominance of management may thus generate leadership practice that is in some way different to desired female leadership practice in a management context. Embedded imperceptible antecedent influences that seek to maintain the male practice are potentially in continual tension for women – hence the salience of gender.

Perhaps the ability of women to deal with the embedded structural gender influences is associated with many issues, namely the management of confidence and self-efficacy; the use of women-only support networks; the balancing of other roles and identities beyond the organisation; and the nature of being seen as unconventional in a male world, interrelated with social marginality. These aspects created a response to cope with embedded perspectives associated with gender. Catherine commented on gender at the end of the interview in terms of looking back over her career and the prominent issues that have affected her:

> When I was working in Hong Kong at that stage the women doctors were working longer hours and paid less than the men and I took it to my PMA representative, who happened to be an obstetrician, and he said 'well I think that's quite right because you're a woman'. I think there are some of my male colleagues in the civil service who certainly have said 'you've got an advantage because you're a female you remind people of their mothers'. But I mean its life isn't it. You are the gender you are and get on with it.

Thus it appears that for women the relationship with notions of leadership is much more complex than for men.

Comparing leadership learning of employed men and women

There are six distinctive themes that standout as having influence on leadership learning of these women. All of these are affected by broad contextual and structural issues associated directly or indirectly with gender. Table 7.2 summarises the key influences shaping leadership learning drawn from both groups of men and the women's group.

Table 7.2 Comparing influences on leadership learning between the men and women groups

Male managers	Women managers
Identity and salience of leadership	Equivocal on identity, but salience of leadership
Career pathways very explicit	Blocked or complicated pathways
Situated leadership practices	Present but with marginalisation issues
Limited discussion on enacted learning	Similar – but linked to maintaining confidence
Low significance of formal training	Similar – but also as a genderised process
Incidents causing reflection	Similar – but oriented to a genderised discussion
Observational learning – notable men	Similar – but with a balance of men and women

Although the women managers shared strong similarities of influences with the male groups, the structural issues surrounding their career experiences have been revealed to be different and suggest that leadership learning for women appears to be qualitatively different from men. The following key influences on leadership learning have been distilled:

- Commonality of influences on leadership learning – there was high congruence between all groups – but the affect was moderated by other structural influences of gender, marginalisation and confidence.
- Dominance of observational learning with notable people prevalent for all groups. Men rarely described notable women; women less frequently used men as positive role models – rather these were invariably notable women.
- Low significance of formal learning – for all three groups formal learning related more to affirmation of identity, confidence and networking along the career path.
- Role enactment common but limited in reflection – infrequent mention of learning through action with examples – rather, role enactment was related to confirmation of self-efficacy and career pathway progression.
- Situated learning through career pathways – implicit learning exhibited through detailed discussion of career pathways. For all three groups the richness of a variety of contexts enhanced the learning of career pathways, a strong sense of 'becoming' a leader through participation. However, situated learning was problematic due to the antecedent male oriented nature of situated practice. For example, in meetings the loudest voice or most physically forceful demeanour was a recognised part of 'masculine' leadership practice.
- Aspired identity and the salience of leadership – the greater the salience and aspired identification with leadership to the individual, the more explicit and detailed the career path and the learning opportunities drawn from such situated learning. The women group recognised the salience of leadership but were more equivocal on a leader identity due to contextual reasons, particularly gender associations of 'leader' as a masculine noun and significant negative notable men observed in their careers.

The story thus far is of the emergence of similar influences on leadership learning within the employed context; although these are

distorted by socially embedded practices that appear to distort learning along career pathways for women managers. However, the self-
employed context is very different. There is a very alternate story to
be told.

Part D: Influences on leadership learning of owner managers

Examination of Parts A, B and C has concluded by summarising the
key themes that appear to be influencing leadership learning. This final
part wishes to commence with a summary to illustrate the immediate
contrasts. This is because emphasis needs to be placed on the contrast.
The broad areas identified to be associated with influencing leadership
learning of the owner-manager group are:

- Low salience and identification with leadership
- Limited significance of notable people
- Restricted participation along career pathways

This is strikingly different to the employed managers. The discussion to
follow will illustrate a very different perspective of leadership learning
compared with the three previous groups. Tom's experiences of leadership learning very much represents the owner-manager group, with one
exception, that of Alan who will be examined briefly at the end of the
chapter.

Tom's Story

Tom (mid-forties) – Co-founder, with his brother, of a maintenance
surveying service of high-rise structures with approximately 75 full-
time employees and a substantial number of consultant associates.
The business has diversified into a number of areas particularly
becoming a market leader in vacuum seal testing and at the time
of the interview had a turnover of £2.8m. Tom has had only one
previous short-term employer before establishing the business at
the age of 24. Tom's lack of employed history is in sharp contrast to
employed managers.

Limited experiences of leadership learning

It was most striking that eight of the ten owner-managers had difficulty is sustaining a conversation on leadership comparable to the
other groups, in terms of revealing antecedent influences on learning.

The available experiences, roles, people and contexts were limited. Tom's timeline illustrates this point:

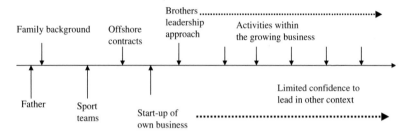

The significance of leadership to Tom in terms of his identity and as a salient phenomenon is captured in the following opening comment on being interviewed about his learning to lead:

> I'll be interested to see how relevant this is for me ... or for you!

Generally the owner-managers had limited salience with leadership and an equivocal sense of themselves as a leader – despite leading successful businesses. Additional aspects common to the owner-manager group were limited organisational experience and organisational roles, limited variety of employed contexts, rejection of authority and avoidance of dedicating themselves to a career ladder within organisations. A corollary of a limited career ladder was the absence of notable people to observe in an employed context. Finally, a most common feature was the dominance of formative influences of schoolteachers and family – particularly parents.

Not an aspired identity

Unlike their employed manager counterparts, 'leadership' as an identity was not personally significant to all but one of the owner-managers and did not form an important element of their identity aspirations. A significant limitation to leadership learning of owner-managers appears to be associated with the nature of their relationship with leadership.

The notion of employed managers aspiring to become the valued identity as a leader in the public and private sectors appears to be an important element of leadership learning. In the lived experiences of these owner-managers it appears to be low in relevance or aspiration, even appearing to have negative associations related to early career experiences in an employed context. Tom reveals much about his limited sense of identity as a leader:

The odd thing is Steve that you have mooted this sort of conversation we are having for a while you know and we never quite got round to organising it, have we? And I think you have mentioned this leadership thing – the funny thing is I don't see myself as leader. If you asked various people in the office or even me – come up with two-dozen sub-adjectives to describe yourself – I don't think leader is one of the adjectives, if it is an adjective, that I would label with myself.

The identities that appear to be much more relevant were described as being associated with a professional or craft skill, or towards being accepted as a successful owner-manager or entrepreneur. The gestalt of the interviews gave them a powerful sense of themselves as independent, in control, and as business builders.

The limited identification or even rejection of leadership as a valued role by the large majority of the owner-manager group is in stark contrast to the three previous groups. What is common about the owner-managers, and distinct from the managers drawn from the large organisations, is the absence of an organisational career.

Limited organisational experience

The importance of career pathways to the learning process of organisational leadership was illustrated in the previous three groups. All but three of the owner-managers had either no experience or severely limited experience within organisations as an employee. The career pathways that have the potential to provide learning through observation and enactment were absent from the experience of these owner-managers.

Tom had no organisational experience as an employee. After graduating from University:

I worked off-shore for a short while – couple of years. And then I was made redundant in '84 or '85. I joined my brother about six months after he had started up himself. My brother started formally in February '85 and I joined him in something like June '85. That was over in Manchester and the business has moved across [now based in Sheffield]. I would be about 24 or 25. I should be able to work it out I guess. The company is 15 years or so – yes about 25 I guess. And the company started from scratch as I say in 1985 and has grown ever since just about.

Tom placed no significance to the years offshore in terms of leadership learning. He was made unemployed and that was the catalyst to set up in business with his brother: 'I needed to do something.' The other owner-managers reflected a similar story. They saw employed experiences in a rather jaundiced way. They did not see themselves on a career pathway. As a consequence notions of situated leadership learning as an employee simply did not occur. Further, the rejection, or absence, of pursuing such a career and avoiding progression along an organisational pathway, may also be significant in terms of personal salience and identification with leadership. Thus learning from organisational contexts was limited in terms of role enactment, associated situational learning and observational learning from notable managers. What was common to all the owner-managers was the dominance of their business as the arena for enacted and situated learning.

Enacted and situated learning in their business

The owner-managers could not identify many events, and certainly few people, that have shaped their learning of leadership. However, the powerful prevalence of the organisation that they had created and developed was dominant in all the interviews. This context had been the crucible forging their approach to leading; it was the centrepiece of their leadership careers. However, there were few leadership incidents that could be articulated. Rather the conversation on leadership frequently migrated into business stories such as survival, marketing, customer relationships or managing finances.

The owner-manager and the business are delicately intertwined and represent a symbiotic example of situated learning. The tacitly acquired knowledge and processes of running the business were expressed through these business stories. As a consequence the practice of leadership in each business is a unique combination of the owner-managers personality, limited prior experiences and sets of continual enactments of managing and leading set within their business. In a sense the leadership practice becomes the accepted or expected approach in this very special context. For the owner-manager the 'becoming', in terms of leadership apprenticeship is relatively isolated from external influences. The leadership practice becomes refined in a potentially restrictive manner. For intergenerational family businesses there is the argument of a type of leadership practice that is passed on from generation to generation if the successor has only known this context.

The notion of the restrictive context in terms of capability to lead outside their business was reflected in the frequent mention of confidence. They showed concern about their ability to lead in other contexts. For example, Tom was unsure what he would do if he sold the business:

If somebody put in the right offer I would say, 'OK then'. I guess the only problem I would have is 'what am I going to next'. I don't know. Could I manage something else?

Tom was lacking in confidence as to whether the business and leadership capabilities he had learnt could be applied to a new context. Moreover, Tom was also not confident that he had developed leadership skills:

> I guess the company does move on and it is funny because some of these things are almost out of your control. You know, business comes through the door and the company grows as a result of that. So the company does move away and onward from some of the skills that I have got and perhaps my brother has got. And I guess there are skills – leadership skills – that I haven't got. Delegation is perhaps one of the things – just one of the skills – just knowing when to pass work on essentially. I'm not convinced that I'm totally good at it. There are probably all sorts of skills out there that I guess come under the umbrella of leadership but I don't see myself at the forefront of these skills. I think it's true to say that the company has moved forward and there are skills out there that I haven't got. I think that's fair to say.

It should be stressed that Tom and his brother do lead a most successful business employing over 75 people. Through the 20 years of managing this business he will have overcome numerous technical, marketing, HR, operational, financial hurdles and many interpersonal issues. He is simply unable to recall aspects of learning which he can relate to leadership. This was similarly echoed with the other owner-managers.

In contrast, and recalling the findings from Parts A, B and C, the employed leaders, both men and women, were more able to describe leadership in nuance ways in a major part as a result of observing and comparing themselves to a variety of people. Further, the variety of contexts and variety of roles provided novel memorable episodes to recall. The experiences and observational models that appeared most dominant to all the owner-managers were from their family contexts.

Notable people and the dominance of parents

For each and all of these owner-managers, family experiences appeared to be the most prominent part of the developmental process that has shaped their leadership practice in terms of values and ethics as well as leadership style. Tom emphasised the impact of his father and mother:

> I think to be honest with you it is my background in terms of family background and my general education. I think that is the thing that has formed me most. I guess I have had a relatively straightforward upbringing. I think you have it drummed in to you to be straight and honest and just make decisions on that basis really. I think by far and away my biggest influence has definitely got to be family and my background. My experiences in my early years.

Tom moved on to explore the notion of leaders being born or made; he very much saw leadership as shaped by genetics and upbringing:

> Leaders are born aren't they? I think. But I think that specific leadership skills can be picked up. I think you pick up those from your early years don't you? Don't you think? The skills you learn start on day one don't they? As soon as you are born you start learning these skills. It's not started when the business started, is it?

The questions posed in the quote are interesting in the sense that Tom is seeking confirmation and perhaps is lacking a sense of confidence and assured authority of perceiving himself as a 'leader'. The nature of his discourse is in striking sharp contrast to the assured confidence expressed by the employed managers. In a conversation that continued after the interview he was most interested in the comparisons with the employed managers and we discussed some of the emerging aspects outlined in this chapter – prominently the impact of notable people. Tom responded and explored the influence of his father:

> I guess first and foremost I would probably have to say my Dad. Yes my father. I guess I am more like my father than my brother or my sister. My Dad is dead straight and I'm not pretending that I'm whiter than white but my Dad has always taught us to play things with a straight bat.

Tom developed his interpretation of the influence from his father through a connection to sport and teams, which Tom valued highly:

> I'm very much a team player in terms of – I guess this is one of the things – I am a team player and in terms of management structures

we always joke that the management hierarchy in this company is nigh on horizontal – that is probably not true if you ask other people – but we like to think of the management structure as being horizontal; we're not into big hierarchies. I think probably because we don't think that they work. I mean we like to involve people and it's a team effort and you can't shout at people and get things done, you have to work with people.

These formative experiences in the family, and the explicit carry over into espoused practice, were attributed with greater significance by the group of owner-managers than was the case with the senior employed men and women. Interestingly, however, with my executive work with junior managers with restricted experience, and in my work with undergraduate students prior to their postgraduate first employment, parents, teachers and sporting contexts are the most prevalent influences. This suggests an important (albeit obvious) point that there is a greater emphasis on early formative influences for those who have had less leadership experience in organisational contexts. The policy implications of this point are explored in Chapter 9.

For Tom, like the other owner-managers with short or no employed history, the impact of notable people outside the family context was severely limited. Tom described no one other than his father and brother. Other owner-managers described one or two bad notable people in their limited career experiences.

What this suggests is a rather restrictive nature to the self-employed context in terms of generating the naturalistic learning experiences that are the lifeblood of leadership learning, namely career pathways in a variety of contexts that provide numerous role enactments that enable engagement with a range of notable people. Running through such participative engagement is the importance of 'becoming' in the sense of situated learning apprenticeship and the associated development of a leader identity. Perhaps the catalyst to engage these influences is the notion of salience – the importance, significance and prominence of leadership. With the employed managers we have seen that this was often associated with circumstances and people.

The interviews with the owner-managers were qualitatively different compared to the employed managers. Different in terms of the duration of the interview: often only 40 minutes at a push for the self-employed; while the employed managers invariably exceeded two hours and could have continued for much longer. Different in terms of stimulants to tease out leadership learning: for the owner-managers there necessitated a continual refocusing on leadership as the interview typically moved to business related issues; the employed managers had an endless supply of people, incidents and related insights. Different in terms of salience and identity: of very low salience and limited desired identification for the owner-managers; compared to high salience and sense of achievement if considered a successful leader. This was an aspirant goal, a career achievement for the employed managers, particularly the men.

However, one of the owner-managers, Alan, had a different tale to tell. His lived experience reflected the owner-manager profile described above until a particular watershed occurred.

Alan – Owner-manager of a retail business

Alan was in his late forties at the time of the interview. He acquired a specialist training college in his early thirties employing approximately 40 people. He sold this business ten years later and became an executive in a construction company, then sold his interest and set up a retail business with a chain of three outlets. Alan had very limited organisational experience prior to the college acquisition in his late twenties. His leadership learning had the same pattern as Tom until a critical watershed. He had the opportunity to work alongside two key notable people: N and B (names removed) as a consequence of winning a competition:

> We won a prize, we won a competition. It was a TV competition that we entered and it was to find the most enterprising company in the north west of England – we won it, which was good for the prize money was £15,000. Quite a lot of money in 1990 and we won lots of other things. One of the things we won was this guy who was from the small business service as business advisor. A guy called N. He was a huge influence on me. We used to meet once a week and he was a real mentor and I very quickly got to be comfortable and leant on him quite heavily and ask 'what do you think I should do about that?' and he would tease all these things out of me. He became a post I would lean against.

This relationship with N led to an opportunity to meet with B. He would become a director and eventually buy Alan out of the business:

> B who I intensely don't like; I don't like his management style. There is very little I like about him at all; although I admire him tremendously. If I was running a business and I was in trouble he would be

the person I would want to talk to because he knew everything. He's not a people person at all, to some extent he is an axe man when it comes to sorting out companies, but he is very good with it – he was a very good and positive influence. No doubt he had a huge influence on me.

The impact of these two notable people was undoubtedly significant to Alan. The opportunity to learn through close engagement with two people at a time when their advice and activity was most required appeared to be the necessary stimulant to wish to become better at leading and greatly extend his leadership learning and development of his leadership practice:

> I knew everything there was to know about training of radio and communications. So I knew everything about it but what I didn't know anything about was how to lead a business. I didn't know anything about business leadership really.

In terms of identification Alan commented:

> I think I'm doing what N helped me with as a sort of mentor and what B helped me with as a fairly tough non-executive director. I think I'm now doing that or attempting to do that with D [colleague] in this company because I saw a real benefit in that.

He saw himself as a leader. He described an identity as a leader outside the working environment as both Deputy Leader of the District Council and Chair of School Governors:

> I got elected and then I became political group leader and then I became Vice-chairman. Since that turnaround point [the relationship with N and B] why do I end up within a year as political group leader for the party when I had only just become a District Councillor? What am I doing that makes people think that I am good leader? I am the Chairman of the School Governors. Can't just be a Governor you know, got to be the Chair!

The observational learning from notable people has been most marked with Alan. The other owner-managers have not had such relationships in the contexts of leading their business. In a sense this raises an issue of the isolation of owner-managers from the leadership learning lifeblood of observation and social comparison. The qualitative difference between the interview with Alan and the other nine owner-managers illustrated a number of issues associated with Alan's lived experience:

- More prominent notable people in the organisational context, particular a mentor:

   I think that 90%, the vast majority of the influences are these leaders, are the people I have worked with.

- Periods of significant hardship linked with notable people
- An opportunity to have structured reflection:

   I've been on leadership courses, and assertiveness courses, MBA ... and they've all been great. But they've all been things I've done to help me adapt and improve or reflect on what I think is right. [Alan undertook an MBA. He commented that this was not significant in terms of content on leadership; rather it acted as an explicit process of reflexive assessment of his career.]

- Confirmation of self-efficacy of leading through a range of associated leadership roles. For example, Alan talked of being Chairman of School Governors, Councillor and Deputy Leader of a local political party and a Non-executive Director.
- A greater explicit value placed on the role of leadership and his identification with this identity

These elements will be explored in comparison to the other owner-managers and the three other groups.

Conclusion – comparing employed and self-employed leadership learning

There are most striking contrasts in the influences on leadership learning between the employed managers and the owner-managers. These have been simplified and captured in Table 7.3.

It is not intended to suggest whether one group or the other operates more or less effectively in their contexts; or whether one group has better leaders than the other. Rather the comparison is towards the identification of different influences and different orientations with regard to their relationship with leadership for these two groups.

Table 7.3 Comparison influences on leadership learning between the employed managers and owner-managers

Employed managers	Owner-managers
High identity and salience of leadership	Very low salience and identity with leadership
Career pathways very explicit	No pathway
Impact of a variety of notable people	Very limited – mostly family and a bad boss
Situated learning of structures and practices	Own structures of own business context
Limited discussion on enacted learning	Similar, but less explicit to leadership learning
Low significance of formal training	Low, but greater emphasis than other samples
Incidents causing reflection	Similar, but limited to leadership learning

Concluding where Part D started the owner-managers contrasted markedly with the employed managers in a number of ways:

- 'Leadership' was much less personally salient and not an aspired identity – no great desire to become a leader.
- Leadership style tended to be attributed to inherent personality characteristics, rather than role or experiences.
- There were strikingly few references to significant individuals as influences on leadership learning.
- Severely limited organisational experiences and limited career pathways with associated leader role responsibilities.
- The 'family' metaphor was very powerful as a framework for leading.

Within Alan's lived experience of leadership was a watershed driven by critical incidents that involved notable people. As a consequence, Alan was the only respondent for whom 'leadership' as an identity had high personal relevance and association.

The predominant influence of notable people shaping leadership also appears significant. Employed managers, and notably Alan, had opportunities to learn leadership, through contextual circumstances. For the employed managers such opportunities were associated with active participation along career pathways where trajectories within organisations offered up notable people and role enactments from which individuals appeared to be able to learn, mostly tacitly, their way towards a valued identity – a gradual process of 'becoming' a leader.

However, this does not fully explain why Alan distinctively began to value leadership. Concurrent with being involved in a critical incident and closely involved with two perceived notable leaders, Alan was also heavily engaged in two different arenas:

- Elected as a Councillor and selected as Deputy Leader of the council
- Studying for an MBA described by Alan as a 'heavily reflective and affirming process'

Perhaps both these dynamics alongside his personal circumstances of a variety of contexts offered up leadership as highly salient and personally significant as an aspirational identity to which he believed he could perform. In some ways this mirrors the career experiences of the employed managers. The contexts shaping career trajectories created a sense of aspirational identification with a valued identity. The senior employed managers aspired to leadership and valued this identity. They described numerous role enactments and engagement with notable others, provided through situated career pathways, affirming their sense of belief in their capabilities to perform.

Yet for all managers, employed or self-employed, the context was the dominant crucible shaping their approaches to leading. For the self-employed, such situations forged a paternal style of leadership. The crucible was not detached from themselves. Rather the owner-manager and the business were inseparable, reflecting a reinforcing and arguably limiting situation in regard to leadership learning. This was distinctively different from the contextual influence on the employed managers. Repeatedly they commented on a range of changing situations, including a broad range of learning stimuli.

On the face of it, there appear to be indications that leadership learning in small businesses might be doubly problematic for entrepreneurs who have limited experience of employment and of management within established organisations. The experience of the employed environment is typically much richer in examples of superiors, peers and subordinates in leadership contexts, creating both opportunities to learn from notable people and to be in roles from which self-efficacy of performance can be ascertained. Such rich variety of experiences and relationships are structurally limited in the owner-manager context, suggesting potential difficulties in addressing issues of greater scale and scope associated with growth and organisational complexity.

Quite simply, these opportunities are unlikely to exist, or are certainly restricted within a self-employment context.

Chapter 8 synthesises the various themes drawn out from Parts A, B, C and D and connects the commonality of influences on leadership learning, notably: observational learning from people; situated and enacted learning through participation in leadership roles; identity development through increasing personal salience of leadership; and capability of leading. Thus there is an emergent sense of becoming a leader within an organisational context over a significant period of time. The notion of apprenticeship begins to be most relevant to leadership learning through lived experience and the development of a manager's relationship with leadership.

8
Towards an Explanation of Leadership Learning

Leadership learning through lived experience

In the conclusion to Chapter 5 I suggested a framework, Figure 5.1, as sufficiently broad and inclusive to integrate and cohere extant theory of informal leadership development and principles of experiential learning. This is important, as it enables a simple argument to be put forward outlining how leadership learning occurs through lived experience. However, such a broad and simple argument fails to explore and illuminate the underlying influences on leadership learning that lie behind the generic headings. The detailed nuances of influences and their interaction in particular contexts are thus the focus of this chapter. To reveal underlying influences and to be able to explain how these operate together in a systemic manner within particular contexts required the use of bodies of theory that had not previously been applied together to the field of leadership learning.

Leadership learning through a range of lenses

I recall presenting a paper at a conference in which I explored ideas from sociology and psychology illustrating how each greatly informed on the other. My mistake was not recognising the heresy of my act. My colleagues appeared to be all sociologists. To these folk I was proverbially mixing oil and water. My view is pragmatic.[1] If knowledge can provide insight wherever it comes from, then it's well worth the risk of 'mixing and matching'. With that justification asserted, the broad areas of literature utilised in this study are:

- Salience – prominence of a phenomenon.
- Social learning – observation, enactment and self-efficacy.

- Situated learning – career pathways and apprenticeship through participation.
- Identity development and the notion of 'becoming' – aspirational identity.
- Structure and agency duality.

It is through the fusion of these five bodies of work into an interrelated whole that a greater illumination and understanding of leadership learning is created and mapped out. This chapter will be structured into two parts:

- Part A – Insights into influences on leadership learning: *What influences shape leadership learning and how do these operate?* Part A will outline a group of interpersonal influences of observed, enacted and situated learning, and intrapersonal influences of identity, salience and self-efficacy. These two groups will be argued to work in an interdependent and systemic manner. A model is illustrated to explain this systemic process of leadership learning through lived experience.
- Part B – Insights into contextual variations of leadership learning: *How does context affect such influences on leadership learning?* Part B adopts a contextual examination of the argument from Part A. Three contrastive insights are drawn between the following groups: public and private sectors; male and female managers; employed managers and self-employed owner-managers.

Through this structure and movement from identifying influences and illuminating contextual variation, the chapter provides an argument to the original puzzle that has shaped this book: *How have managers learnt how to lead?*

Part A – Insights into influences on leadership learning

The underlying influences identified through the four cases in Chapter 7 are interpreted here through the lenses of: salience, situated learning, social learning and identity development – these four areas have been explored in detail in Chapter 3. Such perspectives have not previously been drawn together and integrated to make sense of leadership learning. The antecedents of these bodies of knowledge are perhaps not natural bedfellows – as previously mentioned – in the sense that they originate from two distinct disciplines:

- Social psychology – encompassing social learning, particularly drawing on self-efficacy, observational and enacted learning and self-concepts[2] including salience and schematic conceptualisation.
- Sociology – focusing on structure–agency duality, situated learning and identity development.

The examination of influences on leadership learning is both at the social interpersonal level and at the individual intrapersonal level. Both inter- and intrapersonal perspectives will be argued to occur together as they are seen to have mutuality of influence.

The first influence examined is salience. This is because it will be shown that it powerfully interrelates to all influences and perhaps can be seen as a significant catalyst for leadership learning and a deepening relationship with leadership.

Salience: 'where ever I look there's leadership!'

Salience is argued to be 'a property (or distinctiveness) of a stimulus that makes it stand out in relation to other stimuli and attract attention in that context' (Hogg & Vaughan, 2002: 62). The notion of salience suggests that certain phenomena, such as leadership, are personally more relevant, more significant, more apparent or more prevalent than others in particular contexts: for example, a female manager in an organisation dominated by male managers. Such phenomena interrelate to the circumstances of an individual and are valued higher than other competing phenomena and have the effect of dominating our thoughts (Hogg & Vaughan, 2002). As a consequence of salience people focus their attention towards elements such as objects, identities, artifacts or people, particularly if it is related to personal goals (Fiske & Taylor, 1991). Salience thus becomes a filter or a switch directing our attention.

Salience, however, is temporal in the sense that, for example, leadership competes for attention, relevance and importance at a point in time for some people; while for others it can remain salient for extended part of their careers. Is leadership more or less salient in particular contexts? Certainly in Chapter 7 we have seen that in large organisations the notion of leadership as a career goal is very prominent – most strikingly so with the private sector group. While with the owner-managers there was a very different picture: low salience was predominant. The interrelationship of contexts and salience of leadership appears to be most important to leadership learning.

Within the employed context Bennis and Thomas (2002) argue that events are prominent in shaping leadership development. I argue here that such events within particular personal circumstances are catalytic to stimulating salience of leadership. For example, someone may experience a dreadful bully as a boss but not associate the learning from this experience as developing an understanding of leadership; rather, it lessens the salience of leadership as a valued role. Such a scenario was frequently the case with the owner-manager group.

Understanding of what an organisation holds as salient is learnt explicitly as well as tacitly through participation in organisational life. Learning of contextual practice, such as leadership, may be revealed through the lens of situated learning that provides potentially powerful insights into underlying causes of leadership learning.

Situated learning

Through the lens of situated learning many underlying influences on leadership learning are revealed.

Through all of the interviews there was limited value placed on formal programmes of leadership development. Yet there was minimum description of learning through informal activities. The invisible naturalistic process of emergent learning is most difficult to reveal. Hence the process of situated learning powerfully expresses and captures the essence, as well as providing the nuances, of leadership learning in particular contexts.

Particularly relevant to leadership learning are the notions of legitimate peripheral participation and apprenticeship as central features of situated learning (Lave & Wenger, 1991). The stories from the employed managers illustrated career pathways of participation that provided role opportunities not only to enact leadership and learn through experimentation, but also to provide numerous notable people as indicators of good and bad practice – learning through observation and enactment are described under social learning further on. Such pathways of participation varied in terms of diversity of roles and diversity of contexts. The greater the variety of roles and contexts, the richer and more intricate were the descriptions and approaches to leadership. Such a finding strongly echoes the findings of Davies and Easterby-Smith (1984), who similarly illustrated that diversity of contexts and roles, linked with increasing levels of freedom and responsibility, acted as processes for enhanced management development.

In contrast, the career pathways of participation of the owner-managers were very different and illustrated numerous culs-de-sac of limited role responsibility and severely limited scope for participation in terms of leadership learning. Engagement within organisations, as a pathway of legitimised participation of increasing responsibility in a leadership context, was notably absent.

Although evidence of participation was given by employed managers as episodes and incidents within roles, there was limited recognition that a process of apprenticeship had influenced them or that leadership learning had been acquired through engaged participation. For many, they were unsure how they had learnt leadership skills and, to an extent, struggled to describe their depth of learning.

The notion of situated learning through participation and engagement resembles the apprentice learning knowledge and meaning through participation within communities of common practice (Lave & Wenger, 1991; Wenger, 1998). Such knowledge acquisition can be related to tacit learning (Polyani, 1966) and resembles knowledge and meaning that is directly related to the situational context that is difficult to express (Fox, 1997a). One of the managers from the public sector group provided an example of recognition that his practice and expectations of leading did not conform to a new context:

> Sometimes in [name of new organisation] that is what I'm missing a bit. In the civil service you have the rank and you don't have to win respect when you went into a meeting, whereas in [his new organisation] it is very different, and you have to win that respect in every meeting you go in and you are starting from scratch every time. Although I have the skills to lead these people its just so difficult to have the same impact.

He was not aware of his practice and understanding of leadership until the common practice of this very different situation illustrated to him that he was not in rapport with others – something that he never considered during his fifteen years of leadership 'apprenticeship' in the previous organisation.

If processes of knowledge acquisition are unconscious to the individual, similarly problematic is the ability to describe such knowledge. It is perhaps unsurprising that when managers were asked how they had learnt how to lead, they typically struggled to provide a detailed explanation. In a broader and more generalised perspective, this explanation also provides an insight into the often heralded, notion of leaders being 'born to lead'. On numerous executive development workshops I have posed this question – born or made? The rationale for born leaders often cites no formal development or ability to recall where learning may have occurred ... therefore there's a sense that it must be born.

The notion of situated learning and associated process of legitimate participation within communities of practice provides a powerful explanation to this conundrum. The pathways of participation, provides potential insight into the importance of access to opportunities to acquire knowledge, skills and values of leadership mutually understood within a particular context. This is a most central theory to leadership learning as it explains how both individual and collective leadership practice develops; as well as illustrating how similar and different practices of leadership occur between teams, departments, organisations and sectors. Further, situated learning through engagement with notable people and role activities illustrates an associated link to identity construction, and notions of 'becoming' a leader – more on this shortly.

Prior to an examination of identity aspiration as an influence on leadership learning, we need to step out of a sociological perspective and into the field of social psychology. There is striking coherence between situated and social learning, particularly through the activities of observational learning and role enactment.

Social learning – observed and enacted learning

The work of Bandura (1977, 1986) in the field of social learning provides a pivotal connection between situated learning and identity development in terms of constructing a coherent framework of leadership learning. Social learning theory provides a substantial foundation to build upon in terms of illuminating how observation and enactment influence leadership learning.

Observational learning through notable people

A dominant influence that appears to have been prominent with all groups was the impact of notable people. For the employed managers, there was a greater weight of attention towards notable people within a broad range of organisational contexts. It was noticeable that the greater the salience an individual had towards leadership, the greater the plurality of reported notable people. The owner-managers had fewer examples of notable organisational leaders and placed greater weight on the importance of family and educational influences. This correspondingly appeared to place a low salience on leadership.

Interestingly, and to be developed further in Part B, employed women managers on the one hand, generally recalled learning from notable men as equivocal and typically favoured women as role models. Men on the other hand, rarely ever mentioned women as notables, focusing on good and bad male leaders.

Bandura (1977, 1986) powerfully argues that observational learning is the dominant formative learning process. He states that:

> Learning through action has thus been given major, if not exclusive, priority. In actuality, all learning of phenomena, resulting from direct experience, can occur vicariously by observing other people's behaviour and its consequences for them.
>
> (1986: 19)

Bandura argues that social learning through observation provides invaluable short cuts to knowledge acquisition of complex phenomena such as leadership:

> Some complex skills can be mastered only through the aid of modelling. If children had no exposure to the utterances of models, it would be virtually impossible to teach them the linguistic skills that constitute language.
>
> (1986: 20)

Although Bandura's area of work has established the significance of observational, or vicarious learning (ibid.; McGuire, 1984; Markus & Wurf, 1987), there is a dearth of explicit research focused on observational learning within organisational contexts (see Kempster, 2008). Rather, the focus of this body of work is predominantly towards the transition of children to adults. The closest identified related research is associated with career exploration (Betz & Voyten, 1997) or socialisation (Jones, 1988) or Ibarra's work on professional adaptation (Ibarra, 1999). The value of observational learning and social learning theory to leadership learning has significant potential for the following reasons:

- Notable people were perhaps the single most dominant and common theme of all interviews.
- Observational learning that involved notable people enables the development of global implicit theories of leadership – such as strong, certain, visionary, charismatic.
- Observational learning from notables within organisations enables the development of leadership practice interrelated to specific contexts.

Observational learning can be seen to be interconnected with situated learning and salience. Career pathways within organisations offer varieties of notables. As a manager transcends to increasingly senior levels of responsibility, the salience of leadership is enhanced or affirmed. This appears to provide additional focused attention towards observing notables and perhaps becoming more discerning towards relevant attributes pertinent to particular contexts. Such observation is not as a direct copy or facsimile of these notables but rather as symbols providing general guidance (Bandura, 1986) and a broad framework drawn from, and relevant to, particular contexts – hence the anchoring of observational learning with situated learning.

Learning through enactment

> Enactive experience is a ubiquitous tutor, however toilsome and costly the lessons learned from experience might be at times.
>
> (Bandura, 1986: 106)

The symbolic and guiding nature of observational learning can be seen to be refined through enacted practice. Enactment of leading in particular contexts is offered up through career trajectories in the form of roles and associated responsibilities. These enactments serve to act as a form of experiment in leading; they further stimulate self-reflection on self-efficacy (Bandura, 1977, 1986, 1997) of leading as well as confirmation of identification with becoming a leader. Both aspects of self-efficacy and identity will be developed in detail further on, but are mentioned here to anchor association with situated learning, observational learning and, most notably, learning through enactment.

Roles, as forms of enactments, were the most prominent feature in the narratives of managers' who saw leadership as salient. These were described within an unfolding discussion of their career pathway placing emphasis on explaining the role and the responsibility, rather than experiences that occurred as a result of the roles. Through these roles the managers' emphasised the impact of notables, both good and bad, but did not place emphasis on their own experiences of leading.

Extant literature, most prominently McCall et al. (1988) suggests that experience of enactments is dominant in learning leadership and management. The primacy of enactment is without question the focus of learning within the work of Burgoyne (1977 and 1983 with Hodgson) and Davies and Easterby-Smith (1984). The limited articulation within these managers' experience may relate to the notion of reflection-in-action (Schon, 1983). Schon's argument connects with Polyani (1966) and Nonanka and Takeuchi (1995) and suggests that professional practice develops through immediate reflection-in-action (Schon, 1983), where enactment of leading in action develops knowledge of leadership through tacit acquisition. Burgoyne and Hodgson (1983) illustrated that recall of routine learning events was highly problematic over a short 3–4 week time period; but their research illustrated the cumulative affect of such repetitive routines in terms of acquired learning. Linking tacitly acquired knowledge through enactment with situated learning provides additional emphasis to the notion of leadership learning as a form of apprenticeship (Kempster, 2006).

A further explanation of the limited espoused impact of learning through enactment is interrelated with the work on memory (Tulving, 1983; Nurius, 1993; Walsh, 1995). It is difficult to recall repetitive, non-emotional everyday happenings. Rather, memory is more able to recall transformative learning (Mezirow, 1985) and novel emotive events (White, 1982; Walsh, 1995). For example, events such as hardships trigger a person to reappraise their sense of understanding, confidence and identity (Marcus & Wurf, 1987).[3]

In conclusion, the work of Orr (1996) provides a useful summary to the limited descriptions of enactments in this study. Orr's empirical ethnographic work on service technicians illustrated a significant divergence between what people are able to describe and the practice they enact. Verbal descriptions of a practice were described as 'thin descriptions'; while the observed activity of their practice was characterised as 'thick descriptions'. Orr observed that the practice in action was so much more complex than the technicians were able to describe to him in the interviews. Undoubtedly the 40 managers and owner-managers examined in this study have only been able to provide a glimpse of their learning acquired through enactments.

Summary

The high prevalence of notable people in all the discussions with the interviewees suggested that processes of observational learning should be considered as a key element. It provides a useful explanation to the development of global perspectives of leadership, in terms of popularised leadership figures, and equally provides a building block for understanding of leadership practice in local settings.[4] Enacted learning has been argued to be central to leadership learning despite the counter-intuitive finding of limited explicit empirical evidence in this study. Orr's work, in particular, amplifies the arguments that enactment shapes behaviour beyond the capability of an individual to express (1996). Further, enactment is part of a continual process of reflection-in-action that is difficult to recall unless it forms a central feature of memory formation or alteration (Walsh, 1995). To sum up what must seem axiomatic: experience through role enactment is important to leadership learning; but its importance needs to be placed alongside the other influences notably observational learning and situated learning.

Social learning can be seen to fit closely with situated learning. Through situated learning and participation, managers come in contact with notable people and through such participation they are able to enact a variety of roles; as they proceed along career pathways so that the variety of both observed notables and role enactments extends and deepens leadership learning. The degree to which learning from observation and enactment occurs appears to relate not only to the availability of notables and opportunities to experience leadership through roles, but also to the extent that a manager wants to invest something of themselves in becoming a leader, in association with the value a community holds for the role of leadership.

The discussion will move from the interpersonal perspective associated with situated, observed and enacted learning, to an intrapersonal perspective associated with identity development and self-efficacy performance expectations.

Identity construction – 'becoming' a leader

In Chapter 7 a striking finding emerged through comparing the lived experiences of the employed and the owner-managers associated with the notion of identity. The self-employed identified themselves as owner-managers of their respective businesses or saw themselves through their professional identity as a solicitor, an engineer or perhaps as a joiner or an IT specialist.

In contrast, the employed senior managers who saw leadership as personally salient (reflecting all but three of the 30 interviewed managers) strongly identified with leadership, both as a valued role at the personal level and invariably as a valued role in their organisations and occupations. In many respects the notion of community salience of the social identity of leadership was highly prevalent. Such community salience can be seen as significant in terms of being interrelated with aspirations to become this valued identity, particularly through the role model influence of notable people.

Most relevant to this research is an association made by Bussey and Bandura (1992) who identified an interrelationship of salience with selective information processing once a person has accepted becoming an identity.[5] For example, the greater the identification with leadership, the greater the salience and attentiveness to observe leadership. Thus the construction of an identity as a leader is important to leadership learning.

A review of related theory on identity was outlined in Chapter 3 which presented a clear argument. Although there is limited explicit research on identity construction, a range of commentators (notably Gergen, 1971; Markus & Nurius, 1986; Markus & Wurf, 1987; Yost et al., 1992; Ricoeur, 1992; Ezzy, 1998; Ibarra, 1999; Sparrowe, 2005) have developed similar perspectives that emphasise identity as a continuing ongoing process that links past experiences with future expectations in current situations – usefully captured by Ibarra (1999) in the phrase 'provisional-selves', as outlined in Chapter 3. A critique of Ibarra's work illustrates parallel and comparable research findings to the arguments of this chapter; that the dual processes of observation and experimentation are important to identity construction.

The findings of some employed managers revealed the high salience of a leadership identity to them. Their lived experience illustrated incidents or episodes within particular contexts that highlighted an increasing identification with leadership and a shift away from previous identities. For others there was no sense of an explicit watershed, triggered by an incident that illustrated a realisation of changing identities; rather, the narrative of their lived experience reflected a gradual and imperceptible shift towards a leader identity. Whether it was an incident or an emergent shift, the core common issue was an aspiration to become a leader. This appears to be significant when compared to the absence of such an aspirational identity with the owner-managers, who did not participate along the development pathway of 'becoming' and constructing a 'provisional identity' of a leader. Further, they did not see leadership as salient. However, the example of Alan, in Part D of Chapter 7, exemplifies Ibarra's argument. Alan observed key people and saw the value of leadership. It became salient to him. He talked about seeking to emulate these people – he sought to become a leader.

A desire to become an identity requires commitment and investment by an individual into the desired identity (Wenger, 1998). Of those employed managers who strongly identified with the construction of a leader's identity, they similarly perceived leadership as most salient; they were in roles in which their 'emplotment' provided repeated opportunities to learn how to become this valued identity and this was enacted through their career pathways of legitimate participation (Lave & Wenger, 1991). Again the example of Alan illustrates numerous roles and contexts that provided such repeated opportunities. Because of the structural limitations of the self-employed isolated context, in a sense, he sought out these situations – exemplified with Alan becoming a Councillor and then Leader of the council.

A desire to become an identity and investment of oneself into becoming this identity appears to be a further important underlying influence on leadership learning. It has been shown that identity construction is a gradual and often imperceptible process that links past experiences and future aspirations into the present perspective of an individual's 'provisional' identity (Markus & Nurius, 1986; Ibarra, 1999). In essence, leadership learning can be seen as a continual process of 'becoming'.

Identity construction is closely associated with the salience of an identity within an organisational context. For owner-managers the limited identification with leadership appears to reflect the restricted salience of leadership in their own situation. While for employed managers the career goal to become a leader is highly salient, and active participation along the organisational career pathway, inclusive of enactments and observable notables, reinforces such identification.

Through such participation, evidence is ascertained of a manager's performance of becoming a leader and providing leadership. The final underlying influence to be outlined in Part A is that of self-efficacy – an expectation of performance as a leader.

Self-efficacy of leading

The notion of self-efficacy expresses individuals' expectations of their level of performance in achieving a particular outcome (Bandura, 1977, 1986, 1997) – in this instance a manager's expectations of his/her performance to lead in a particular context. There is very limited academic application of self-efficacy in the field of management research, with only two citations associated with leadership learning. Nevertheless the opportunity provided by utilising self-efficacy to illuminate underlying influence on leadership learning will be argued to be most central.

Self-efficacy has been examined in Chapter 3 within the context of social learning. In short, self-efficacy assumes that an individual interprets feedback on their behaviour in a particular environment, which in turn shapes cognition that subsequently modifies behaviour. The environment provides essential sources of information from either vicarious experience of notable others, or from immediate experience of role enactment or within career pathways of legitimate participation. Within the environment are certain challenges:

> To succeed at easy tasks provides no new information for altering one sense of self-efficacy, whereas mastery of challenging tasks conveys salient evidence of enhanced competence.
>
> (Bandura, 1986: 201)

The importance of this quote is to emphasise the necessity of variety and complexity to enhance expectations and confidence of being able to perform and master leadership; Bandura says that:

> The more varied the circumstances in which threats are mastered, the more likely are the success experiences to authenticate personal efficacy and to impede formation of discriminations that insulate self-perceptions from disconfirming evidence.
>
> (1986: 210)

Rich experience of leading in a variety of contexts is thus seen to greatly enhance an individual's belief in his/her capability to lead.[6] The cases in Chapter 7 illustrated this point by a comparison between the employed managers and the variety of role opportunities for enactment and people to observe, in contrast to the owner-managers who had severely limited sets of experiences related to leadership. The owner-managers were greatly restricted in developing their performance expectation of leading as they had no confirmatory evidence from alternative contexts or benchmarks.

Self-efficacy provides a most useful and relevant framework for understanding the impact of contextual experience, shaped by observed, enacted and situated learning, on a manager's cognition and beliefs about his/her capability and understanding of being able to lead. Inference from the evidence across the groups suggests that confirmation of performance capability from a rich set of sources of feedback is more available in the employed context than the self-employed. The associated influences of identity construction and salience are argued to work congruently alongside role enactments and observed benchmark comparisons from notable others, to enhance confirmatory evidence of being able to perform as a leader. As such, I argue that self-efficacy is a further underlying influence on leadership learning.

Self-efficacy is important to an understanding of leadership learning; but in itself it is only a partial explanation. This is perhaps equally applicable to all the influences on leadership learning. Significance may lie in the interrelationship with salience and identity, along with observed, enacted and situated learning.

Theoretical insights explaining leadership learning

Drawing together the preceding discussion a set of theoretical interpretations and explanations are proposed that provide insights on leadership learning. The research theme that has run throughout the book is: how have managers learnt to lead? The answer is towards a set of underlying influences made up from the following:

- An interpersonal configuration – observed, enacted and situated learning.
- An intrapersonal configuration – identity development, salience and self-efficacy.
- A systemic configuration that integrates the inter- and intraperspectives.

Each of these will be examined and then drawn together as a holistic and integrated explanation of leadership learning.

Interpersonal influences on leadership learning

It is intended that this discussion creates a coherent explanation of identified influences on leadership learning through an illustration of how dynamics of situated, observed and enacted learning are interrelated, and how all three sit within the broader notion of interpersonal leadership learning through lived experience. Such an interrelationship is captured in Figure 8.1. The diagram seeks to represent a reciprocal relationship of observed and enacted learning generated along the career pathway, shown as the wavy line running though the context.

The below diagram illustrates the crucible (Bennis & Thomas, 2002) of the context of lived experience in which the three processes of situated, observed and enacted learning operate. Situated learning is the emphasised processes of meaning and practice acquired through interaction and the dominance of career pathways; thereby providing opportunities to participate and, through such participation, managers come into

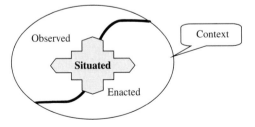

Figure 8.1   Interpersonal influences on leadership learning

contact with the formative influence of observational learning from notable people. Equally, career pathways provide roles of leadership enactment that enables observed learning to be applied in particular contexts, thereby refining knowledge through repeated applications. Through observation, enactment is guided. Through the processes of enactment practice is refined, and situated practice is developed. Observational learning of notable people similarly transmits practices and meanings of leadership.

Thus the interrelationship of all three is significant. In light of the discussion thus far, it can be seen that in the employed context these elements are in great abundance, creating a sense of reinforcement and act as an emergent property – more than the sum of their parts. In the self-employed owner-manager context there is significantly less reinforcement as a result of limited variety of enactment opportunities and restricted presence and the variability of notables to observe.

Identity, salience and self-efficacy – an intrapersonal helix

The interrelationship of identity, salience and self-efficacy appears to be significant to leadership learning and a metaphor of an intrapersonal helix is introduced to illustrate the strength of this interrelationship. Please note, however, I am not suggesting a DNA of leadership learning! Rather, the metaphor of the helix is to illustrate the intertwining of three connected stands, namely salience, identity and self-efficacy. First, I wish to elaborate on the mutuality of connection between these three intrapersonal underlying influences, illustrated in Figure 8.2.

The mutuality of the cycle reflects arguments from the following scenarios:

- Salience led – if leadership is personally salient to a manager then he/she invests personal effort and commitment to become the

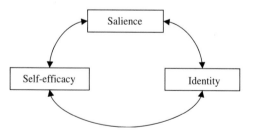

Figure 8.2   Mutual cycle of salience, identity and self-efficacy

identity of a leader. Through such investment he/she seeks out evidence of the self-efficacy of their performance of this salient identity.

- Self-efficacy led – if a manager receives confirmation of his/her ability in leading, this may raise the salience of leadership and consequently begin to relate more towards the identity of a leader.
- Identity led – if a manager identifies himself/herself as a leader, then he/she seeks out evidence to confirm the identity through performance capability. Similarly he/she is much more attentive to salient information on leadership – recognising leadership out of the milieu of stimuli.

Anchoring these scenarios into the evidence from the study, the managers who strongly identified themselves as leaders talked about the personal importance of leadership to themselves. Through the interviews, there was a depth and richness of experience related to leadership as evidenced through numerous episodes of learning, both from observation of notables and role enactment that appeared to provide a strong sense of self-efficacy, of being able to lead. Through the legitimate participation of role enactment at increasing levels of seniority, there was a sense of confirmation of increasing the self-efficacy of leading. As a manager's career became increasingly associated with leadership, so leadership became more salient, and thus there was an increased investment into becoming the social identity of a leader.

Such an interrelationship of identity, salience and self-efficacy was illustrated in a contrasting and opposite manner. The owner-managers generally perceived leadership to be of low salience to themselves and certainly identified appreciably less with 'becoming' a leader. Rather, this was negatively associated with organisational leadership and a career they had rejected. Numerously their lived experiences had a paucity of leadership episodes and certainly there was a dearth of notables. There was very little evidence of a strong sense of self-efficacy of leading. For many they raised questions as to their confidence, competence and capability to lead in contexts other than their own business.

Figure 8.3   Helix of intrapersonal influences on leadership learning

The argument shows a strong interrelationship between identity, salience and self-efficacy. In a sense these three influences on leadership learning can be seen to be intertwined as an intrapersonal helix forming a rope, as illustrated in Figure 8.3.

The final section of Part A draws together the intra- and interpersonal influences into a systemic conceptualisation that links a processual and temporal perspective to leadership learning through lived experience.

A systemic model of leadership learning

The explanation of the interdependence of identity, salience and self-efficacy has been developed along with situated, observed and enacted learning. In fact without these associated interpersonal influences, the 'helix' on leadership learning would be severely restricted, arguably non-existent. Thus it is to situations and the learning that these provide, and that the helix must be embedded with. It is argued that the intrapersonal helix is the line that can be seen to run through the context in which situated, enacted and observed learning occurs, as illustrated in Figure 8.4.

All managers, employed or self-employed, experienced a number of situations. The employed managers placed greater emphasis on organisational situations and these were more numerous. While the self-employed managers placed greatest emphasis primarily on two contexts: the family and the associated formative experiences, such as schools and their own business.

If we now add successive contexts that the managers experience through their careers we can create a temporal perspective, as illustrated in Figure 8.5.

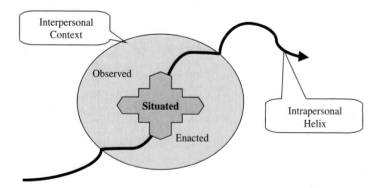

Figure 8.4 Leadership learning in a single context

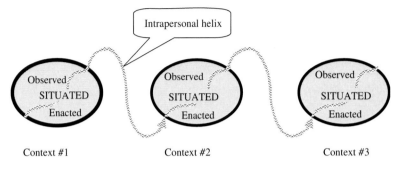

Figure 8.5 Temporal perspective of leadership learning

This temporal and processual perspective seeks to illustrate a number of themes:

- A sense of ongoing development through successive contexts.
- Situations providing stimulus to the helix – in terms of learning drawn from situated, observed or enacted learning.
- The helix subsequently accentuates attentiveness to learning from the situation in terms of observed notables and enacted roles.

Although three contexts have been illustrated, the range and diversity of contexts is most central to an understanding of leadership learning. Further, managers are often active in serial and parallel contexts. The description by Daniel (given earlier in his case study) illustrates his serial career moving from one context to another. This is most typical of the employed managers:

> And I went from Warwick to Leeds and Leeds just blew my mind. From G. who was an appalling man, Machiavelli would have felt at home, to C., who became director in Northumberland, he was a very good role model for me; and I learnt a tremendous amount from that. S. was the director who was much more staid but he was very stubborn. In Warwickshire I worked with M. who became director in Solihull and he was energetic but he wasn't in the same league really as a leader as S.

However, the comment from Phillip (a senior partner in a firm of solicitors) about locations and experiences since practicing as a solicitor, exemplifies the dominant owner-manager perspective:

> But I'm very insular. I haven't had any other job. I've been self-employed for donkeys years, I haven't had a boss. I have only worked in two offices in all these years.

Summary of influences on leadership learning

Part A of this chapter has sought to address the questions that were set in Chapter 1:

- *What influences shape leadership learning?* The identified influences shaping leadership learning are suggested to be interpersonal occurring within the context through situated, observed and enacted learning; and intrapersonal within the individual as illustrated by a 'helix' of salience, identity and self-efficacy.
- *How do these influences shape leadership learning?* A strong relationship appeared to occur between all of the underlying influences producing a system. The power to shape leadership learning of this system is influenced by the context of the manager. It has been shown that an employed manager experienced situations that provided situated learning opportunities of participation and the generation of common meanings and identification. Through social learning, employed managers experienced role enactments and observational learning from notable people. In contrast the self-employed managers illustrated the absence of influence of the 'helix' in leadership learning and there were very different situational experiences, such as the absence of a career pathway and legitimised participation, limited variety of salient notable people and role enactments.

The arguments have thus been outlined to answer the first two questions. Building upon the explanation of these underlying influences, it is essential to explore further and seek to illuminate the contextual variations that have been identified within Chapter 7. This is the focus of Part B.

Part B: Insights into contextual variation on leadership learning

Part A has outlined an explanation of leadership learning through lived experience; but how does context influence the interaction and effect of the intra- and interpersonal processes? Hence the third question: *How does context influence leadership learning?*

In Chapter 7 the relationship with leadership was illustrated as varying considerably between the groups, most notably comparing women and men managers and employed and self-employed. Part B seeks to draw upon these findings by exploring and revealing why such variations may occur through the use of 'influence configurations'. An influence configuration is adapted from the work of Fleetwood (2004) as a method for moving away from the catch-all notion of context to create a more specific explanatory framework. This framework will be employed throughout Part B, highlighting contextual variation between men in the public and private sectors, men and women managers, employed managers and owner-managers.

Prior to elaborating on such contrastive discussions a final theoretical lens is introduced that links Parts A and B together: the role of the individual (as agent) interacting within specific contexts (structures).

Context shaped by structures and agency

A context can be seen as an amalgam of numerous influences and from an organisational perspective such influences, which are both external and internal, form a complex influence configuration (Fleetwood, 2004), which is able to have an affect on outcomes. Such an influence configuration would be developed over many years and reflects antecedent structure–agency interaction.

Within a context, structures in the form of embedded practices are sustained or elaborated through people. Some people have greater power than others and thus have potentially greater influence within organisations to shape practices. This proposition introduces the work of Archer (1995, 2000) and adds a important additional interpretation to leadership learning through the lens of structure–agency interaction.[7]

Her argument is that embedded practices pre-exist individuals and, as a consequence, individuals are influenced by such practices.[8] Certain individuals who have access to influence and power, in this case leaders, can elaborate (or sustain) leadership practices and meanings, causing influence on their colleagues leadership learning within a specific organisation – particularly direct reports. I consider this notion of structure–agency interaction a most powerful insight into the development of underlying influences shaping leadership learning and practice, and most helpful in providing an illumination of contextual variety.

The arguments of Part A are thus extended by Archer's work, which places the inter- and intrapersonal influences into a structural context that is continuously in flux, being either sustained or elaborated by the actions of individuals. For example (and to be elaborated in detail below), the prominence in this study towards the role of notable people influencing leadership learning needs to be connected to the role of individuals to sustain or elaborate pre-existing practices of leadership.

Arguably through such structure–agency interaction the differentiation of practices of leadership between the groups occurs and can, in part, be explained. Part B will thus explore how different practices, in the form of 'influence configurations', differ between the public and private sectors, between men and women, and between the employed and the self-employed. I will show how the intra- and interpersonal underlying influences on leadership learning are affected by other context-based influences.

To achieve this goal we need to first understand the process of contrasting 'influence configurations'. An influence configuration seeks to make explicit influences that appear to be shaping the occurrence of a particular outcome in a specific context. The influences are divided between internal and external. The internal influences, such as the intra- and interpersonal influences on leadership learning identified in Part A, may be present in a number of contexts; but this does not mean that leadership learning will occur, or that there is any regularity in the form of learning. This is because other influences are likely to be present. Further any notion of regularity is further undermined by the numerous external influences that affect all contexts, or affect specific contexts. In essence, the most that can be shown in an influence configuration are internal influences, mediated by external influences, to generate a 'tendency' to stimulate leadership learning, the outcome of which is leadership practice.

To help simplify this description we need an example; Figure 8.6 outlines a method of illustrating how this works. For this example the intra- and interpersonal influences are shown as A's; while other influences are B's (drawn from Context 1) and C's (drawn from Context 2). Some influences can be common to many contexts, or bespoke to one single context. In the example shown in Figure 8.6, Context 2 includes influences in Context 1 but also distinct influences only present in Context 2 – identified here as C's. The external influences on leadership learning are assumed in this example to be media images of leaders and texts, such as this book! These influences directly affect an individual's leadership learning but may also influence the context. Finally, the

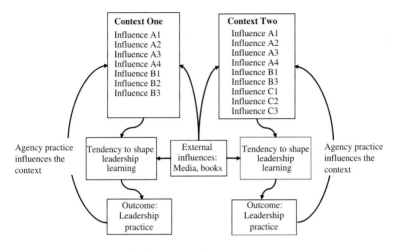

Figure 8.6   Comparison of influence configurations

example shows that the context is itself sustained or elaborated by the agency actions of a leader's practice.

Figure 8.6 illustrates two patterns of contextual influence. Both contexts share some influences, while additional influences are seen to be prevalent in one context and different in another. Both contexts have external influences and the affect of such influences will vary in each context. For example, a change of government may be more influential on the public sector than in the private. Equal opportunities legislation may have more impact on women's leadership learning than men's.

This notion of contextual variation is a most fundamental principle that has guided the epistemology behind this book: what is known can only be explained as a 'tendency' for influences to produce a similar outcome. Contexts, or 'influence configurations', change all the time. Prediction that certain influences will shape leadership learning in all contexts is a fallible notion. At best certain influences, if present and influential in a particular context, will have a 'tendency' for leadership learning to produce a certain situated leadership practice.

We shall now compare the three different groups: the private and public sectors; men and women; and employed and owner-managers. Through such comparison the contextual variations and the influences that appear to shape such differences will be illuminated.

Comparing public and private sector leadership learning

The intra- and interpersonal influences on leadership learning were prominent in both public and private sectors, but varied in the manner of their affect on individuals, for example:

- Career pathways more pronounced in the private sector.
- Intrinsic purpose of public sector activities.
- Espoused importance of ethics was dominant in the public sector but less explicit in the private sector.
- Greater value placed on team orientation in the private sector.
- Abuse of power was commonly described in the private sector.

The varying influences generated from the respective sectors have been drawn into a comparative influence configuration shown in Figure 8.7 to allow comparison between the groups. The intra- and interpersonal influences are identified as 'C'; the influences drawn out from the public sector annotated as 'PS' – one of which, career pathway to the goal of being a leader, is shared with the private sector; while the influences distinct to the private sector are shown as 'P'.

What is shared between both groups is the dominance of the earlier identified intra- and interpersonal influences shaping leadership

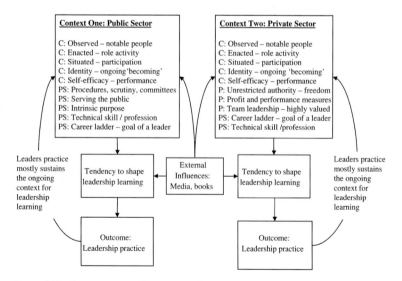

Figure 8.7 Contrastive influence configuration of private and public sector managers

learning. However, the nature and characteristics of leadership were different between the private and public sector groups as a consequence of additional contextual influences that reflect the historic antecedent of the embedded practices of the previous generations.

For example, in the public sector group, managers frequently commented on the influence and salience of organisational purpose and on the ethos of public service. Combined with these influences was the affect of public scrutiny, use of public money and associated bureaucracy ensuring public access to information, policy and performance measurement. Such embedded practices and associated relationships create contexts that are distinctive from the private sector. For the public sector leader, these influences appear to limit freedom of action, autonomy and restrict personal use of power. Rather, power was more associated with position in the hierarchy.

In contrast, managers from the private sector frequently mentioned the abuse of power by notable individuals reflecting greater freedom of action and the notion of 'fiefdoms' within organisations. There was a distinction between the two sectors with regard to purpose, particularly a lack of implicit societal purpose within the private sector in contrast to the public sector group. Discussion of societal purpose was most central to the public sector managers; Harry, a Director of an NHS Trust, exemplifies this point:

Something I did meant that patients got a better deal, a better service.

It appeared that the private sector managers saw purpose through the value of teams of which there was frequent mention, particularly the recognised value of being a team leader. Finally, a further distinction can be drawn between the sectors relating to the economic imperative of profit in the private sector and economic scrutiny in the public sector.

The intra- and interpersonal influences on leadership learning were present in both the groups. However, historic embedded practices can be seen to have distorted the nature of the leadership practice between the private and the public sectors generating a different emphasis and practice of leadership. The explanation of leadership learning between the public and private sector groups has similarities with the group of women drawn from each sector in terms of the common intra- and interpersonal influences. However, for the women there are also striking additional influences on learning that appear to create a different perspective to leadership learning and associated leadership practice.

Women and leadership learning

At the outset of this study into how managers learn leadership, it was not the intention to develop a contrastive discussion between men and women. However, findings emerged that illustrated a potential rich area of contrast. The similar and contrasting influences are illustrated in Figure 8.8. The previous notations will continue to be used adding 'W' for the influences that appeared to have affected the women managers. Additionally some of the previous notations are amended with '/W' to show how the previous influences are altered in affect on the women. The increased complexity of describing women's leadership learning in part exemplifies the increased complexity of leadership learning for women. To try to simplify such increasing complexity we will only compare men and women managers from the private sector.

There are strong similarities to the male employed managers particularly with respect to the presence and influence of generative intra- and interpersonal influences of leadership learning. Most significant was the role and impact of notable people. An emphasis in the female

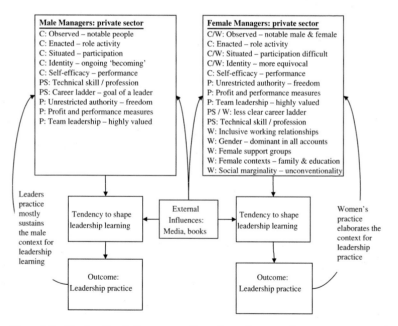

Figure 8.8 Contrastive influence configuration of men and women managers in the private sector

group was balanced between genders but with a prominence of role model influence towards women drawn from inside and outside the employed context. However, a deeper exploration reveals significant differences.

Perhaps the most explicit was gender. Gender was predominant and highly salient to the female group, significantly shaping their lived experience of leadership learning in striking contrast to the men. Phillips and Imhoff (1997) undertook a review of literature examining women and their career development and summarised that much has been learnt over the last ten years about structural influences on women's careers in terms of identity, occupational choices, barriers to entry into particular careers and experiences of organisational life. In their review of vocational experiences, the gender-related issues echoed the emergent themes from this study, that there is an historic structural phenomenon that greatly influences vocational careers of women and reflects elements of the following gender-oriented factors:

- Dissuading women from entering non-traditional roles, such as management (Phillips & Imhoff, 1997: 39 – citing the work of Chatterjee & McCarrey, 1989; and similarly Mazen & Lemkau, 1990).
- Women have held low self-efficacy expectations in non-traditional careers – such as management (Bridges, 1988; Lauver & Jones, 1991; Matsui et al., 1994).
- Negative attribution through marginalisation – 'Men, currently in higher ranking positions, prefer to promote other men' (Phillips & Imhoff, 1997: 46). Similarly, and most striking, Saal and Moore (1993) suggested that the promotion of a same-sex candidate over an opposite-sex candidate was perceived as more fair than was the reverse!
- Problematic career pathways (Betz & Fitzgerald, 1987), associated with marginality and negative attribution – women have experienced difficulties progressing along career trajectories. Melamed (1995), for example, identified that sexual discrimination accounted for between 55 per cent and 62 per cent of variance in career success.
- Multiple roles – associated with career progression is the impact of career breaks and multiple roles. Expectations on women to balance work and home, roles and identities; balancing of roles and identities made more difficult through career breaks that resulted in issues of maintaining confidence.

However, some aspects of structural gender discrimination have been used by the women managers as influences to help mitigate or overcome such dominant structural effects. These were identified as:

- Female contexts – descriptions were given of situations in which females were dominant. These were often family or educational contexts, such as a single-sex schools.
- Social support groups – contexts in which deliberate groups were sought out or formed to provide support in terms of sharing experiences, providing advice and encouragement, thereby building or sustaining confidence.
- Social marginality – the non-traditional role of being a female manager provided structural opportunities of being less embedded in organisational culture. This enabled a perceived sense of freedom of action and independence of mind greater than that of their male counterparts. Further, the unconventionality of having a woman as a leader in a male world appeared to create a sense of charismatic attribution towards the women.
- Multiple roles – plurality of roles appeared to generate a balanced perspective to work/life priorities, role modelling an emerging structural change in employee expectations. Broadening of perspectives beyond the organisation was described by some of the women managers as providing a richer personal identity.
- Inclusive working relations – a desire by organisations for a team focus was described by a number of the women as suiting their gendered perspective of relationships. A feminine perspective to leadership may link to espoused desirable leadership qualities of emotional awareness and individualised consideration (Bass & Avolio, 1990a).

Influences of these gender-associated effects are perhaps best seen as an interrelated influence configuration. For example, the formative female context provided role models to observe and enact opportunities and for leading which often created high efficacy aspirations for employment in management careers. Such formative experiences may have been a catalyst for women to subsequently seek out female support groups in organisational contexts to provide assistance and encouragement, provide further role model guidance and help sustain confidence, particularly following career breaks. Equally, issues of marginalisation could be explored and advice offered to assist overcoming structural obstacles along the career path.

This discussion reflects identified research and recommendations for interventions, such as the use of social support groups (South et al., 1987), exposure to role models (Bailey & Nihlen, 1990), the use of other women as agents to reduce barriers to career advancement (Betz & Hackett, 1987) and the provision of mentors, particularly female mentors (Dreher & Ash, 1990).

The ever increasing prominence of women in management careers, and at increasing levels of seniority, is perhaps most salient not only to a discussion specifically on women's leadership learning, but also more generally significant to potential changes, albeit imperceptible, to leadership practice. In essence, the historic perspective of leadership as a masculine phenomenon (Grint, 2005), sustained through structural powers, may be on the cusp of becoming feminised (Billing & Alvesson, 2000).

The work of Phillips and Imhoff (1997) not only described gender structures inhibiting women's vocational careers, but also referred to changes occurring to structures around gender and careers. For example, they cite Gerstein et al. (1988) who identified that women's self-efficacy expectations have substantially increased over the preceding two decades with regard to careers in non-traditional occupations, such as management. Similarly they cite Tangri and Jenkins (1986) who suggested that women's career patterns are changing, reflecting higher numbers of employed women and greater numbers of women in non-traditional careers. Alongside these changes is the increasing role innovation more suited to flexible working, greater education of women, smaller families and starting families later in careers (Phillips & Imhoff, 1997). Further, the increase in experience of men working with women is seen to be changing male expectations of women in non-traditional roles (Palmer & Lee, 1990; Fandt & Stevens, 1991). Thus research has begun to illustrate that women's career expectations of management careers have risen as a result of improving career experiences of a greater number of women role models (Elliott & Stead, 2008).

Drawn together, these 'green shoots' provide indications of change and reflect Archer's (1995) notion of morphogenesis, where the pre-existing structural influences are becoming modified by actions of influential individuals. In this case, the individuals are an ever-increasing number of women managers who are, alongside women employees, in increasingly prominent and numerous leadership roles. Thus Archer's model may give light and focus to an emerging structural change to leadership and an argument for the feminisation of leadership.

To elaborate lets consider the inter- and intrapersonal influences. The greater the number of women managers the more prominent will be processes of observational learning of women managers and salience of women's leadership. The increasing number of women at senior positions will begin to reshape and modify the practices of leadership through processes of situated learning. Associated with modified practices will be the potential for a greater sense of personal identification with the role of a leader for women and their enhanced expectation of being able to perform this role due to the changed nature of leadership practice.

Billing and Alvesson (2000) argue that the qualities and characteristics associated with leadership are becoming decreasingly associated with masculinity. However, the prominence of literature on the pre-existing structural antecedents and influences of gender discrimination suggest at best that the arguments outlined regarding the feminisation of leadership reflects these very early 'green shoots'. Phillips and Imhoff (1997) concluded with a call for greater research into the processes shaping a woman's career path:

> We know little about a woman's efforts to enter the workforce and about what helps her negotiate this transition well.
>
> (1997: 50)

Save for the recent work of Elliott and Stead (2008) that explored how leadership is experienced and constructed by women, we know even less about how women leaders in particular contexts have learnt how to lead. The illuminations from this study will help to map out areas of further research and hopefully policy implications for effective intervention to assist women's leadership learning.

Owner-managers and leadership learning

Although the two previous explanations have revealed different influence configurations shaping leadership learning, the contrast between the employed and self-employed groups is starkly different by comparison. It is through this comparison that the significance of influences on leadership learning is exhibited. Figure 8.9 illustrates the comparison. The same notations are used as with the two previous configurations plus two additional influences, annotated as 'OM', for the owner-managers: their purpose for running their businesses, and the crucible of learning that is their business. What is striking is the absence of most of the intra- and interpersonal influences.

Unlike the previous groups, the dominant underlying intra- and interpersonal influences on leadership learning are either absent or certainly very low in effect. Rather, the self-employed group has an influence configuration that in part draws on elements of the other three

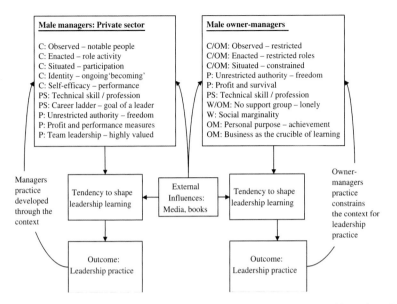

Male managers: Private sector

C: Observed – notable people
C: Enacted – role activity
C: Situated – participation
C: Identity – ongoing 'becoming'
C: Self-efficacy – performance
PS: Technical skill / profession
PS: Career ladder – goal of a leader
P: Unrestricted authority – freedom
P: Profit and performance measures
P: Team leadership – highly valued

Male owner-managers

C/OM: Observed – restricted
C/OM: Enacted – restricted roles
C/OM: Situated – constrained
P: Unrestricted authority – freedom
P: Profit and survival
PS: Technical skill / profession
W/OM: No support group – lonely
W: Social marginality
OM: Personal purpose – achievement
OM: Business as the crucible of learning

Managers practice developed through the context

Tendency to shape leadership learning

External Influences: Media, books

Tendency to shape leadership learning

Owner-managers practice constrains the context for leadership practice

Outcome: Leadership practice

Outcome: Leadership practice

Figure 8.9 Contrastive influence configuration of employed and self-employed managers

groups and illustrates influences distinct to the owner-manager context. The similarities are, for example:

- Marginalisation – similar to the women managers, the self-employed managers described situations of being on the periphery of organisational life (Goffee & Scase, 1985; Curran, 1986);[9] being somehow different from their colleagues in terms of independence and social fit (Gray, 1990).
- Confidence – again similar to the women group, a common issue for the self-employed related to a questioning of their ability to perform in other contexts and their capacity to lead a larger organisation (Gray, 1990). Unlike the women, the self-employed managers did not provide coping mechanisms, such as support groups – they were very much alone.
- Technical excellence – similar to all the groups the self-employed managers anchored their confidence in their professional or technical skill, for example, as a solicitor. Such technical excellence appeared as a source of power and confidence for leading in their specific organisation.

- Abuse of power – those self-employed with organisational experience commented on the abuse of power of notable managers. This abuse of power perceived by the owner-managers appeared to be linked to marginalisation and limited independence, generating a stimulus for leaving organisational life and becoming self-employed. There was a strong similarity here with a number of the women managers.
- Economic imperative – a dominant focus of survival and growth (echoed in the work of Gray, 1990).

Although similar to the private sector, such a focus belies the motivations of the individual owner-manager. The influences explicit to the self-employed owner-managers were:

- Personal purpose – in contrast to public sector group, where there was a common purpose, for the owner-managers the business was a vehicle for self-achievement or independence, for early retirement, for control or as a vehicle for simply making a living with no alternatives available (see Gartner, 1989 or Gray, 1998), for a review of the commonality of these elements).
- The business as a dominant context – the lived experience of the owner-manger group was dominated by the business. This was the crucible in which role enactment and leadership responsibility occurred.

The above distinct influences, in particular the limitations of such a single context, have had a prominent impact on the leadership practice of the self-employed group. Often this is because the owner's business is the first prominent context for situated and enacted leadership learning in a managerial context. Such learning appears relatively limited in terms of nuance appreciation of leadership practice for changing circumstances – for example, a growing business. I am not suggesting owner-managers are not learning – far from the case. Entrepreneurial learning has been shown to occur throughout the life cycle of becoming an owner-manager and coping with the challenges that constantly face survival and growth (Cope, 2005). Rather it is the absence of intra- and interpersonal influences on leadership learning within the self-employed context that inhibits the development of their leadership practice. Arguably this is most significant in relation to issues of organisational growth.

The striking low-level presence of the suggested intra- and interpersonal influences on leadership learning can be explained by the lived experience of the self-employed, most notably their rejection of organisational careers. Such a rejection often reflected unfavourable and negative experiences caused by a few notable people in their short formative employed careers. The truncated length of organisational careers severely restricted situated learning and associated opportunities to observe and enact leadership. Sometimes there was a complete absence of any experiences in organisations other than their own self-employed context. An outcome of such antecedent influences and experiences resulted in:

- Very limited career pathway – no opportunities for a leadership learning apprenticeship.
- Low enactment responsibilities – absence of role opportunities for learning through line responsibility.
- Minimal influence of observational learning in an organisational context – few people observed as only few were available to observe due to limited career pathway.
- Low salience of leadership – further compounding the limited observation of leadership, as the phenomenon was not prominent to them.
- No identification with leadership – rather a sense of positive discrimination of organisational leadership as a surrogate of organisational life which they had rejected.

The comparison of employed and self-employed managers illustrates a striking contrast in the manifestation of leadership learning. The limited presence of the suggested inter- and intrapersonal influences shaping leadership learning within the influence configuration of the owner-managers group may have important implications on the practice of leadership in these contexts and the potential consequential impact on the development of their businesses. However, the configuration can change. The example of Alan, in the last section of Chapter 7, provides a powerful illustration of such change and the consequential impact it had on his leadership learning, and subsequent leadership practice, by stimulating the underlying intra- and interpersonal influences of leadership learning. For Alan it was the mentor relationships and the observational learning that occurred with two notable people that made leadership salient to him. The story of Alan's experience opens up the possibilities for intervention.

And the role of formal development?

It has been the deliberate intent of the structure of this chapter to leave all discussions on the role and impact of formal intervention processes on leadership learning to the final comments of this chapter. Common to all of the employed managers was an experience of formal leadership development programmes. It has been most striking that a common perspective of such intervention was its limited impact. Certainly, little acknowledgement was given to the developmental nature of formal education in terms of curriculum impact. However, formal education did have significant associated consequences influencing leadership learning. Often, formal programmes were considered of minimal relevance, yet powerful in terms of: identity confirmation; being recognised by the organisation; or an affirming process through comparison to other managers on the programme; or perhaps a form of networking. The single most dominant influence of being on an educational programme and away from work was the opportunity to reflect and make sense of experiences (Kempster & Bailey, 2007). As a finding this was not surprising, as the literature in Chapter 4 was relatively unequivocal on a consensus that informal leadership development interventions were seen as most relevant. The best practice review of leadership development by James and Burgoyne (2001) confirms this perspective and went further to synthesise organisational interventions in leadership development, examples of which were mentoring, leadership coaching and providing a rich diversity of contexts and responsibilities in which to enact leadership (ibid.; Burgoyne et al., 2004; Conger, 2004).

However, there was very limited recognition or understanding of the underlying influences on these informal activities and the complexity of intervening. Further, an appreciation of the naturalistic and apprenticed perspective of leadership learning raises significant question marks related to efficacy of interventions. The naturalistic development process of leadership learning through lived experience may not be capable of being condensed into a development programme. The evidence from these managers suggests that their experience of leadership development thus far is highly problematic in terms of being congruent to their circumstances and thus being efficacious in terms of influencing leadership learning. The final chapter draws together the arguments of this study and addresses this thorny issue of how to intervene in this complex phenomenon.

9
Conclusion

The need for the study

The necessity for understanding leadership learning has been outlined in the opening chapter, where it was argued that a clear disquiet exists towards the efficacy and effectiveness of formal leadership development interventions as a means to enhance leadership learning. Further, it was established that informal development as part of an individual's lived experience, and not formal development, has been found to be significant and dominant in accounts broadly described as leadership learning. Yet there is a dearth of studies into leadership learning at the level of the individual and, in particular, limited detailed understanding and explanation of underlying influences on leadership learning, and the development of leadership practice, interrelated to the contingent effect of contexts.

In light of the need for research into leadership learning, the study aims its focus on two questions:

- What influences shape leadership learning and how do these operate?
- How does context affect such influences on leadership learning?

So ... how do managers learn to lead?

Certainly the dominance of informal and naturalistic influences shaping leadership learning has been confirmed. The cycle of leadership learning through lived experience, introduced in Chapter 5 integrates together important themes at a very general level of explanation. The model has been modified to incorporate a central argument from Chapter 8, that of identity construction and the notion of 'becoming' a leader, shown as Figure 9.1.

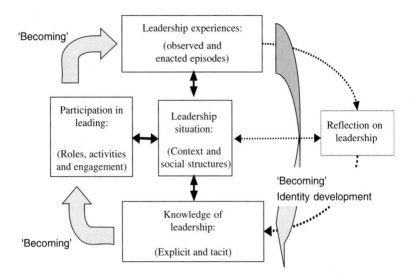

Figure 9.1 Leadership learning through lived experience – a cycle of becoming (Kempster, 2006)

The arguments outlined in Chapter 8 reveal depth to this cycle of learning by applying theories of learning to this model that have not been integrated together before, namely situated learning, observational and enacted learning, identity construction, salience and self-efficacy. These very different elements form a systemic and integrated explanation of underlying influences on leadership learning.

A systemic perspective of leadership learning – an emergent power

Chapter 8 outlined two sets of common influences on leadership learning: Intrapersonal in the form of salience, identity construction and self-efficacy; and interpersonal formed from observed, enacted and situated learning. Taken together, these intra- and interpersonal underlying influences on leadership learning appear to take the form of an interrelated system that has an emergent power – a power drawn out of the sum of the parts working as a cohesive whole. A reprise of Figure 8.5 from Chapter 8 illustrates such a system.

The system illustrates a series of contexts which are connected through the suggested intrapersonal helix: hence a temporal and processual perspective of leadership learning. This system has an evolving nature that is enhanced or constrained by unfolding contexts. The example given of Alan at the end of Chapter 7 exemplifies the importance of this temporal perspective to the processual impact of leadership learning. Alan's context

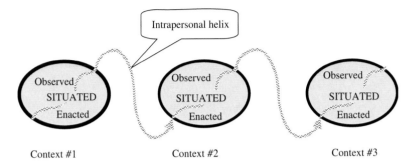

Reprise of Figure 8.5 Consolidated explanation of leadership learning through lived experience

changed and, as a consequence, the presence of influences on leadership learning became enacted. Most prominent to Alan was the impact of a notable person making leadership salient to him at the moment when he desperately needed assistance to survive near insolvency.

The central argument is that both the intra- and interpersonal influences on leadership learning are interdependent to each other. Sayer (1992) argues that interdependent causes can create an emergent power. An emergent power is similar to the notion of teamwork where the whole is greater than the sum of the parts. Such an emergent influence on leadership learning is argued to exist only as a consequence of the other elements and reflects a system shaped by successive contexts, shown as Figure 8.5.

The central contribution that this book makes is through identifying and explaining how common intra- and interpersonal influences interact from both a temporal and processual manner on leadership learning within and through successive contexts. Although these influences appear to be significant to the process of leadership learning, their presence and impact is contingent to particular contexts.

The significance of context to leadership learning

Chapters 7 and 8 have illustrated the significance of context and its contrasting affect between employed managers and self-employed owner-managers, and between men and women managers. Most notably the study has shown:

- *Limited differences between private and public sectors:* At the sectoral level of analysis, the common intra- and interpersonal influences were most evident and similar in affect. There were additional influences and these were associated with sectoral contexts such as organisational purpose and bureaucratic control in the public sector, and the abuse of power and centrality of teams in the private sector. The influence of varying additional influences in the respective sectors fashioned differential perspectives to leadership conceptions and leadership practice – as might be expected.

- *Significant differences between employed men and women:* The study identified a striking difference in the leadership learning experiences of employed men and women. Although the common intra- and interpersonal influences were evident in both groups, the women appeared to experience additional influences that affected their leadership experiences and learning. The intrapersonal differences affected self-efficacy expectations of non-traditional careers, a greater range of identities and maintaining confidence. With regard to interpersonal differences these were broadly associated with gender such as: masculine symbols of leadership; gender attribution of notable people and impediments to situated learning; career pathways through career breaks; social expectations of women's roles; and masculine practices as barriers to situated leadership learning.
- *Very significant differences between employed and self-employed:* A further most striking and notable aspect of the study was the difference between employed managers and self-employed owner-managers. The experiences of the self-employed is dominated in the interpersonal realm by extended formative familial influence (particularly parents and teachers), the owner-managers' business context, severely limited pathways of organisational participation, limited observational learning through notables and similarly limited role enactment. While intrapersonally there was low salience and identification with leadership, as well as limited self-efficacy expectations of being able to lead in a context other than their business.

The identification of common underlying intra- and interpersonal influences on leadership learning and illumination of the differential impact of contexts on leadership learning has occurred through the utilisation of a broad range of theories drawn from fields that are not commonly connected together.

Building a theoretical base of leadership learning – an interdisciplinary perspective

By removing boundaries that are artificially constructed around particular fields of study there is the potential to make significant insights in our understanding of how leadership is learnt. Remaining within traditional fields does give greater critical depth and a sense of scholarly command but a phenomenon, such as leadership learning, does not neatly fit into our academic disciplines. This study has shown that by using theories as lenses we can begin to see aspects of leadership learning in different ways. By connecting these perspectives together into a systemic appreciation I argue we obtain a more rounded and realistic connection to lived experience. The four areas that this study has drawn together will be briefly reprised.

The first area draws from social psychology and social cognition from the established work of Bandura. This research found that managers frequently mentioned notable people and role enactments, echoing Bandura (1977, 1986, 1997), who argued for the prominence of observational learning from which enactments refine learning. Concurrent, and shaped by observational and enacted learning, is Bandura's notion of self-efficacy – (ibid.). The findings in this research illustrated a growing sense of increased self-efficacy of leading through role enactments.

Similarly, narratives of the sampled managers' lived experience revealed a deepening investment of themselves into an identity as a leader. Drawing on the collective works of Gergen (1971), Ricoeur (1992), Ezzy (1998), Ibarra (1999) and Markus and Wurf (1987) such investment reflected theoretical discussions of 'aspirational', 'possible' and 'provisional-selves' associated with identity construction. Such learning was complementary to and catalysed by observations and enactments. Thus the study linked both social learning theory to identity construction illustrating how each provides a fuller account of the other as an understanding of leadership learning.

Additionally, the study illustrated that personal salience of leadership, leader identity and self-efficacy of leading, were not only shaped by observational and enacted learning, but were also fashioned within the crucible of particular contexts. Thus an explicit link to the ideas of Lave and Wenger (1991), Fox (1997a) and Gherardi et al. (1998) and a body of work collectively known as situated learning, and associated notion of 'legitimate participation' (Lave & Wenger, 1991: 34) was established. Lave and Wenger (1991) argue that learning is constructed and continually shaped in the interaction between people, thus creating meaning through participation in the form of activities in particular situations. In essence, an individual's pathway of participation was seen to have shaped access to, and meaning of, observation, role enactment, identity development and self-efficacy of leading.

The final element through which leadership learning has been revealed was through Archer's work of social morphogenesis (1995, 2000). The findings illustrated how lived experience is shaped by implicit theories of leadership, drawn generally from society, and, more specifically, shaped within organisational contexts. Such implicit theories have influenced notable people and subsequently were exhibited through the actions of these notable people. Archer (1995) argues for the existence of social structures, interpreted here as embedded practices and meanings of leadership that have pre-existed leaders and shape current leadership practice. Yet key people (often leaders) have the ability, dependent on the access and usage of power, to sustain or elaborate such embedded practices and meanings through their conscious or unconscious behaviours. In this case local leadership practice can be sustained or moderated by notable people.

The linkage of all four of the above bodies of knowledge powerfully extends and anchors leadership learning into a cohesive picture. Rather than exploring leadership learning through the lens of either social learning, situated learning, identity construction or social interaction of structures and agents, a richer interpretation is drawn from incorporating arguments of each into a more holistic appreciation enabling a deeper, systemic explanation of underlying influences.

Future directions of research into leadership learning

A greater depth of exploration and explanation of leadership learning would be desirable within discrete populations and in particular situations, for example:

- *Specific organisations* – in both the private and public sectors there is a need to examine how, for example, within a single organisation, situated learning influences leadership practice. Such a specific focus would also reveal changing influences of the structure–agency interactions over time, reveal career pathways, role enactments and observed notables and seek to explain in-depth nuances of leadership learning within a single organisational context.
- *Comparing organisations* – expanding on from a single organisational study is the potential to compare organisations within the same sector, and between sectors, and perhaps conduct a more extensive and intensive study comparing public and private contexts in a similar way to this study.
- *Women managers* – there is a need for greater rigour to explore the different influences on leadership learning of women managers compared with men. In particular, a specific study on the impact of gender on leadership learning drawing upon a deeper review of extant theory would help to illuminate the intricacies that have perhaps been overlooked thus far in this work. This would potentially reveal many additional influences on a women manager's leadership learning through lived experience.

- *Comparing lived experiences of leadership learning of women and men in the same organisation* – linked to the themes above is a rich opportunity to highlight differential leadership learning experiences between men and women in the same organisation and between organisations.
- *Owner-managers* – although a clear contribution of this study is towards identifying a marked difference in leadership learning between employed and self-employed managers, the scope for further research is extensive. For example, do owner-managers who commence self-employment later in their careers tend to have a greater salience, identity and self-efficacy of leading compared to those commencing their businesses early in their careers? How do owner-managers, without an employed career, learn leadership? Is this a different form of leadership to the employed managers? If there is to be intervention to affect leadership practices in small businesses, how should such intervention interact with influences present in the self-employed context?
- *Sports contexts* – the study has limited its scope to organisational contexts. It is not known whether the identified common intra- and interpersonal influences that appear to have a tendency to shape leadership learning are common in a sports context. The example of Sir Chris Bonnington in the introduction provides a glimpse that the contributions of this book might be most applicable in revealing the leadership learning of, say, a football manager or team captain. There is much scope to be explored in this sector as well as comparing leadership learning between business and sports contexts.
- *Methodology* – this study has outlined an approach to eliciting narratives of leadership learning. The approach may have extended benefits beyond the academic research domain. As a result of the interview process, a number of respondents have explored whether the timeline process could be utilised within their organisations as a tool for both recruitment and succession planning. Is it compatible to other instruments? Does a narrative provide details that would reveal greater depth of insight on an individual's perspective of leadership than, for example, through the use of a psychometric instrument? Could it be utilised within an assessment centre? I will elaborate on this practical application later in terms of 'what next for the practicing leader'.

Before an examination of the implications for practicing leaders, I wish to look at the policy and educative implications of this books' explanation of leadership learning.

So what are the implications for policy, educative practice and personal leadership practice?

The importance of understanding the underlying influences on leadership learning is significant from a number of perspectives. Firstly, there are major policy implications that can be drawn from this explanation. Secondly, and associated with shaping policy, is the impact that this explanation has on the design of intervention programmes. Thirdly, and perhaps most importantly the study has immediate implications for leaders at the start of their journey and for practicing leaders. The chapter concludes with recommendations in this respect.

Policy development

A range of notable commentators have signalled a clear recognition of favouring interventions that are oriented towards informal activity within organisational contexts (Lowe & Gardner, 2000; James & Burgoyne, 2001; Burgoyne et al., 2004; and Conger, 2004). Importantly though, a distinction needs to be made when comparing informal activities and the underlying naturalistic influences identified in this study. Informal leadership development interventions are organised activities (such as mentor relationships and action learning projects), while naturalistic influences may exist regardless of intervention and can be catalysed to have affect. In many ways these naturalistic and underlying influences are congruent to interventions recommended. For example, mentor relationships provide notables for observation, extend salience of leadership, provide feedback for self-efficacy and assist the process of identification. Thus from a policy intervention perspective, best practice (James & Burgoyne, 2001) may be greatly enhanced through designed congruence with underlying influences.

Of particular focus within the CEML findings was the situation of leadership development in the SME sector. Research identified that the SME sector was severely limited in effective intervention activity, yet it is doubly needed (Perren & Grant, 2001). This is partly because of the demand-side being disadvantaged from accessing available interventions and not seeking appropriate support; and partly from a supply-side issue of inappropriate provision not tailored to needs and perspectives of owner-managers (ibid.). Policy recommendations in this regard were to stimulate demand and refocus the supply-side provision towards informal activities, similar to the above large organisational interventions. The arguments from this book suggest that intervention in this sector is likely to be much more problematic than for large organisations, for the following reasons:

- Stimulating demand-side may be more difficult than anticipated due to the low salience and identification that owner-managers appear to have with leadership. Communications to stimulate demand for development need to be most carefully constructed and certainly should not echo assumptions drawn from large organisational experiences.
- Limited pathways of participation suggest limits to enactment opportunities for role and context diversity that exists in large organisations.
- Owner-manager is a notable person – self-employment limits opportunities to learn leadership from a variety of notables in salient contexts. Can interventions create the complex naturalistic learning dynamics that are grist to the leadership learning and the development of contextualised leadership practice?

In summary, a cautionary note needs to be emphasised. Leadership learning is a complex temporal process. It appears to occur over the long term and reflects a form of apprenticeship learnt over many years, in a range of contexts triggered by episodes and incidents that may not be possible, or even desirable, to replicate through intervention, and probably not within an accelerated timescale.

Finally, whether the naturalistic development process (Burgoyne & Stuart, 1977) shaped by underlying influences can be measured is a major question mark, particularly as any intervention occurs in an open system responding to the milieu of events and over an extended time period. Thus measuring causality would be highly problematic. However, if policy intervention adopted a process to explain different outcomes shaped by prevailing influences in specific contexts on a longitudinal basis, there might be significant opportunity to further inform on practice and policy of interventions. Burgoyne et al. (2004) have argued that evaluation undertaken at the end of an intervention is likely to be of minimal use. They argue that evaluation needs to be considered throughout the life cycle of an intervention, especially during the design stages, if performance of the intervention related to a specific context is to be improved. It is to this call for evaluation-led intervention that the next section addresses, with a specific example of the LEAD programme.

Educative practice

If leadership learning were a form of apprenticeship influenced by underlying influences, within particular and often multiple contexts over an extended period of time, this would have a significant influence on the design of leadership development programmes. This may explain, in part, the significant criticism of intervention approaches in terms of their efficacy of affecting leadership practice (Wexley & Baldwin, 1986; Conger, 1998; Burgoyne, 2001).

In light of the findings and explanation within this study, the scope of educative intervention is encouraged to be towards stimulating both the intra- and the interpersonal influences. To give an insight as to what a leadership development intervention might look like I will outline a specific programme that utilised the knowledge from this study: the LEAD Programme.

Owner-manager development – the 'LEAD' programme

Responding to the recommendations of CEML in regard to leadership intervention in the SME sector of the UK, the North West Development Agency funded a programme specifically for established businesses with no more than 20 employees. The number of owner-managers who participated in the programme that ran for two years were 67 and the programme had two explicit aims: business growth and leadership development. The programme was evaluated against quantitative business growth measures and qualitative leadership measures, which were salience, identification and self-efficacy of leading.

The design reflected a programme that could be moulded to the situational needs of the owner-managers and the business. It sought to create a situated curriculum based on the identified intra- and interpersonal influences to compensate for the structural absence of these in the SME environment. For example, the owner-mangers had a form of situated learning through engagement on the programme over an extended period; they had specific roles, such as the exchanges, that sought to maximise opportunities for enactment. They came into contact with numerous notables, both peers and mentors, as well as distinguished leaders. The programme explicitly sought to make leadership highly salient to the owner-managers from the outset. It sought to explore their sense of identity and gauge their level of self-efficacy of leading in their business context and other situations. In-depth feedback was designed to be provided by coaches, mentors and importantly their peers in action learning sets and by many informal social interactions. Although many aspects of the programme drew upon recognised best practice features of leadership development (James & Burgoyne, 2001), the guiding underpinning philosophy and design lay below the surface, shaping the pedagogy and learning curriculum towards the everyday contextual circumstances of the owner-managers. The design is represented in Figure 9.2.

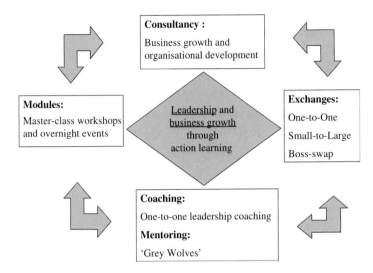

Figure 9.2 Structure of the LEAD programme

A major feature of the design was the integration of evaluation. The participants were interviewed prior to enrolling; they completed a diary throughout the programme; were interviewed at two specific points (after the coaching and after the first exchange), and were interviewed at the end of the programme following the 'boss-swap'.

The programme has been formally evaluated by Newcastle University Business School to identify whether it has had impact on the performance of the businesses:

> The conclusion of the evaluation is that the LEAD programme has had substantial effects on business outcomes (achieved or expected), and that these outcomes have been induced by changes to business operations, which are due to the programme. While some aspects of the LEAD programme appear more important in generating these changes, the overall conclusion is that the programme has been successful in achieving its objective of promoting business development and growth.
>
> (Wren & Jones, 2006)

The qualitative examination of changes in leadership practice was undertaken by the Institute of Entrepreneurship and Enterprise Development at Lancaster University Management School:

> Increased confidence in, and awareness of, individuals' leadership roles was widely observed. This was often accompanied by elevated

abilities to delegate effectively, leading in turn to staff empowerment and to protection of owner-managers' strategic space for further enterprise development.

(Peters, 2006)

The evaluation has led the North West Development Agency to roll-out of this programme as a major strand of their response to the Leitch Report (2006) – it is intended that the programme may reach approximately 2000 small business owners across the North West of England.

In essence, the evaluation has shown that intervention can be designed to be linked with underlying intra- and interpersonal influences on leadership learning and by doing such it does appear that this makes a significant difference. We have been able to address the efficacy question that has been the elusive aspect and heralded weakness of numerous interventions. The 'Newcastle' evaluation even entertained the notion of a return on investment in terms of Gross Value Add benefits of the £861,000 investment – the 'Holy-grail' of leadership development practitioners. The final section of the book seeks to apply this understanding of leadership learning to both the practicing leader and to someone yet to practice organisational leadership.

Becoming better at leading

It is possible that someone may be thinking: 'So what am I meant to do with this explanation of underlying influences? If leadership learning is a complex imperceptible process can I do anything about my learning?' For people commencing their apprenticeship there is much that can be suggested. For those who have already travelled far along their journey the ability to change leadership practice is more complex but much can be gained by applying the ideas in this book in a reflective manner – not least a legacy issue that a leader's current practice can influence the leadership practice of the next generation of leaders.

So what does all this tell me at the beginning of my journey?

If you are starting out in your managerial career there are many ways you can shape your leadership learning apprenticeship. The fact that this book is being read suggests that a journey has already begun. If you have not explored your lived experience using the timeline process outlined in Chapter 6, a first step might be to consider undertaking this exercise; it would greatly enhance insight, reflection and subsequent structuring of the six identified intra- and interpersonal influences to guide the ongoing apprenticeship. A useful second step might be to address some of the following questions associated with these six influences:

1. *Observational learning* – Who have you observed? Are there opportunities for you to observe many different people? How can you create opportunities to engage with a variety of leaders?
2. *Enactments* – What leadership roles have you performed? How varied were these roles in terms of activity and context? Can you create an opportunity to lead a team? Can you create a pathway that provides a variety of roles in a variety of contexts?
3. *Situated learning* – Are you aware of the leadership practice around you? Can you identify how this practice is performed? What are the valued aspects of this practice and the weaknesses of this practice? Can you make explicit the situated aspects of the culture that appear to be shaping leadership practice? Begin to make visible the situated curricula; for example, the way meetings are conducted, the loudness of voices, the language used, the interpretation of titles and hierarchy, the clothes people wear in such meetings, the places they sit, who they talk to and what they talk about, the type of notes taken and by whom.
4. *Identity* – How do you describe yourself to others? Can you imagine others identifying you with being a capable leader? What form of leader identity do you aspire to have?
5. *Self-efficacy* – What is your sense of competence in leading? How confident are you in leading? What activities are available for you to test your leadership skills? How do you judge whether you are good at leading?
6. *Salience* – How important is leadership to you? Why is it important? If you were to watch a film (such as 'Apollo 13', 'A Night at the Museum' or perhaps 'Twelve Angry Men') do you see leadership roles throughout?

When concluding sessions on executive leadership programmes I often finish with the phrase: 'Up your salience!' Perhaps the most important underlying influence is salience; it acts as a catalyst to leadership learning. Once leadership is salient to managers they seek it in all aspects of life. They study their boss and their bosses' boss. They observe and compare the way meetings are chaired, or the way disappointments or a crisis are dealt with. In their private lives they take greater recognition to the differing styles of political leaders presented in the media. Such people identify actors in films as metaphors for how to lead.

With salience on the up it is likely to affect recognition of leadership roles that we are presented with. Rather than simply conducting the task it can become an opportunity to apply the observed learning. Conscious of seeking to lead better, feedback is then most readily sought which becomes an increasingly positive re-enforcing cycle. As careers progress the increasing identification as an aspirant leader stimulates a desire for new roles and differing contexts in which to perform. The continuing feedback allows a sense of gauging identity construction and self-efficacy at leading.

Mentors are an important element of leadership development. They connect to many of the underlying influences. Perhaps most prominently to observational learning, but the influences of salience, identity construction and self-efficacy are very much present. For example, the mentee may use the mentor as an aspirant identity and a reference against which to compare. In terms of self-efficacy the mentor and leadership coach can provide candid feedback and advice to guide enhancement of the practice of leading in specific situations. By having a mentor and investing time and energy into the relationship, the result is the raising of the salience of leadership. To obtain these types of benefits requires a high degree of respect and trust in the relationship (Stead, 2005). Stead argues that mentor–mentee relationships that are organised by a formal system appear to be much less successful than relationships that are created and managed through the efforts of the mentee.

Consider forming an action learning support group. In Burgoyne and James's (2001) review of best practice, it was identified that groups provide an important function. In this study we have seen how the women leaders have formed groups to provide the much needed support and encouragement. Additionally the discussion on the structural issues of owner-manager development has revealed a strong sense of isolation. For example, the action learning groups have been most successful within the LEAD programme – previously described. In fact we have discovered that they have grown much more in significance than we expected. The owner-managers have driven the process to extend the role of these groups both within the programme and after the programme has concluded.

Action-learning support groups enable the enactment of the influences on leadership learning. They keep the salience of leadership constantly in the consciousness of managers; conversations provide a reflexive process to explore an individual's sense of self-efficacy. The process allows people to benchmark themselves against their peers through observing their colleagues style, and learn vicariously from the situations that their colleagues describe. Through the stories they tell of the situations in which they are 'emplotted' they continually develop a clearer narrative identity of themselves as a leader – since it is leadership practice that the action learning sets are exploring. Again success from such a process depends on trust and the level of commitment. For example, consider forming a group from peers who are at a similar stage in their careers. It was shown in this study that the women managers formed peer groups as a shared experience that addressed issues of confidence and marginalisation.

In essence, there are a number of ways of organising a structured approach to developing leadership practice that draws on the intra- and interpersonal underlying influences. The key at the beginning or early stage of a journey of leadership apprenticeship is to be much more consciously aware of these underlying influences and shape the occurrences and impacts on the development of our leadership practice through our ongoing lived experience.

So what can I do as a practicing leader?

As an experienced leader who has been practicing for many years the development opportunity is initially a reflexive process. Looking back and applying the six underlying influences to the lived experience will illuminate many insights into leadership practice; a practice that reflects characteristics drawn from the situation. Often managers see a practice of leadership that has echoes of the behaviours exhibited from past managers they had close contact with. In many instances this has been a great surprise and for others it can be unsettling. The surprise appears to centre on an assumption that their approach to leading is theirs, it's unique, and in many instances reflects something of 'nature' rather than 'nurture'. Unsettling in terms of echoing practices that they had observed and experienced themselves and to which they recall how much this was disliked: 'Is this part of my own leadership practice? Am I becoming a notable "bad" person in others leadership learning?'

With 'nurture' firmly in the ascendancy a manager can begin to explore the antecedent influences and the contexts in which these had an affect. For example, masculine styles of leadership practice may have been most prominent in a particular context, at a period of time; these aspects have been learnt from a range of notable people prominent in a manager's timeline. However, the needs of the current context may require leadership practice that stimulates learning, problem solving and a greater sense of supportive encouragement than had been prominent at the early formative stage of the managers 'nurturing'.

The experience of using the tents exercise with over 300 managers (outlined in detail in Chapter 6) suggests that this process of reflexive sense making of antecedent influences appears to give personal validity to addressing current practice. This does not necessarily mean a change in practice. What it does mean is an increased conscious awareness of leadership practice and how it has been constructed. The salience of the influences sustaining practice development is palpable and visible. A manager is thus more able to take control of the affect of these influences on their leadership practice.

Discussions with managers after the 'tent' reflections generates a recognition of a growing sense of responsibility for the influence they have on the future leadership practice of direct reports. For example, the nature of the discussion I have had with participant managers has evolved typically around the following:

> Consider for a moment that you are the notable person within a junior leaders lived experience. How do you wish to be remembered? What influence do you wish to have? If you are aware that you will be leaving a legacy of influencing their leadership practice would this affect your daily practice? What changes would you make?

In this sense leadership learning becomes an active and continuous process that is less of a mystery and much more of a malleable phenomenon. The responsibility of being an active participant in others leadership development can be seen to link to Senge's (1990) notion of leader as teacher. The difference is not that the teacher is suggesting a way to lead, but rather the teacher is enacting a way to lead.

Selecting better leaders?

A final aspect to be explored here is the potential to utilise the underlying influences as a lens through which leadership experience of prospective applicants can be screened to identify their relationship with leadership. If leaders learn how to lead but are unconscious to the cause (and the source of the cause) of the learning, it is a corollary that job applicants will not be able to recall the nuances of this learning – unless they have read this book! A solution to this lack of recall has been the use of psychometrics to provide an 'expert' insight into the leadership potential of the applicants. However, psychometric instruments fail to reveal the depth of understanding an individual has acquired through experiencing leadership and the importance of contextualisation to leadership practice. The universality of the instrument suggests a 'house' theory that purports to know what leadership is: if the applicant matches up well against the criteria of this theory then they should be a leader!

This book has argued that leadership is learnt through complex processes of social participation. Simply put, there cannot be a universal theory of leadership. Thus a psychometric instrument fallibly assumes dimensions of leadership to measure what may be out with the practice of the organisation. Further, if leadership practice is difficult to identify and articulate how do we select 'house' theories of leadership against which to judge someone's leadership practice and fit to the employing organisation? How do we know if a psychometric instrument is a useful insight into someone's leadership practice or understand how far someone has developed in terms of his/her leadership practice?

An alternative is to ask someone to tell his/her story. If the individual has to talk their way through their lived experience, the story can be deconstructed against the underlying influences. For example, the lived experience might show depth of salience on leadership, degree of identification and self-efficacy expectations of performance. These aspects could be cross-examined for association with enacted roles, and observed from the lived experience of notable people. Additionally the insights drawn from situated learning might reveal many useful hints as to the nature of the contextualised learning and the sense of practice that may emerge from a candidate if given a leadership role. If someone has been employed for many years within a single context, a particular practice is likely to be very much eschewed to that organisation. Would a different practice of leadership be useful for the organisation? Or is the scope of change required of the person an unrealistic expectation?

Can candidates make up a story? On one level of course a story can be stretched or finessed to present oneself as a socially desirable leader – usually the case when answering questions of psychometric instruments. However, this becomes most apparent to the interviewer when the story lacks verisimilitude; that is it evokes in the listener a feeling that the experience described is not lifelike, not believable and simply not plausible – it seems inauthentic. A story's authenticity is readily detected. Storytelling, and the assessment of others authenticity of their stories, is a daily occurrence in our everyday lives. The process of storytelling follows a clear structure that is common to the orator and the receiver. We are all thus experts in appreciating the authenticity and verisimilitude of a story.

Further, a skilled interviewer can dig into aspects of a story and, for example, triangulate a candidate's definition of leadership, their lived experience and their rules of thumb for leading. A coherent story illustrates a strong connection between these three elements. If a candidate is constructing an inauthentic story it is very obvious.

The impact on an organisation of appointing a leader is surely worth the considerable extra effort I am suggesting. Examining a candidate's lived experience in a structured manner can enable a contextualised appreciation of the likely leadership practice in a way that simply cannot occur through the use of psychometric instruments.

Final comments

This study has looked at leadership learning at the level of lived experience with the aim of revealing influences affecting such learning within particular contexts.

The explanation, drawn from the 40 interviews, builds on previous research suggesting that leadership learning occurs predominantly through informal, systemic influences within organisational contexts, particularly notable people and problematic experiences (Burgoyne & Hodgson, 1983; Davies & Easterby-Smith, 1984; McCall et al., 1988; Cox & Cooper, 1989; McCall, 1998, 2004; Jackson & Parry, 2001; Hill, 2003; Conger, 2004). The contribution of this study was to go beyond the general headings and reveal more detail on influences, namely salience, identity and self-efficacy and observed, enacted and situated learning; it sought to explain how these underlying influences integrate together to generate an emergent property of leadership learning.

It has been shown that common intra- and interpersonal influences of leadership learning were contingent on particular contexts and that additional influences were present that modify learning outcomes. The two most striking examples were the impact of gender on women's leadership learning and the potential limitations of the self-employed environment to the development of organisational leadership.

It is acknowledged that the findings and explanations are not intended to be exhaustive, and generalisation is limited to seeing the identified common influences as having only a tendency to shape leadership learning. Contextualised consideration will always dominate any detailed understanding and explanation of leadership learning and leadership practice.

The main contribution of the study is in going beyond broad statements that we learn leadership from experience, most notably relationships and activities. It is perhaps not surprising that there is a dearth of evaluation on the efficacy of leadership development interventions (Conger, 1993; Burgoyne et al., 2004), when the process of leadership learning appears to be a phenomenon that is complex, long term, emergent and opaque. Basically, it is both difficult to reveal and too simple to isolate to one particular theory. The naturalistic and informal process of leadership learning through lived experience reflects elements that may be highly problematic to replicate in an effective and efficient manner through formal interventions, unless the programme designs seek congruence with naturalistic underlying influences and extend over a considerable period of time. The notion of leadership learnt as an emergent informal apprenticeship, offered in career pathways of participation, should cause us to rethink interventions if we are to gain greater returns on the billions of pounds invested each year.

So how have managers learnt to lead? The answer is that they have been shaped by common influences that are more or less influential, dependent on the situation and the individual. The influences appear to work on two dimensions, intra- and interpersonal, and the congruence and integration of these two produce an emergent property that is enhanced or weakened, but certainly moderated in affect by the variety of contexts experienced by an individual.

Epilogue

A personal example is used to conclude the study that hopefully exemplifies my argument of how we learn to lead. At the start of my explorations into leadership learning, back in 1999, I asked my two sons what they thought leadership was. My eldest son Chris, then ten, commented: 'The best person, the most skilled, like a football captain.' My youngest son Robert, at the age of seven, described leadership as: 'Going somewhere you want to get to, like Jesus.'

Finally at the end of writing this book, I asked Chris, now 17, the same question. He initially sent me away as I was disrupting something, but then found me and described leadership as:

> Helping others achieve a goal by role modeling and encouraging even if they don't believe they can achieve the goal. Helping bring the best out of people.

Explaining how he knows this:

> I think it's mostly through things I've led, like in tennis or football. I guess also you see it in films don't you where the leader has encouraged people to achieve goals beyond all odds.

For Robert, now fourteen, he is questioning what he believed it is:

> Leadership is a skill, isn't it? It's difficult to explain though. It's very complicated. I guess it's someone leading people to do something, able to motivate them, help them achieve their goals.

His explanation of how he has learnt this is also more equivocal:

> I don't know really. Watching films, watching the leaders on films. Also it's people who lead you; for example we had a school trip in the Lakes and some good people doing gorge scrambling were leading us.

It's interesting for me to see how their definitions have evolved – some elements the same and other aspects changed. Particularly fascinating is the increasing sense of seeing leadership as more complicated and increasingly more difficult to describe than was the case for their earlier definitions – certainly more nuance in their interpretation. For some strange reason, leadership has become increasingly salient to them both!

Notes

1 Introduction: How Do Managers Learn to Lead?

1. *Business Week's* executive education survey (1999) was explicit: 'The unquenchable thirst for learning means that it's a great time to be in the executive education market. The average company spent about $10 million on internal and external executive development in 1998. Overall spending up 17% from last year' (Reingold, Schneider & Capell, 1999: 76). A search for current expenditure on leadership and management development was undertaken but no estimates were available at the time of writing.
2. Notable people is a phrase used by McCall et al. to describe the learning an individual gains through contact with particular individuals. Bandura (1986) clarifies processes of learning from people and observational learning – developed in Chapter 3.
3. It needs to be stressed that this book differentiates learning from development. Learning is seen as the acquisition of knowledge, skills and attitudes from environmental interaction. Development is seen as an intervention to stimulate learning. A full exploration of learning is in Chapter 3 and leadership development in Chapter 4.
4. John Hunt was the leader of the expedition that enabled Hillary and Tensing to reach the summit of Everest.
5. CEML was set up by David Blunkett MP and Stephen Byers MP in April 2000 to advise on action needed to improve the quality of management and leadership in the country. CEML was asked to present a report with recommendations to the Secretaries of State for Education and Skills and Trade and Industry by March 2002.
6. 'Quasi formal' reflects designed interventions based in organisational contexts; mentoring or job rotation are examples of such quasi-formal leadership development interventions. Leadership commentators often refer to such activities as 'informal'. There is much confusion as to whether informal happens as part of unplanned lived experience or as designed contextualised intervention. Burgoyne and Hodgson (1983) are helpful in this respect and add the term 'naturalistic' to informal unplanned activities to emphasise a sense of accidental happenings, part of the milieu of everyday events.
7. Within the field of strategy, the strategy-as-practice group has established a perspective of practice as an 'understanding of human agency in the construction and enactment of strategy which addresses the actions and interactions of the strategy practitioner' (Jarzabkowski et al., 2007: 6). In essence they argue that strategising, like leadership, can be understood as the 'doing of strategy' (Johnson et al., 2003) or how an individual actor (rather than organisations as a whole) *does* strategy on a day to day basis.

2   What Is Leadership? Can It Be Learnt?

1. Positivism, as a philosophy of science, seeks to discover universal truths or laws. Positivism has been most productive in the natural sciences in being able to measure the natural world. The application of this philosophy to leadership studies, a social phenomenon, has been much less successful. The desire of positivists to prove or falsify a claim as to what leadership is, or is not, has led to endless and inevitable cul-de-sacs. Nevertheless this approach to studying leadership has dominated leadership studies.
2. Hunt and Dodge (2001) have argued that particular research groups, through historic legacy and stakeholder dominance in publications, have greater influence on the process of understanding the phenomenon of leadership than other groups.
3. There were originally three characteristics but inspirational motivation was separated from charisma.
4. It is interesting to note that Masi and Cooke (2000) identified that the transactional leadership style has a greater negative impact on organisational performance than the positive impact of transformational leadership, and that investment is better directed at identifying and reducing unproductive leadership activities rather than aspire to developing transformational leaders.
5. At the time of writing there appears to be no empirical longitudinal grounded data to give insight to a more holistic examination of trait combinations in different contexts (Bryman, 1996; Parry, 2001).
6. For example, Yukl (1998) has consolidated previous taxonomies through factor analysis, judgmental classification and theoretical deduction (1998: 59) into a taxonomy of 14 behaviour categories illustrated as: (1) Planning and organising (2) Problem solving (3) Clarifying roles and objectives (4) Informing (5) Monitoring (6) Motivating and inspiring (7) Consulting (8) Delegating (9) Supporting (10) Developing and mentoring (11) Managing conflict and team building (12) Networking (13) Recognising others (14) Rewarding.
7. Criticisms of the two-factor model have centred on the methodological weakness that the research did not consider, the fusion of these two behaviours together to form a behaviour that is both task and relations oriented (Blake & Mouton, 1982; Yukl, 1989). Similarly, the descriptive studies of managerial work (Mintzberg, 1973; McCall & Sergist, 1980; Kotter, 1982; Kanter, 1983) suggest that complementary behaviours are woven together into a tapestry such that the whole is greater than the sum of the parts (Kaplan, 1986).
8. It is interesting to note that followers consider personal power more important than position power due to the associations of identification and self-esteem; followers want to be valued by people that they value (Bass et al., 1961). For Fiedler et al. (1976) the combination of the leader's position power and personal power applied to task and relationship behaviours determines whether the leader will be effective.
9. LMX grew out of a leader subordinate transactional relationship where leaders differentiated between subordinates in the way that they supervised them (Brower et al., 2000) leading to the creation of in-groups and out-groups

(Dansereau et al., 1975). Attribution theory, associated with LMX, identifies that with 'in' groups, a leader and followers perceive poor performance as a result of external factors, while individuals in 'out' groups will be seen to be the cause of poor performance by the leader, and the out-group attributes the cause for poor performance to the leader (Graen & Scandura, 1987).

10. For example, within a group or department there may be a common task; some members may experience charismatic leadership and share common goals while others experience transactional management where self-interest and reward/punishment exchanges are predominant.

3   How Do We Learn?

1. The importance of context and variety of contexts and learning opportunities was found by Davies and Easterby-Smith (1984) to be significant to the informal process of a manager's development – elaborated in Chapter 4.

2. Hill (2003) similar to McCall et al. (1988) and Cox and Cooper (1989) did not seek to be specific about leadership or management. Here, and their focus, was on general principles or events that shaped the learning process of becoming a manager.

3. The field of cognitive leadership development is emerging and draws from positivist traditions of social and cognitive psychology as a scientific investigation (Hogg & Vaughan, 2002); however the social construction of individual cognition has not been extensively explored from a phenomenological socially constructed perspective (Gergen, 1993). Gergen questions the epistemological traditions of the field of social psychology and outlines relevance of a constructionist standpoint and in particular argues that individual cognitive learning processes are set within relationships that have been forged through symbols, most predominant being that of language. Gergen argues that 'when cognition is replaced by language as the major means for representing the world, then the individual is replaced by the social relationship as the central focus of concern' (1993: 145).

4. The interaction of the short-term working memory with the long-term declarative memory is argued to retrieve abstract or semantic knowledge and episodic knowledge that is domain relevant to the phenomenon under examination and stores subsequent episodic and semantic knowledge in declarative memory (Tulving, 1983; Srull & Wyer, 1989; Wofford & Goodwin, 1994). Episodic memory (Tulving, 1983; Srull & Wyer, 1989) is seen to draw on general semantic memory to translate and infer meaning to events and semantic memory is argued to develop through the accumulation and abstraction of information obtained through episodic events. This conversion of experiences into abstracted declarative memory can be seen to be central to domain specific schema development and may be most central to illuminating understanding of how managers have learnt how to lead.

5. Nonaka and Takeuchi (1995) encapsulated a dynamic movement between tacit and explicit knowledge. Each informs on the other through a cyclical process of socialised knowledge being externalised into explicit knowledge, and enactment of explicit knowledge in a community becomes socialised knowledge.

4 What Is Understood about Leadership Learning and Development?

1. It should be emphasised that the Centre for Creative Leadership (CCL) has considerable influence in the current field of 'on-the-job' leadership development cited in two dominant leadership texts: Bass (1990) and Yukl (2001). Further, Day (2000), reviewing the field of leadership development, places considerable emphasis on the work of academics from CCL: 'One of the most notable offerings is the work by the Centre for Creative Leadership and the "Handbook of Leadership Development" (McCauley et al., 1998) which summarises much of what the centre researchers have learnt about leadership development over the past 30 years' (2001: 582).

2. The research constituted four separate studies encompassing 191 executives from six major corporations who responded to some version of the following question: *'When you think about your career as a manager, certain events or episodes probably stand out in your mind – things that led to a lasting change in you as a manager. Please identify at least three key events in your career that made a difference in the way that you manage now. What happened? What did you learn from it (for better or worse)?'* (McCall et al., 1988: 5). A total of 616 'events' were identified from which executives related 1,547 corresponding lessons, perceived as skills and ways of thinking (1988: 6) that were thematically grouped into three key areas of development.

7 Exploring Leadership Learning: Four Case Profiles

1. This finding echoes the discussion of implicit leadership in the literature reviewed in Chapter 2, as well as reflecting much of the process of the social construction of leadership argued by Sjostrand et al. (2001) – also in Chapter 2. The notion of a legitimised pathway and a sense of becoming have been previously amplified most notably by the work of Lave and Wenger (1991) – described in detail in Chapter 3.

8 Towards an Explanation of Leadership Learning

1. Actually my philosophic position is that of a critical realist. I am persuaded that a real world exists independent of my imagination and perception of it – real ontology. However, difficulties lie in viewing and understanding the world, independent of our sense interpretation. We see the world through socially constructed language; language that has generated knowledge of the world. As humans err then such knowledge must be fallible – truth of knowledge claims are thus problematic as the justification is humanly constructed – relative epistemology. The goal then is to seek a practically useful understanding of the world. A sense that the knowledge claim appears to resonate with peoples lived experience. The test of the arguments of this book is that a manager would say: 'you know this makes sense to me. It connects to my experience and helps me understand my leadership learning'. For critical realists, at best claims of knowledge explaining the world

are as tendencies for causal powers (or influences) to exist that have influence in some contexts but whose influence is contingent to other influences in particular contexts.

2. There is a strong similarity between self-concepts and identity; simply put, they both examine the individual's understanding of self in relation to others.

3. The work of McCall (1998 – outlined in detail in Chapter 3) highlighted that a common feature of the lived experience of the managers in his sample was hardship in the form of feedback received through demotion, dismissal or project failure. The affect of such personal hardship was to cause a radical review of personal schemas. In essence, their behaviour, previously seen as strength, had evolved through enactment to become inappropriate, and the gravity of the situation forced schemata reassessment hence being recalled as a transformative episode (Cope & Watts, 2000). Similarly, Cox and Cooper (1989) identified that their sample of chief executives recalled common hardships of working overseas in cultures that triggered a reappraisal of their tacitly learnt approaches.

4. The significance of leadership partly as a locally learnt process specific to particular contexts is the central argument of Sjostrand, et al. (2001), known as 'invisible leadership'. A full exploration of localised leadership is to be found in Chapter 2.

5. In work related to gender development, Bussey and Bandura (1992) illustrated that gender behaviours were not adopted until children had labelled themselves unalterably as a boy or a girl. Perhaps, this is the same with leadership but this study is unable to provide examples.

6. A variety of experiences have been similarly shown to be significant in terms of management development as initially reported by Davies and Easterby-Smith (1984).

7. Archer's (1995 and 2000) work appears to interrelate to a range of constructionist and realist commentators (notably Berger & Luckmann, 1966; Bhaskar, 1978, 1986 and 1989a; Giddens, 1984; Sayer, 1992) and elaborates on a theory entitled 'morphogenesis' (1995: 294).

8. Archer refers to individuals with low power as primary agents. They are unaware of the existence of structures and are unconsciously influenced by these structures and, through their ongoing action, sustain such structures of practices and meanings. Such people with power are referred to as corporate agents; they may or may not be aware of the structures but through their actions are able to modify or sustain practices and meanings within organisational life.

9. The work of Ram (1992a) has explored the associated issues of social marginalisation and ethnic minorities in a self-employed context.

References

Ackerman, P. O. (1992) Predicting Individual Differences in Complex Skill Acquisition: Dynamics of Ability Determinants. *Journal of Applied Psychology*, 77 (5), pp. 598–614.

Adair, J. (1983) *Effective Leadership*. London: Pan.

Armstrong, S. J. and Mahmud, A. (2008) Experiential Learning and the Acquisition of Managerial Knowledge. *Academy of Management Learning and Education*, 7 (2), pp. 189–208.

Alheit, P. (1994) *Taking the Knocks. Youth Unemployment and Biography: A Qualitative Analysis*. London: Cassell.

Alverson, M. (1996) Leadership Studies: From Procedure and Abstraction to Reflexivity and Situation. *The Leadership Quarterly*, 7 (4), pp. 455–85.

Alvesson, M. and Wilmott, H. (1996) *Making Sense of Management: A Critical Introduction*. London: Sage Publications.

American Society for Training and Development (1995). National HRD Executive Survey. In D. Day (2000) Leadership Development in the Context of On-going Work (p. 586). *The Leadership Quarterly*, 11(4), pp. 581–613.

Anderson, S. M. and Cole, S. T. (1990) Do I Know You? The Role of Significant Others in General Social Perception. *Journal of Personality and Social Psychology*, 59 (3), pp. 384–99.

Anderson, W. A. (1943) The Family and Individual Participation. American Sociological Review, 13, 239–42. In B. Bass (1990), *Bass and Stogdill's Handbook of Leadership* (p. 809), New York: Free Press.

Archer, M. S. (1995) *Realist Social Theory: The Morphogenetic Approach*. Cambridge: Cambridge University Press.

Archer, M. S. (2000) *Being Human: The Problem of Agency*. Cambridge: Cambridge University Press.

Argyris, C. (1991) Teaching Smart People How to Learn. *Harvard Business Review*, May–June, pp. 99–109.

Argyris, C. and Schon, D. A. (1978) *Organisational Learning: A Theory of Action Perspective*. Reading, MA: Addsison-Wesley.

Arlin, P. K. (1990) Wisdom: The Art of Problem Finding. In R. J. Sternberg (ed.), *Wisdom: Its Nature, Origins and Development* (pp. 142–59). New York: Cambridge University Press.

Ashforth, B. E. and Mael, F. (1989) Social Identity Theory and the Organisation. *Academy of Management Review*, 14 (1), pp. 20–39.

Avolio B. J. and Gardner, W. L. (2005) Authentic Leadership Development: Getting to the Root of Positive Forms of Leadership. *The Leadership Quarterly*, 16 (3), pp. 315–38.

Avolio, B. and Luthans, F. (2006) *The High Impact Leader: Moments Matter in Accelerating Authentic Leadership Development*. New York: McGraw Hill.

Bailey, B. A. and Nihlen, A. S. (1990) Elementary School Children's Perception of the World of Work. *Elementary School Guide Counselling*, 24, pp. 134–45.

Bandura, A. (1977) *Social Learning Theory*. Englewood Cliffs, New Jersey: Prentice-Hall.

Bandura, A. (1986) *Social Foundations of Thought and Action: A Social Cognitive Theory*. Englewood Cliffs, New Jersey: Prentice-Hall.

Bandura, A. (1997) *Self-efficacy: The Exercise of Control*. New York: Freeman.

Barker, R. A. (1997). How Can We Train Leaders if We Do Not Know What Leadership Is? Human Relations, 50 (4), pp. 343–60.

Barker, R. A. (2001) The Nature of Leadership. *Human Relations*, 54 (4), pp. 469–94.

Bass, B. M. (1960) *Leadership, Psychology and Organizational Behavior*. New York: Harper.

Bass, B. M. (1985) *Leadership and Performance Beyond Expectations*. New York: Free Press.

Bass, B. M. (1990) *Bass and Stogdill's Handbook of Leadership*. New York: Free Press.

Bass, B. M. (1995) Theory of Transformational Leadership. *The Leadership Quarterly*, 6 (4), pp. 463–78.

Bass, B. M. and Avolio, B. J. (1990a) Developing Transformational Leadership: 1992 and Beyond. *Journal of European Industrial Training*, 14, pp. 21–7.

Bass, B. M. and Avolio, B. J. (1993) Transformational Leadership: A Response to Critiques. In M. Chemers and R. Ayman (eds), *Leadership Theory and Research: Perspectives and Directions* (pp. 49–80). New York: Academic Press.

Bass, B. (1997) Does the Transactional-Transformational Leadership Paradigm Transcend Organizational and National Boundaries? *The American Psychologist*, 52 (2), pp. 130–9.

Bass, B. M., Waldman, D. A., Avolio, B. J. and Bebb, M. (1987) Transformational Leadership and the Falling Dominoes Effect. *Group & Organisation Studies*, 12, pp. 73–87.

Bass, B. M. and Yokochi, N. (1991) Charisma Among Senior Executives and the Special Case of Japanese CEO'S. *Consulting Psychological Bulletin*, Winter/Spring, pp. 31–8.

Bateson, G. (1973) *Step to an Ecology of Mind*. New York: Ballantine Books.

Beck, J. (1988) Expatriate Management Development: Realizing the Learning Potential of Overseas Assignments. In proceedings of the Academy of Management 48th Annual Meeting, pp. 112–16. In C. D. McCauley, and S. Brutus (1998), *Management Development through Job Experience: An Annotated Bibliography* (p. 31). Greensboro, NC: Center for Creative Leadership.

Bell, N. E. and Staw, B. M. (1988) People as Sculptors Versus Sculpture: The Roles of Personality and Personal Control in Organizations. In M. B Arthur, D. T. Hall and B. S. Lawrence (eds), *Handbook of Career Theory* (pp. 232–59). Cambridge: Cambridge University Press.

Belling, R., James, K. and Ladkin, D. (2004) Back to the Workplace: How Organisations Can Improve Their Support for Management Learning and Development. *Journal of Management Development*, 23 (4), pp. 234–55.

Bennis, W. (1989) *On Becoming a Leader*. Reading, MA: Addison–Wesley.

Bennis, W. and Nanus, B. (1985) *Leaders: The Strategies for Taking Charge*. New York: Harper & Row.

Bennis, W. G. and Thomas, R. G. (2002) Crucibles of Leadership. *Harvard Business Review*, 80 (9), pp. 39–46.

Berger, P. L. and Luckmann, T. (1966) *The Social Construction of Reality*. London: Penguin, Harmondsworth.

Bess, J. L. and Goldman, P. (2001) Leadership Ambiguity and K-12 Schools and the Limits of Contemporary Leadership Theory. *The Leadership Quarterly*, 12 (4), pp. 419–50.

Betz, N. B. and Voyten, K. K. (1997) Efficacy and Outcome Expectations Influence Career Exploration and Decidedness. *The Career Development Quarterly*, 46, pp. 179–89.

Betz, N. E. and Fitzgerald, L. F. (1987) *The Career Psychology of Women*. New York: Academic.

Betz, N. E. and Hackett, G. (1987) Concept of Agency in Educational and Career Development. *Journal of Counselling Psychology*, 34, pp. 299–308.

Biggart, N. W. and Hamilton, G. C. (1987) The Power of Obedience. *Administrative Science Quarterly*, 29, pp. 540–49.

Billing, Y. D. and Alvesson M. (2000) Questioning the Notion of Feminine Leadership: A Critical Perspective on the Gender Labelling of Leadership. *Gender, Work & Organization*, 7 (3), pp. 144–57.

Blake, R. R. and Mouton, J. S. (1982) Management by Grid Principles or Situationalism: Which? *Group and Organization Studies*, 7, pp. 207–10.

Blumer, H. (1969) *Symbolic Interactionism: Perspective and Method*. Englewood Cliffs, NJ: Prentice-Hall. In R. L. Boot and M. Reynolds (1983), Issues of Control in Simulations and Games. *Simulations and Games for Learning*, 13 (1), Spring, pp. 3–9.

Bouchard, T., Lykken, D. T., McGue, A., Segal, N. L., and Tellegen, A. (1990) Sources of Human Psychological Differences: The Minnesota Study of Twins Reared Apart. *Science*, 250, pp. 223–8.

Bourdieu, P. (1980) *Le Sens*. Paris: Le Minuit. In S. Sjostrand, J. Sandberg and M. Tyrstrup (2001), *Invisible Management: The Social Construction of Leadership* (pp. 28–49). London: Thompson Learning.

Bradford, D. L. (1983) Some Potential Problems with the Teaching of Managerial Competences. *The Organizational Behavior Teaching Journal*, 8 (2), pp. 45–9.

Brett, J. (1983) Job Transitions and Personal and Role Development. In K. M. Rowland and G. R. Ferris (eds), *Research in Personal and Human Resources Management* (vol. 2, pp. 155–85). Greenwich, CT: JAI Press.

Bridges, J. S. (1988) Sex Differences in Occupational Performance Expectations. *Psychology of Women Quarterly*, 12, pp. 75–90.

Broderick, R. (1983) How Honeywell Teaches it's Managers to Manage. *Training*, January, pp. 18–23.

Brower, H. H., Schoorman, F. D. and Tan, H. H. (2000) A Model of Relational Leadership: The Integration of Trust and Leader-member Exchange. *The Leadership Quarterly*, 11 (2), pp. 227–50.

Brown, A. (1999) *The Six Dimensions of Leadership*. London: Random House Business Books.

Brown, J. S. and Duguid, P. (1991) Organizational Learning and Communities of Practice: Toward a Unified View of Working, Learning, and Innovation. *Organization Science*, 2 (1), pp. 40–57.

Bryman, A. S. (1996) The Importance of Context: Qualitative Research and the Study of Leadership. *The Leadership Quarterly*, 7(3), pp. 353–70.

Bryman, A. S. (2004) Qualitative Research on Leadership: A Critical but Appreciative Review. *The Leadership Quarterly*, 15 (6), pp. 729–69.

Bryman, A. S., Stephens, M. and Campo, C. (1996) The Importance of Context: Qualitative Research and the Study of Leadership. *The Leadership Quarterly*, 7(3), pp. 353–70.

Bunker, K. and Webb, A. (1992) *Learning How to Learn from Experience. Impact of Stress and Coping*. Greensboro, NC: Center for Creative Leadership.

Burgoyne, J. G. (1977). Self-development, Managerial Success and Effectiveness: Some Empirical Evidence. *Management, Education and Development*, 8, pp. 16–20.

Burgoyne, J. G. (1995). Learning from Experience: From Individual Discovery to Meta-dialogue Via the Evolution of Transitional Myths. *Personnel Review*, 24 (6), pp. 61–72.

Burgoyne, J. (2001) Tester of Faith. *People Management*, 7 (4), pp. 33–4.

Burgoyne, J. G. and Stuart, R. (1976) The Nature, Use and Acquisition of Managerial Skills and Other Attributes. *Personnel Review*, 5 (4), pp. 19–29.

Burgoyne, J. G. and Stuart, R. (1977) Implicit Learning Theories as Determinants of the Effect of Management Development Programmes. *Personnel Review*, 6 (2), pp. 5–14.

Burgoyne, J. G. and Hodgson, V. E. (1983) Natural Learning and Managerial Action: A Phenomenological Study in the Field Setting. *Journal of Management Studies*, 20 (3), pp. 387–99.

Burgoyne, J., Hirsh, W. and Williams, S. (2004) *The Development of Management and Leadership Capability and Its Contribution to Performance: The Evidence, the Prospects and the Research Need*. DfES Research Report RR560. London: DfES.

Burns, J. M. (1978) *Leadership*. New York: Harper & Row.

Bussey, K. and Bandura, A. (1992) Self-regulatory Mechanisms Governing Gender Development. *Child Development*, 63, pp. 1236–50.

Cabinet Office (2000) *Leadership in Delivering Public Services*. London: Performance Improvement Office.

Calder, B. J. (1977) An Attribution Theory of Leadership. In B. M. Staw and G. R. Salancik (eds), *New Directions in Organisational Behaviour*. Chicago: St. Clair.

Cammack, I. (2003) *Response to the Zeitgeist: The (de)construction of Shackelton's Leadership*. Proceedings of British Academy of Management, 15–17 September.

Catrambone, R. and Markus, H. (1987) The Role of Self-schemas in Going Beyond the Information Given. *Social Cognition*, 5 (4), pp. 349–68.

Centre for Excellence in Management and Leadership (2002) *Joining Entrepreneurs in Their World: Improving Entrepreneurship, Management and Leadership in the UK*. London: CEML. Report from the SME working group.

Chatterjee, J. and McCarrey, M. (1989) Sex Role Attitudes of Self and Those Inferred of Peers, Performance and Career Opportunities as Reported by Women in Non-traditional vs. Traditional Programs. *Sex Roles*, 21, pp. 653–69.

CIMA (2000) *Success Beyond 2005: A Global Survey of Business Leaders*. London: Chartered Institute of Management Accountants.

Collinson, D. (2003) Identities and Insecurities: Selves at Work, *Organization*, 10 (3), pp. 527–47.

Collinson, D. and Collinson, M. (2005) *The Nature of Leadership: Leader-led Relationships in Context*. Lancaster: Centre for Excellence in Leadership, Working Papers.

Conger, J. A. (1989) *The Charismatic Leader: Behind the Mystique of Exceptional Leadership*. San Francisco, CA: Jossey-Bass.

Conger, J. A (1992) *Learning to Lead*. San Francisco: Jossey-Bass.

Conger, J. A. (1993) The Brave New World of Leadership Training. *Organisational Dynamics*, Winter, pp. 46–58.

Conger, J. A. (1996) Can We Really Train Leadership? *Strategy and Business*, 2, pp. 52–65.

Conger, J. A. (1998) Qualitative Research as the Cornerstone Methodology for Understanding Leadership. *The Leadership Quarterly*, 9 (1), pp. 107–21.

Conger, J. A. (2004) Developing Leadership Capability: What's Inside the Black Box? *Academy of Management Executive*, 18 (3), pp. 136–9.

Conger, J. and Kanungo, R. (1987) Toward a Behavioral Theory of Charismatic Leadership in Organizational Settings. *Academy of Management Review*, 12, pp. 637–47.

Cooke, R. A. and Szumal, J. L (1993) Measuring Normative Beliefs and Shared Behavioral Expectations in Organizations: The Reliability and Validity of the Organizational Culture Inventory. *Psychological Reports*, 72, pp. 1299–330.

Cope, J. (2005) Toward a Dynamic Learning Perspective of Entrepreneurship. *Entrepreneurship: Theory and Practice*, 29 (4), pp. 373–98.

Cope, J. and Watts, G. (2000) Learning by Doing: An Exploration of Critical Incidents and Reflection in Entrepreneurial Learning. *International Journal of Entrepreneurial Behaviour and Research*, 6 (3), pp. 104–24.

Cox, C. J. and Cooper, C. L. (1989) The Making of the British CEO: Childhood, Work Experience, Personality, and Management Style. *The Academy of Management Executive*, 3 (3), pp. 241–5.

Cunliffe, A. (2001) Reflexive Dialogical Practice in Management Learning, *Management Learning* 33 (1), pp. 35–61.

Cunliffe, A. (2002) Managers as Practical Authors: Reconstructing our Understanding of Management Practice, *Journal of Management Studies*, 38 (3), pp. 351–71.

Curran, J. (1986) The Width and Depth: Small Enterprise Research in Britain 1971–86. *Paper Presented to the Ninth National Small Firms Policy and Research Conference*, University of Stirling.

Dansereau, F., Yammarino, F. J. and Markham, S. E. (1995) Leadership: The Multiple-level Approaches. *The Leadership Quarterly*, 6 (2), pp. 97–109.

Daudelin, M. W. (1996) Learning from Experience Through Reflection. *Organizational Dynamics*, 24(3), pp. 36–48.

Davidson, M. and Burke, R. (2004) Women in Management. In M. Davidson and R. Burke (eds.), *Women in Management: Current Research Issues*, 11 (pp. 1–8). London: Sage.

Davies, J. and Easterby-Smith, M. (1984) Learning and Developing from Managerial Work Experience. *Journal of Management Studies*, 21 (2), pp. 169–83.

Day, D. D. (2000). Leadership Development: A Review in Context. *Leadership Quarterly*, 11(4), pp. 581–613.

Dewey, J. (1938) *Experience and Education*. Chicago: Kappa Delta Pi.

Drath, W. H. (1998) Approaching the Future of Leadership Development. In C. McCauley, R. S. Moxley and E. Van Velsor. *Handbook of Leadership Development* (pp. 403–32). San Francisco: Josey-Bass Publishers.

Drath, W. H. and Palus, C. J. (1994) *Making Common Sense. Leadership as Meaning Making in a Community of Practice.* Greensboro, NC. Center for Creative Leadership.

Dreher, G. F. and Ash, R. A. (1990) A Comparative Study of Mentoring Among Men and Women in Managerial, Professional and Technical Positions. *Journal of Applied Psychology*, 75, pp. 539–46.

Eckert, P. (1993) The School as a Community of Engaged Learners. Palo Alto, CA: IRL Working Paper. In S. Gherardi, D. Nicolini and F. Odella (1998) Toward a Social Understanding of How People Learn in Organisations: The Notion of Situated Curriculum. *Management Learning*, 29 (3), pp. 273–97.

Ehn, P. (1988) Work Oriented Design of Computer Artefacts. Stockholm: Arbetlivscentrum. Cited in S. Gherardi, D. Nicolini and F. Odella (1998). Toward a Social Understanding of How People Learn in Organisations: The Notion of Situated Curriculum. *Management Learning*, 29 (3), pp. 273–97.

Elliott, C. and Stead, V. (2008) Learning from Leading Women's Experience: Towards a Sociological Understanding. *Leadership*, 4 (2), pp. 159–80.

Emrich, C. G. (1999) Context Effects in Leadership Perception. *Personality and Social Psychology Bulletin*, 25, pp. 991–1006.

Engle, E. M. and Lord, R. G. (1997) Implicit Theories, Self-schemas and Leader Member Exchange. *Academy of Management Journal*, 40 (4), pp. 988–1013.

Eraut, M. (2000) Non-formal Learning and Tacit Knowledge in Professional Work. *British Journal of Educational Psychology*, 70, pp. 113–36.

Ezzy, D. (1998) Theorizing Narrative Identity: Symbolic Interactionism and Hermeneutics. *The Sociological Quarterly*, 39 (2), pp. 239–52.

Fandt, P. M. and Stevens, G. E. (1991) Evaluation Bias in the Classroom: Evidence Relating to the Effects of Previous Experiences. *Journal of Psychology*, 125, pp. 467–77.

Ferry, N. M. and Ross-Gordon J. M. (1998) An Inquiry into Schon's Epistemology of Practice: Exploring Links Between Experience and Reflective Practice. *Adult Education Quarterly*, 48 (2), pp. 98–113.

Fiedler, F. E. (1967). *A Theory of Leadership Effectiveness*. New York: McGraw-Hill.

Fiedler, K., and Bless, H. (2002). Social Cognition. In M. Hewstone and W. Stroebe (eds), *Introduction to Social Psychology*. Oxford: Blackwell Publishers Ltd.

Fiedler, F. E., Chemers, M. M. and Mahar, L. (1976) *Improving Leadership Effectiveness: The Leader Match Concept*. New York: Wiley.

Fiske, S. T. and Taylor, S. E. (1991) *Social Cognition* (2nd edn.). New York: McGraw-Hill.

Fleetwood, S. (2004) The Ontology of Organisation and Management Studies. In S. Fleetwood and S. Ackroyd (2004, eds), *Realism in Action in Management and Organisation Studies* (pp. 27–53). London: Routledge.

Fox, S. (1997a) Situated Learning Theory Versus Traditional Learning Theory: Why Management Education Should Not Ignore Management Learning. *Systems Practice*, 10 (6), pp. 727–47.

Freedman, R. D. and Stumpf, S. A. (1982) Learning Style Theory: Less than Meets the Eye. *Academy of Management Review*, 5 (3), pp. 445–7.

French, J. and Raven, B. H. (1959) The Bases of Social Power. In D. Cartwright (ed.), *Studies of Social Power* (pp. 150–67). Ann Arbor, MI: Institute for Social Research.

Fulmer, R. M. and Wagner, S. (1999) Leadership: Lessons From the Best. *Training and Development*, March, 53 (3), pp. 28–32.

Ganellen, R. J. and Carver, C. S. (1985) Why Does Self-reference Promote Incidental Encoding? *Journal of Experimental Psychology*, 21, pp. 284–300.

Gardner, W. L. and Avolio, B. J. (1998) The Charismatic Relationship: A Dramaturgical Perspective. *Academy of Management Review*, 23 (1), pp. 32–58.

Garrison, R. (1991) Critical Thinking and Adult Education: A Conceptual Model for Developing Critical Thinking in Adult Learners. *International Journal of Lifelong Education*, 10 (4), pp. 287–303.

Gartner, W. (1989) 'Who Is an Entrepreneur' is the Wrong Question. *Entrepreneurship: Theory and Practice*, 13 (4), pp. 47–67.

Gemmill, G. and Oakley, J. (1992) Leadership: An Alienating Social Myth? *Human Relations*, 1992, 45, pp. 953–75.

George, J. M. (1990) Personality, Affect and Behavior in Groups. *Journal of Applied Psychology*, 75, pp. 107–16.

George, J. M. and Brief, A. P. (1992) Feeling Good – Doing Good: A Conceptual Analysis of the Mood at Work-organization Spontaneity Relationship. *Psychological Bulletin*, 112, pp. 31029.

George, J. M. and James, L. R. (1993) Personality, Affect and Behavior in Groups Revisited: Comment on Aggregation, Levels of Analysis, and a Recent Application of Within and Between Analysis. *Journal of Applied Psychology*, 78, pp. 798–804.

Gergen, K. J. (1971) *The Concept of Self*. London: Holt, Rinehart and Winston, Inc.

Gerstein, M., Lichtman, M. and Barokas, J. U. (1988) Occupational Plans of Adolescent Women Compared to Men: A Cross-sectional Examination. *Career Development Quarterly*, 36, pp. 222–30.

Gherardi, S., Nicolini, D. and Odella, F. (1998) Toward a Social Understanding of How People Learn in Organisations: The Notion of Situated Curriculum. *Management Learning*, 29 (3), pp. 273–97.

Gibbons, T. C. (1986) Revisiting the Question of Born *vs*. Made. Toward a Theory of Development of Transformational Leaders. Doctoral Dissertation, Fielding Institute, Santa Barbara, CA. In B. Bass (1990), *Bass and Stogdill's Handbook of Leadership* (p. 844). New York: Free Press.

Gibson, D. E. (2003) Developing the Professional Self-concept: Role Model Construals in Early, Middle and Late Career Stages. *Organization Science*, 14 (5), pp. 591–610.

Gibson, D. E. (2004) Role Models in Career Development: New Directions for Theory and Research. *Journal of Vocational Behavior*, 65, pp. 134–56.

Gioia, D. A. (1986) Conclusion: The State of the Art in Organizational Social Cognition: A Personal View. In H. P Sims and D. A. Giora (eds), *The Thinking Organisation: Dynamics of Organisational Social Cognition*. San Francisco: Jossey-Bass.

Glaser, B. G. and Strauss, A. (1967) *The Discovery of Grounded Theory*. London: Weidenfeld and Nicholson.

Goffee, R. and Scase, R. (1985) *Women in Charge: The Experience of Female Entrepreneurs*. London: HarperCollins.

Goffman, E. (1969) *The Presentation of Self in Everyday Life*. London: Penguin Press.

Graen, G. B. and Uhl-Bien, M. (1991) The Transformation of Work-group Professionals into Self-managing and Partially Self-designing Contributors: Toward a Theory of Leadership-making. *Journal of Management Systems*, 3 (3), pp. 33–48.

Graen, G. B. and Uhl-Bien, M. (1995) Relationship-Based Approach to Leadership. Development of Leader-Member Exchange LMX Theory. *The Leadership Quarterly*, 6, pp. 219–47.

Gray, C. (1990) *Business Independence: Impediment or Enhancement to Growth*. 13th National Small Firms Policy and Research Conference.

Gray, C. (1998) *Enterprise and Culture*. London: Routledge.

Grint, K. (2000) *The Arts of Leadership*. Oxford: Oxford University Press.

Grint, K. (2005) *Leadership: Limits and Possibilities*. Oxford: Palgrave Macmillan.

Gronn, P. (1997) Leading for Learning: Organizational Transformation and the Formation of Leaders. *Journal of Management Development*, 16 (4), pp. 1–9.

Hall, D. T. and Seibert, K. W. (1992) Strategic Management Development: Linking Organizational Strategy, Succession Planning and Managerial Learning. In D. H. Montross and C. J. Shinkman (eds), *Career Development: Theory and Practice* (pp. 255–75). Springfield, IL: Charles C. Thomas.

Hall, L. K. (1983) *Charisma: A Study of Personality Characteristics of Charismatic Leaders*. Doctoral Dissertation, University of Georgia, Athens. In B. Bass (1990), *Bass and Stogdill's Handbook of Leadership* (pp. 809–10). New York: Free Press.

Hall, R. J. and Lord, R. G. (1995) Multi-level Information Processing Explanations of Followers' Leadership Perceptions. *The Leadership Quarterly*, 6 (3), pp. 265–87.

Hanges, P. J., Lord, R. G. and Dickson, M. W. (2000) An Information-processing Perspective on Leadership and Culture: A Case for Connectionist Architecture. *Applied Psychology: An International Review*, 49, pp. 133–61.

Hater, J. J. and Bass, B. M. (1988) Supervisor's Evaluations and Subordinates Perceptions of Transformational and Transactional Leadership. *Journal of Applied Psychology*, 73, pp. 695–702.

Hersey, P. and Blanchard, K. H. (1982) Leadership Style: Attitudes and Behaviors. *Training and Development Journal*, 36 (5), pp. 50–2.

Higgins, E. T. (1987) Self-discrepancy: A Theory Relating to Self and Affect. *Psychological Review*, 94, pp. 319–40.

Higgins, E. T. and Bargh, J. A. (1987) Social Cognition and Social Perception. *Annual Review of Psychology*, 38, pp. 369–425.

Hill, L. A. (2003). *Becoming a Manager: How New Managers Master the Challenges of Leadership*. MA: Harvard Business School Press.

Hoffman, F. O. (1985) Is Management Development Doing the Job? *Training and Development Journal*, 35 (6), pp. 34–9.

Hoffman, L., Rosen, S. and Lippitt, R. (1960) Parental Coerciveness, Child Autonomy and the Child's Role at School. Sociometry, 23, pp. 15–22. In B. Bass (1990), *Bass and Stogdill's Handbook of Leadership* (p. 810). New York: Free Press.

Hogg, M. A. (2001) A Social Identity Theory of Leadership. *Personality and Social Psychology Review*, 5 (3), pp. 184-200.

Hogg, M. A. and Terry, D. J. (2000) Social Identity and Self-categorization Processes in Organizational Contexts. *Academy of Management Review*, 25, pp. 121–40.

Hogg, M. A. and Vaughan, G. M. (2002) *Social Psychology* (3rd edn). Harlow: Prentice-Hall.

Hollander, E. P. (1979) Leadership and Social Exchange Processes. In K. Gergen, M. B.Greenberg and R. H. Willis (eds), *Advances in Experimental Social Psychology*, vol. 5. New York: Academic Press.

Honey, P. and Mumford, A. (1992) *The Manual of Learning Styles*. Maidenhead: Peter Honey.

Hooks, B. (1994). Teaching to Transgress. (New York: Routledge). In S. Fox (1997a) Situated Learning Theory Versus Traditional Learning Theory: Why Management Education Should not Ignore Management Learning (p. 5). *Systems Practice*, 10 (6), pp. 727–47.

House, R. J. (1971) A Path-goal Theory of Leader Effectiveness. Administrative Science Quarterly, 16, pp. 321–39.

House, R. J. (1977) A 1976 Theory of Charismatic Leadership. In J. G Hunt and L. L. Larson (eds), *Leadership the Cutting Edge* (pp. 189–207). Carbondale, IL: Southern Illinois University Press.

House, R. J. (1996) Path-goal Theory of Leadership: Lessons, Legacy, and a Reformulated Theory. *The Leadership Quarterly*, 7, pp. 323–52.

House, R. J. and Mitchell, T. R. (1974) Path-goal Theory of Leadership. *Contemporary Business*, 3 (Fall), pp. 81–98.

House, R. J. and Howell, J. M. (1992) Personality and Charismatic Leadership. *The Leadership Quarterly*, 3 (2), pp. 81–108.

House, R. J., Hanges, P. J., Javidan, M., Dorfam, P. W., Gupta, V. and Associates (2004) *Leadership, Culture, and Organizations: The GLOBE Study of 62 Societies*. Thousand Oaks, CA: Sage.

Huber, V. L. (1985) Training and Development: Not Always the Best Medicine. *Personnel*, 62 (1), pp. 12–15.

Hunt, J. G. (1999). Transformational/Charismatic Leadership's Transformation of the Field: An Historical Essay. *The Leadership Quarterly*, 10 (2), pp. 129–44.

Hunt, J. G. and Dodge, G. E. (2001) Leadership Déjà Vu All Over Again. *The Leadership Quarterly*, 11 (4), pp. 435–58.

Hunt, J. G. and Ropo, A. (1995) Multi-level Leadership: Grounded Theory and Mainstream Theory Applied to the Case of General Motors. *The Leadership Quarterly*, 6 (3), pp. 379–412.

Hycner, R. H. (1985) Some Guidelines for the Phenomenological Analysis of Interview Data. *Human Studies*, 8, pp. 279–303.

Ibarra, H. (1999) Provisional selves: Experimenting with Image and Identity in Professional Adaptation. *Administrative Science Quarterly*, 44 (4), pp. 764–92.

Idson, L. C. and Mischel, W. (2001) The Personality of Familiar and Significant People: The Lay Perceiver as a Social-cognitive Theorist. *Journal of Personality and Social Psychology*, 80 (4), pp. 585–96.

Jackson, B. and Parry, K. (2001) *The Hero Manager: Learning from New Zealand's Top Chief Executives*. Auckland: Penguin Books.

Jackson, B. and Parry, K. W. (2008) *A Very Short, Fairly Interesting and Reasonably Cheap Book about Studying Leadership*. London: Sage.

James, K. and Burgoyne, J. G. (2001) *Leadership Development: Best Practice Guide for Organisations*. London: Centre for Excellence in Management and Leadership (CEML).

Janesick, V. J. (1998) The Dance of Qualitative Research Design. Metaphore, Methodolatry, and Meaning. In N. K. Denzin and Y. S. Lincoln (eds), *Strategies of Qualitative Inquiry* (pp. 33–55). Thousand Oaks: Sage.

Janson, A. (2008) Extracting Leadership Knowledge from Formative Experiences. *Leadership*, 4 (1), pp. 73–94.

Jarvis, P. (1987a) Meaningful and Meaningless Experience: Towards an Analysis of Learning Life. *Adult Education Quarterly*, 37 (3), pp. 164–72.

Jenkins, R. (1996) *Social Identity*, London: Routledge.

Jennings, H. H. (1943) Leadership and Isolation. New York: Longmans Green. In B. Bass (1990), *Bass and Stogdill's Handbook of Leadership* (p. 807). New York: Free Press.

Jones, E. (1953) The Life and Works of Sigmund Freud. vol. 1. New York: Basic Books. In B. Bass (1990), *Bass and Stogdill's Handbook of Leadership* (p. 809). New York: Free Press.

Jones, G. (1988) Socialization Tactics, Self-efficacy and Newcomers' Adjustments to Organizations. *Academy of Management Journal*, 29, 2, pp. 262–79.

Kanungo, R. N. (2001) Ethical Values of Transactional and Transformational Leaders. *Canadian Journal of Administrative Science*, 18 (4), pp. 257–65.

Kanungo, R. N. and Mendonca, M. (1996) *Ethical Dimensions of Leadership*. London: Sage.

Katz, D. and Kahn, R. L (1978) *The Social Psychology of Organizations* (2nd edn). New York: John Wiley.

Keller, T. (1999) Images of the Familiar: Individual Differences and Implicit Leadership Theories. *The Leadership Quarterly*, 10 (4), pp. 589–607.

Kelly, G. A. (1955) *The Psychology of Personal Constructs*. New York: Norton.

Kelman, H. C. (1958) Compliance, Identification and Internalisation: Three Processes of Attitude Change. *Journal of Conflict Resolution*, 2, pp. 51–6.

Kempster, S. J. (2006) Leadership Learning Through Lived Experience. *Journal of Management & Organization*, *12*(1), pp. 4–22.

Kempster, S. J. (2007) Echoes from the Past: An Exploration of the Impact of 'Notable People' on Leadership Learning. *Academy of Management Annual Meeting Proceedings – Best Papers: 67*, Aug 3–8.

Kempster, S. J. (2009) Observing the Invisible: Examining the Role of Observational Learning in the Development of Leadership Practice. *Journal of Management Development*, 28 (5), forthcoming.

Kempster, S. J. and Bailey, A. (2007) Learning the Dance of the Strategist: The Importance of an Experienced Partner. *EGOS Conference*, July.

Kets de Vries, M. F. R. (1988) Prisoners of Leadership. *Human Relations*, 41 (3), pp. 261–80.

Kets de Vries, M. F. R. and Millar, D. (1985) Narcissism and Leadership: An Object Relations Perspective. *Human Relations*, 38, pp. 583–601.

Kim, D. H. (1993) The Link Between Individual and Organizational Learning. *Sloan Management Review* (Fall), pp. 37–50.

Kirkpatrick, S. A. and Locke, E. A. (1991) Leadership: Do Traits Matter? *The Academy of Management Executive*, 5, pp. 48–60.

Klonsky, B. G. (1983) The Socialisation and Development of Leadership Ability. *Genetic Psychology Monographs*, 108, pp. 95–135.

Kolb, D. (1984) *Experiential Learning*. London: Prentice Hall.

Kolb, D. A. and Fry, R. (1975) Towards an Applied Theory of Experiential Learning. In C. L. Cooper (ed.). *Theories of Group Processes* (pp. 33–57*)*. London: Wiley.

Konst, D., Vonk, R. and Van der Vlist, R. (1999) Inferences About Causes and Consequences of Behavior of Leaders and Subordinates. *Journal of Organizational Behavior*, 20, pp. 261–71.

Kotter, J. P. (1982) *The General Managers*. New York: The Free Press.

Kotter, J. P. (1988) *The Leadership Factor*. New York: The Free Press.

Kuhnert, K. W. and Russell, C. J. (1990) Using Constructive Developmental Theory and Biodata to Bridge the Gap Between Personnel Selection and Leadership. *Journal of Management*, 16 (3), pp. 595–607.

Labov, W. and Waletsky, J. (1967) Narrative Analysis: Oral Versions of Personal Experience. *Journal of Narrative and Life History*, 7, pp. 3–38.

Lapping, B. (1985) End of Empire. London: Granada. In B. Bass (1990), *Bass and Stogdill's Handbook of Leadership* (p. 811). New York: Free Press.

Latham, G. (1988) Human Resource Training and Development. *Annual Review of Psychology*, 39, pp. 545–82.

Lauver, P. J. and Jones, R. M. (1991) Factors Associated with Perceived Career Options in American Indian, White and Hispanic Rural High-school Students. *Journal of Counselling Psychology*, 38, pp. 156–66.

Lave, J. and Wenger, E. (1991) *Situated Learning: Legitimate Peripheral Participation*. Cambridge: Cambridge University Press.

Levinson, D. (1978) *The Seasons of a Man's Life*. New York: Knopf.

Leitch Report (2006) *Prosperity for All in the Global Economy – World Class Skills*. Norwich: HMSO.

Lindsey, E., Homes, V. and McCall, M. W. (1987) *Key Events in Executives Lives* (Technical Report No.32). Greensboro, NC: Center for Creative Leadership.

Linville, P. W. (1987) Self Complexity as a Cognitive Buffer Against Stress Related Depression and Illness. *Journal of Personality and Social Psychology*, 52, pp. 663–76.

Lord, R. G. and Emrich, C. G. (2001) Thinking Outside the Box by Looking Inside the Box: Extending the Cognitive Revolution in Leadership Research. *The Leadership Quarterly*, 11 (4), pp. 551–79.

Lord, R. G. and Maher, K. J. (1990) *Leadership and Information Processing. Linking Perceptions and Performance*. Boston: Unwin-Hyman.

Lord, R. G., Brown, D. J., Harvey, J. L and Hall, R. J. (2001) Contextual Constraints on Prototype Generation and Their Multilevel Consequences for Leadership Perceptions. The Leadership Quarterly, 12 (3), pp. 311–38.

Lord, R. G., Foti, R. J. and DeVader, C. L. (1984) A Test of Leadership Categorization Theory: Internal Structure, Information Processing, and Leadership Perceptions. *Organisational Behavior and Human Performance*, 34, pp. 333–78.

Louis, M. R. and Sutton, R. I. (1991) Switching Cognitive Gears: From Habits on Mind to Active Thinking. *Human Relations*, 44, pp. 55–76.

Lowe, K. B. and Gardner, W. L. (2000) Ten Years of *The Leadership Quarterly*: Contributions and Challenges for the Future. *The Leadership Quarterly*, 11(4), pp. 459–514.

Lurgio, A. J. and Carroll, J. S. (1985) Probation Officers Schemata of Offenders: Content, Development and Impact on Treatment Decisions. *Journal of Personality and Social Psychology*, 48, pp. 1112–26.

Markus, H. and Nurius, P. S. (1986) Possible Selves. *American Psychologist*, 41, pp. 954–69.

Markus, H. and Wurf, E. (1987) The Dynamic Self-concept: A Social Psychological Perspective. *Annual Review of Psychology*, 38, pp. 299–337.

Marserick, V. J. (1988) Learning in the Workplace: The Case for Reflectivity and Critical Reflectivity. *Adult Education Quarterly*, 38 (4), pp. 187–98.

Marserick, V. J. and Watkins, K. E. (1990) *Informal and Incidental Learning in the Workplace*. London: Routledge.

Masi, R. J. and Cooke, R. A. (2000) Effects of Transformational Leadership on Subordinate Motivation, Empowering Norms, and Organizational Productivity. *International Journal of Organizational Analysis*, 8 (1), pp. 16–47.

Matsui, T., Ikeda, H. and Ohnishi, R. (1994) Relations of Sex Typed Socializations to Career Self-efficacy Expectations of College Students. *Journal of Vocational Behavior*, 35, pp. 1–16.

Mazen, A. M. and Lemkau, J. P. (1990) Personality Profiles of Women in Traditional and Non-traditional Occupations. *Journal of Vocational Behavior*, 37, pp. 46–59.

McAlister, D. T. and Ferrell, O. C. (2005) Corporate Governance and Ethical Leadership. In R. A. Peterson and O. C. Ferrell, *Business Ethics* (pp. 56–81). London: W.E Sharpe.

McCall, J. (1978) Conjecturing About Creative Leaders. *Journal of Creative Behavior*, 14, pp. 225–34.

McCall, M. W. (1998) *High Flyers: Developing the Next Generation of Leaders*. Harvard Business School: Boston.

McCall, M. W. (2004) Leadership Development Through Experience. *Academy of Management Executive*, 18: pp. 127–30.

McCall, M. W., Lombardo, M. M. and Morrison, A. (1988) *The Lessons of Experience*. Lexington, MA: Lexington Books.

McCauley, C. D. and Douglas, C. A. (1998) Developmental Relationships. In C. McCauley, R. S. Moxley and E. Van Velsor (1998) *Handbook of Leadership Development* (pp. 160–93). San Francisco: Josey-Bass Publishers.

McCauley, C. D. and Brutus, S. (1998) *Management Development Through Job Experience: An Annotated Bibliography*. Greensboro, NC: Center for Creative Leadership.

McCauley, C., Moxley, R. S., and Van Velsor. E. (1998) *Handbook of Leadership Development*. Josey-Bass Publishers: San Francisco.

McGuire, W. J. (1984) Search for the Self: Going Beyond Self-esteem and the Reactive Self. In R. A Zucker, J. Aronoff and A. I. Rabin (eds), *Personality and the Prediction of Behavior*. New York: Academic.

Mead, G. H. (1934) *Mind, Self and Society*. Chicago: University of Chicago Press.

Medin, D. L. (1989) Concepts and Conceptual Structure. *American Psychologist*, 44, pp. 1469–81.

Meindl, J. R. (1995) The Romance of Leadership as a Follower Centric Theory: A Social Constructionist Approach. *The Leadership Quarterly*, 6, pp. 329–41.

Meindl, J. R., Ehrlich, S. B. and Dukerich, J. M. (1985) The Romance of Leadership and the Evaluation of Organizational Performance. *Academy of Management Journal*, 30, pp. 90–109.

Melamed, T. (1995) Career Success: The He-Moderating Effect of Gender. *Journal of Vocational Behavior*, 47, pp. 35–60.

Mezirow, J. (1981) A Critical Theory of Adult Learning and Education. *Adult Education*, 32 (1), pp. 3–24.

Mezirow, J. (1985) A Critical Theory of Self Directed Learning. In S. Brookfield (ed.), *Self-directed Learning: From Theory to Practice* (pp. 17–30). San Francisco: Josey-Bass.

Millar, M. G. and Tesser, A. (1986) Effects of Affective and Cognitive Focus on the Attitude-behaviour Relation. *Journal of Personality and Social Psychology*, 51, pp. 270–6.

Mintzberg, H. (1973) *The Nature of Managerial Work*. New York: Harper & Row.

Mischel, W. (1973) Toward a Cognitive Social Learning Reconceptualization of Personality. *Psychological Review*, 80 (4), pp. 252–83.

Mischel, W. (2004) Toward an Integrative Science of the Person. *Annual Review Psychology*, 55, pp. 1–22.

Morgan, G. (1986) *Images of Organizations*. Beverly Hills: Sage.

Morrison, A. M., White, R. P. and Van Velsor, E. (1987) The Narrow Band. *Issues and Observations*, 7 (2), pp. 1–7.

Moxley, R. S. (1998) Hardships. In C. McCauley, R. S. Moxley and E. Van Velsor. (1998), Handbook of Leadership Development (pp. 194–214). San Francisco, CA: Josey-Bass Publishers.

Mumford, M. D., Zaccaro, S. J., Harding, F. D., Jacobs, T. O. and Fleishman, E. A. (2000) Leadership Skills for a Changing World: Solving Complex Social Problems. *The Leadership Quarterly*, 11(1), pp. 11–36.

Neisser, U. (1976) *Cognition and Reality: Principles and Implications of Cognitive Psychology*. San Francisco, CA: Freeman and Company.

Neisser, U. (1982) *Memory Observed: Remembering in Natural Contexts*. San Francisco, CA: Freeman and Company.

Nicholson, N. (1998). How Hardwired is Human Behaviour? *Harvard Business Review*, 76, pp. 134–47.

Nicholson, N. (2000). Managing the Human Animal. London: Texere Books.

Nicolini, D. and Mesnar, M. B. (1995) The Social Construction of Organizational Learning: Conceptual and Practical Issues in the Field. *Human Relations*, 48 (7), pp. 727–47.

Nonaka, I. and Takeuchi H. (1995) *The Knowledge-creating Company*. Oxford: Oxford University Press.

Nurius, P. S. (1993) Human Memory: A Basis for Better Understanding the Elusive Self-Concept. Chicago: University of Chicago.

Offerman, L. R., Kennedy, J. K. and Wirtz, P. W. (1994) Implicit Leadership Theories: Content, Structure and Generalizability. *The Leadership Quarterly*, 5 (1), pp. 43–58.

Orr, J. E. (1996) *Talking About Machines: An Ethnography of a Modern Job*. Ithaca, NY: Cornell University Press.

Orwoll, L. and Perlmutter, M. (1990) The Study of Wise Persons: Integrating a Personality Perspective. In R. J. Sternberg (ed.), *Wisdom: Its Nature, Origins and Development* (pp. 142–59). New York: Cambridge University Press.

Osborne, R. H., Hunt, J. G. and Jauch, L. R. (2002) Toward a Contextual Theory of Leadership. *The Leadership Quarterly*, 13 (6), pp. 797–837.

Overman, E. S. (1996) The New Sciences of Administration: Chaos and Quantum Theory. *Public Administration Review*, 56, pp. 487–91.

Palmer, H. T. and Lee, J. A. (1990) Female Workers Acceptance in Traditionally Male Dominated Blue-collar Jobs. *Sex Roles*, 22, pp. 607–26.

Parry, K. W. (1998) Grounded Theory and Social Process: A New Direction for Leadership Research. *The Leadership Quarterly*, 9 (1), pp. 85–105.

Parry, K. W. (2001) Could Leadership Theory be Generalized? In R. Wiesner and B. Millett (eds), *Management and Organizational Behavior: Contemporary Challenges and Future Directions* (pp. 161–73). Brisbane: John Wiley & Sons.

Parry, K. W. and Fischer, R. (2003) *Gender Balance in the Workplace: Implications for Leadership*. Australian and New Zealand Academy of

Management (ANZAM) Annual Conference, Fremantle, Western Australia, 2–5 December.

Parry, K. W. and Hansen, H. (2007). The Organizational Story as Leadership. *The Leadership Quarterly*, 3 (3), pp. 301–24.

Parry, K. W. and Sinha, P. A. (2005) Researching the Trainability of Transformational Organizational Leadership. *Human Resource Development International*, 8 (2), 165–83.

Pedler, M., Burgoyne, J., and Boydell, T. (2004). A Managers Guide to Leadership. Maidenhead, UK: McGraw-Hill.

Perren, L. J. and Grant, P. (2001) *Management and Leadership in UK SME's: Witness Accounts from the World of Entrepreneurs and SME Managers*. London: CEML. Report.

Peters, S. (2006) *LEAD Evaluation Report*. Institute for Entrepreneurship and Enterprise Development, Lancaster University.

Pfeffer, J. (1977) The Ambiguity of Leadership. *Academy of Management Review*, 2, pp. 104–12.

Phillips, J. S. and Lord, R. G. (1982) Schematic Information Processing and Perceptions of Leadership in Problem-solving Groups. *Journal of Applied Psychology*, 67, pp. 486–92.

Phillips, S. D. and Imhoff, A. R. (1997) Women and Career Development: A Decade of Research. *Annual Review of Psychology*, 48, pp. 31–59.

Pillemer, D. B., Rinehart, E. D. and White, S. H. (1986) Memories of Life Transitions: The First Year of College. *Human Learning*, 5, pp. 109–23.

Piotrowski, C. and Armstrong, T. R. (1987) Executive Leadership Characteristics Portrayed on CNN'S Pinnacle. Behavioral Science Newsletter, Book XVI, 23. In B. Bass (1990), *Bass and Stogdill's Handbook of Leadership* (p. 809). New York: Free Press.

Polyani, M. (1966) *The Tacit Dimension*. London: Routledge & Keegan.

Price, T. L. (2000) Explaining Ethical Failures of Leadership. *Leadership and Organisational Development Journal*, 21 (4), pp. 177–84.

Pye, A. (2005) Leadership and Organizing: Sense-making in Action. *Leadership*, 1 (1), pp. 31–50.

Raelin, J. A. (1997) A Model of Work-based Learning. *Organization Science*, 8 (6), pp. 563–78.

Ready, D. and Conger J. A. (2003) Why Leadership Development Efforts Fail. *MIT Sloan Management Review*, 44 (3), pp. 83–8.

Reynolds, M. (1997) Learning Styles: A Critique. *Management Learning*, 28 (2), pp. 115–33.

Reynolds, M. (1998) Reflection and Critical Reflection in Management Learning. *Management Learning*, 29 (2), pp. 183–200.

Ricoeur, P. (1992) Oneself as Another (K. Blamey, Trans.). Chicago: University of Chicago Press. In D. Ezzy (1998), Theorizing Narrative Identity: Symbolic Interactionism and Hermeneutics (p. 241). *The Sociological Quarterly*, 39 (2), pp. 239–52.

Ritchie, J. and Lewis, J (2003) *Qualitative Research Practice: A Guide for Social Sciences and Students and Researchers*. London: Sage.

Rothwell, W. J. and Kanzanas, H. C. (1994) Management Development: The State of the Art as Perceived by the HRD Professionals. *Performance Improvement Quarterly*, 4 (1), pp. 40–59.

Saal, F. E. and Moore, S. C. (1993) Perceptions of Promotion Fairness and Promotion Candidates Qualifications. *Journal of Applied Psychology*, 78, pp. 105–10.

Saari, L. M., Johnson, J. C., McLaughlin, S. D. and Zimmerle, D. M. (1988) A Survey of Management Training and Education Practices in US Companies. *Personnel Psychology*, 41, pp. 731–43.

Salancik, G. R. and Meindl, J. R. (1984) Corporate Attributions as Strategic Illusions of Management Control. *Administrative Science Quarterly*, 29, pp. 238–54.

Salancik, G. R. and Pfeifer, J. (1977a) Who Gets Power and How do They Hold Onto It: A Strategic Contingency Model of Power. *Organizational Dynamics*, 5, pp. 3–21.

Sayer, A. (1992) *Method in Social Science: A Realist Approach* (2nd edn). London: Routledge.

Schatzki, T. R. and Knorr-Cetina, K. (2001) *The Practice Turn in Contemporary Theory*. London: Routledge.

Schon, D. (1983) *The Reflective Practitioner: How Professionals Think in Action*. New York: Basic Books.

Schriesheim, C. A. and Neider, L. L. (1989) Leadership Theory and Development: The Coming 'New Phase'. *Leadership and Organisational Development*, 10 (6), pp. 17–26.

Senge, P. M. (1990) *The Fifth Discipline: The Art and Practice of the Learning Organization*. London: Century Business.

Shamir, B., Dayan-Horesh, H. and Adler, D. (2005) Leading by Biography: Towards a Life-story Approach to the Study of Leadership. *Leadership*, 1 (1), pp. 13–29.

Shamir, B. and Howell, J. M. (1999) Organizational and Contextual Influences on the Emergence and Effectiveness of Charismatic Leadership. *The Leadership Quarterly*, 10 (2), pp. 257–83.

Shamir, B., House, R. J. and Arthur, M. B. (1993) The Motivational Effects of Charismatic Leadership: A Self-concept Based Theory. *Organization Science*, 4, pp. 1–17.

Silverman, D. (1997) *Qualitative Research: Theory, Method and Practice*. London: Sage.

Sjostrand, S., Sandberg, J. and Tyrstrup, M. (2001) *Invisible Management: The Social Construction of Leadership*. London: Thompson Learning.

Slife, B. D. and Rychlak, J. F. (1982) Role of Affective Assessment in Modeling Aggressive Behavior. *Journal of Personality and Social Psychology*, 43, pp. 861–8.

Smircich, C. and Morgan, G. (1982) Leadership: The Management of Meaning. *The Journal of Applied Behavioral Science*, 18 (3), pp. 257–73.

Smith, E. R. and Zarate, M. A. (1992) Exemplar-based Model of Social Judgment. *Psychological Review*, 99, pp. 3–21.

Smither, J. W. and Reilly, R. R. (1989) Relationships Between Job Knowledge and the Reliability of Conceptual Similarity Schemata. *Journal of Applied Psychology*, 3, pp. 941–50.

South, S. J., Markham, W. T., Bonjean, C. J. and Corder, J. (1987) Sex Differences in Support for Organizational Advancement. *Work Occupation*, 14, pp. 261–85.

Sparrowe, R. (2005) Authentic Leadership and the Narrative Self. *The Leadership Quarterly*, 16 (3), pp. 419–39.

Srull, T. K. and Wyer, R. S. (1989) Person, Memory and Judgment. *Psychological Review*, 96, pp. 58–83.

Stark, A. (1992) *Because I Said So*. New York: Pharos Books.

Stead, V. (2005) Mentoring: A Model for Leadership Development? *International Journal of Training and Development*, 9 (3), pp. 170–84.

Steers, R. M., Porter, L. W. and Bigley, G. A. (2000) *Motivation and Leadership at Work* (6th ed.). Boston: McGraw-Hill.

Sternberg, R. J. (1985) Implicit Theories of Intelligence, Creativity and Wisdom. *Journal of Personality and Social Psychology*, 49, pp. 607–27.

Sternberg, R. J. (1990) Wisdom and Its Relations to Intelligence and Creativity. In R. J. Sternberg (ed.), *Wisdom: Its Nature, Origins and Development* (pp. 142–59). New York: Cambridge University Press.

Stewart, A. J., Sokol, M., Healy, J. M. Jr., Chester, N. L. and Weistock-Savoy, D. (1982) Adaptation to Life Changes in Children and Adult Self: Cross Sectional Studies. *Journal of Personality and Social Psychology*, 43, pp. 1270–81.

Tajfel, H. (1974) Social Identity and Intergroup Behavior. *Social Science Information*, 13, pp. 65–93.

Tangri, S. S. and Jenkins, S. R. (1986) Stability and Change in Role Innovation and Life Plans. *Sex Roles*, 14, pp. 647–62.

Trice, H. M. and Beyer, J. M. (1986) Charisma and Its Routinization in Two Social Movement Organizations. In L. L. Cummings and B. M. Staw (eds), *Research in Organization Behavior* (pp. 113–64). Greenwich, CT: JAI Press.

Tsoukas, H. and Chia, R. (2002) On Organizational Becoming: Rethinking Organizational Change. *Organizational Science*, 13 (5), pp. 567–82.

Tulving, E. (1983) *Elements of Episodic Memory*. Oxford: Oxford University Press.

Turner, J. C. (1985) Social Categorization and the Self-concept: A Social Cognitive Theory of Group Behaviour. In M. A. Hogg and G. M. Vaughan (2002), *Social Psychology* 3rd edn (pp. 55–7). Harlow: Prentice Hall.

Uhl-Bien, M. (2003) Relationship Development as a Key Ingredient for Leadership Development. W. Barbara and B. Murphy (eds), *The Future Leadership Development* (pp. 129–45). Mahwah, NJ: Lawrence Erlbaum Associates.

Uhl-Bien, M. (2006) Relational Leadership Theory: Exploring the Social Processes of Leadership and Organizing. *The Leadership Quarterly*, 17 (6), pp. 654–76.

Usher, R. S. (1985) Beyond the Anecdotal: Adult Learning and the Use of Experience. *Studies in the Education of Adults*, 7 (1), pp. 59–74.

Vaill, P. (1983) The Theory of Managing in the Managerial Competency Movement. *The Organizational Behavior Teaching Journal*, 8 (2), pp. 50–4.

Van Fleet, D. D. and Yukl, G. (1986a) A Century of Leadership Research. In D. A. Wren (ed.), *One Hundred Years of Management* (pp. 12–23). Chicago: Academy of Management.

Velsor, E. and Guthrie, V. A. (1998) Enhancing the Ability to Learn from Experience. In C. McCauley, R. S. Moxley and E. Van Velsor (1998), *Handbook of Leadership Development* (pp. 242–61). San Francisco: Josey-Bass Publishers.

Vroom, V. H. and Jago, A. G. (1988) *The New Leadership: Managing Participation in Organizations*. Englewood Cliffs, NJ: Prentice Hall.

Waller, W. (1932) The Sociology of Teaching. New York: Wiley. In K. J. Gergen (1971), *The Concept of Self* (p. 55). London: Holt, Rinehart and Winston, Inc.

Walsh, J. P. (1995) Managerial and Organizational Cognition: Notes From a Trip Down Memory Lane. *Organization Science*, 6 (3), pp. 280–321.

Waters, J. A. (1980) Managerial Skill Development. *Academy of Management Review*, 5, pp. 449–53.

Watson and Wyatt Worldwide Survey Report (2000) *Leadership in the Global Economy*. London: Watson and Wyatt Worldwide Research.

Watson, T. J. (2001) *In Search of Management: Culture, Chaos and Control in Managerial Work*. London: Thomson Learning.

Weber, M. (1947) The Theory of Social and Economic Organizations (T. Parsons, Trans.). New York: Free Press. In B. M. Bass (1990), *Bass and Stogdill's Handbook of Leadership* (pp. 184–6). New York: Free Press.

Weick, K. E. (1979) *The Social Psychology of Organizing* (2nd edn). Reading, MA: Addison-Wesley.

Weick, K. E. (1995) What Theory is Not, Theorizing Is *Administrative Science Quarterly*, 40 (3), pp. 385–90.

Wenger, E. (1998) *Communities of Practice: Learning, Meaning, and Identity*. Cambridge: Cambridge University Press.

Wengraf, T. (2001) *Qualitative Research Interviewing*. London: Sage.

Wexley, K. N. and Baldwin, T. T. (1986) Management Development. *Journal of Management*, 12 (2), pp. 277–94.

White, R. T. (1982) Memory for Personal Events. *Human Learning*, 1, pp. 171–83.

Whitehead, A. (1933) *Adventure of Ideas*. New York: Macmillan.

Williams, S. (2001). Upstream, Downstream: The Flow and Stock of UK Managers. London: CEML.

Williams, S. (2002). Characteristics of the Management Population in the UK: An Overview. London: CEML.

Willner, A. B. (1984) *The Spellbinders: Charismatic Political Leadership*. New Haven: Yale University.

Wofford, J. C. and Goodwin, V. L. (1994) A Cognitive Interpretation of Transactional and Transformational Leadership Theories. *The Leadership Quarterly*, 5 (2), pp. 161–86.

Wood, R. and Bandura, A. (1989) Social Cognitive Theory of Organizational Management. *Academy of Management Review*, 14 (3), pp. 361–84.

Wren, C. and Jones, J. (2006) *Ex-post Evaluation of the LEAD Programme*. Business School, University of Newcastle upon Tyne.

Yost, J. H., Strobe, M. J. and Bailey, J. R. (1992) The Construction of the Self: An Evolutionary View. *Current Psychology: Research and Reviews*, 11, pp. 110–21.

Yukl, G. (1989) Managerial Leadership: A Review of Theory and Research. *Journal of Management*, 15 (2), pp. 251–89.

Yukl, G. (1989) *Leadership in Organizations* (2nd ed.). Englewood Cliffs, NJ: Prentice Hall.

Yukl, G. (1998) *Leadership in Organizations* (4th edn). Upper Saddle River, NJ: Prentice Hall.

Yukl, G. (2001) *Leadership in Organizations* (5th edn). Upper Saddle River, NJ: Prentice Hall.

Yukl, G. and Falbe, C. M. (1991) The Importance of Power Sources in Downward and Lateral Relations. *Journal of Applied Psychology*, 76, pp. 416–23.

Zaccaro, S. J., Gilbert, J., Thor, K. K and Mumford, M. D. (1991) Leadership and Social Intelligence: Linking Social Perceptiveness and Behavioral Flexibility to Leader Effectiveness. *The Leadership Quarterly*, 2, pp. 317–31.

Zaccaro, S. J., Rittman, A. L and Marks, M. A. (2001) Team Leadership. *The Leadership Quarterly*, 12(4), pp. 451–83.

Zemke, R. (1985) The Honeywell Studies: How Managers Learn to Manage. *Training*, August, pp. 46–51.

Index